MANIFESTO

MANIFESTO

MICHAEL D. HALLIDAY

Matador
9 Priory Business Park,
Wistow Road, Kibworth Beauchamp,
Leicestershire. LE8 0RX
Tel: 0116 279 2299
Email: books@troubador.co.uk
Web: www.troubador.co.uk/matador
Twitter: @matadorbooks

ISBN 978 1789013 184

British Library Cataloguing in Publication Data.
A catalogue record for this book is available from the British Library.

Typeset in 13pt Adobe Garamond Pro by Troubador Publishing Ltd, Leicester, UK

Matador is an imprint of Troubador Publishing Ltd

CONTENTS

INTRODUCTION

'Manifesto' is a book about politics. Yes, I know, yet another one. As though there weren't too many of the bally things already. Well, I don't think so. Even though I live in a country where the electorate is mostly politically disengaged. And where politics is widely regarded as beyond the pale and politicians the lowest of the low. Because the subjects potentially, and sometimes actually, dealt with by politics matter. They matter profoundly. It is true, of course, that it is much, much easier to write about these things than to engage meaningfully and with significant effect in a practical way. So the challenge to the next generation is a critical one.

This work has been long in the gestation. Even now thoughts are offered here only in a tentative and incomplete way about some of the multifold political reforms I would like to have brought about in the land of my birth. I find the cumulative weight of things as they are well-nigh intolerable.

My book grew out of initial flirtations with the so-called social media. The old traditions of letters and e-mails to institutions seemed to be giving way rapidly to such platforms as Twitter and Facebook, though considerably limited in practice by the trivial preoccupations of users and the small number of words. What finally decided me against blogging either was a lack of desire to engage in unstructured debate, and possibly attract unsavoury elements with dark motives to the site. And there again, a lot of people shout, but how many listen?

Another motive to write the book was my career experience, the constant interference of central government, their crushing budget cuts, the lack of trust, the unseemly haste of badly thought out plans for change, the cult of ideology over evidence. I started out with bushy tail and wide-eyed eagerness, only to observe the slow decline by propaganda of our public-spirited ideals in the face of an ill-informed and increasingly indifferent, later hostile, community. Too late did I come to realize that a nation without much interest in politics gets the rank politicians it deserves.

'Reformation' was my original title, but it is more optimistic than I felt. Various other possibilies were considered: 'reclamation', with its connotations of waste, the moralistic 'restitution', even the pretentious 'renaissance'. 'Reformation' was better, serving both its literal sense of making something again, and also the cultural notion of improvement thorough new and more enlightened ideas. In the end I decided to call the book simply 'Manifesto'. We are all familiar with the idea that the political parties publish 'manifestos' in the run up to general elections. Though most of us never see any of them, because they aren't in the shops. We vaguely know that they set out programmes which the parties hope to implement if/when in power. The Wikipedia definition states that 'A manifesto is a published verbal declaration of the intentions, motives, or views of the issuer, be it an individual, group, political party or government'. So my 'Manifesto' is within the normal scope of meaning: it sets out in writing my main political views as an individual, though I like to think I hold them provisionally and would change them if the evidence was persuasive enough.

'Manifesto' operates in various places on quite a high level of abstraction and some generality, as is required in order to transcend the detail and fragmentation to be found in policy. Quite a few of the items in the book are relatively small concerns in themselves in the grand scheme of things. Taken together, however, they form a much more formidable agenda. The author has not wished to go over his old ground again, so that the larger socio-political issues covered in his books 'Radical Bureaucracy', 'Outside the Outcrowd' and 'Memoirs of an Educationalist' are not revisited here, except maybe in passing. Nevertheless, they remain very relevant, and are arguably matters deserving to be taken up by wider society.

It is possible to characterize my approach in broad terms as, say 'democratic', or 'nationalist', or 'capitalist with a human face', in other words, general positions adopted by many other political commentators and members of the public. But my 'worldview' is my own and hopefully influential for others.

'Manifesto' is utopian, at least in the sense that it deals mainly in ideas and ideals unlikely to be realized anywhere in totality. This, in my belief, is far from an indication that the ideas are poor ones; rather, it is a hard-nosed assessment that fundamental political change, even in these speeded-up days, is a slow and piecemeal, unsystematic process and that the values adopted are rarely the most noble. In one important sense utopia is a concept foolish to contemplate, since no kind of perfection could possibly hold for long in a world that inevitably changes. Nevertheless, it can provide the stuff of dreams, a flame of hope that life on earth may become better, whatever that might mean for us in practice.

What are the prospects of even remotely approaching the kind of country I would be prepared to concede was decent and civilized and that I would enthusiastically want to live in? Unfortunately, it is a chimera; the chances are virtually nil. That is not to say that it could not be improved in part, which it is not out of the question to hope, whilst, almost inevitably, the rest of it deteriorates, or remains mired in mediocrity. So what to do? To get out, I say, is the only option, early in life when not too old to have prospects. And before they do you down and take your money off you. But as to where to go, I regret I do not know. Somewhere in Scandinavia, perhaps, which has always impressed me on visits and has a humane welfare umbrella. We are brainwashed here, of course. They try to drum it in from a tender age that ours is the best country in the world. Well, it is far from that, except for the lucky, privileged few, and never will be, I fear, for the many. This country is not so impressive in international terms. Just look at history to glimpse its present and prevailing horrors, its ceaseless warmongering, callous institutional treatment of ordinary citizens, inadequate laws that protect the rich and powerful and where justice for victims seems so elusive. The cheap appeals to nationalism we are regularly fed do not fool me or make me feel a part of it.

Apart from the heroic few, by and large, the British people do not engage with the determination and degree of mass organization needed to make a substantial difference to the behaviour of the political classes. When they are not being hidebound by family tradition, or brainwashed by the popular media, people are mostly too bogged down in the never ending struggle for economic survival in our jungle of a country, where standards of living are frequently quite high, yet the quality of life merely indifferent to poor for most.

In this characterization of the subject matter let me explain that 'Manifesto' is not particularly concerned with the journey from A to B, the process by which a plan is turned into action, or a policy implemented. After a lifetime of administration in the service of politicians, the author knows better than to belittle, or in any wise underestimate, the invariable difficulties, even once 'agreement' is reached, in the attainment of political objectives. This is only partly because goals can sometimes be achieved by myriad means. It is also a recognition that objectives are seldom pursued consistently when they are pursued at all. More likely, most of what I desire will moulder on the back burner for donkeys' years, or never make the priority list for action, should it even receive general assent as something to be desired. So we would be talking of patience, persuasion, and above all the long game. It has to be admitted, of course, that it is far easier to prescribe outcomes than ways of reaching them. Policy aims have always to vie with each other under the political context of the moment. This heady mix of aspiration, current realities, and external pressures almost always ensures failure. Ultimately every regime comes up short in public estimation, its successes modest in comparison with its targets. The leaders we sometimes enthusiastically adopt, even the rare good ones, all fail after a while, or otherwise lose popularity.

It could be argued that it was an unusually problematic time to be writing a book on politics because of the turmoil in that world serving as a backdrop with very uncertain outcomes. I refer mainly to Donald Trump's unique Presidency of the United States, the British referendum decision to leave the European Union, and the snap calling of a general election by Teresa May. All these events were in the nature of surprises. Where it suited my purpose I made reference. The book was, however, never intended to be a topical pot-boiler such as you can read in the press every day, but one of lasting relevance and significance for many years to come. So I was largely able to continue writing un-deflected by the commotion, so to speak.

The approach adopted in the book is firstly to show and deplore the shortcomings in the British claim to be a proper democracy. Political structures and practice in the United Kingdom context are then examined, and radical proposals made for reform of their many faults and democratic deficits. Thus politics is the broad subject-matter of chapter 2. Dreams are the main theme in chapter 3, with broad discussion of directions we may go in and outcomes I would like to have come to pass, drawing on a wide-ranging sample of worthy contemporary political texts for potential insights to evaluate. Chapter 4 sets our international context, including the issue of Brexit. In chapter 5 I grapple with the big ogre of Capitalism and how it might be regulated and humanized whilst retaining its better features. I look next in chapter 6 for some solutions to our environmental plight, though the familiar science and politics of the subject are not reworked here. Finally in chapter 7 I discuss our wellbeing, which is supposed to be what politics strives to bring about instead of being so often merely its excuse and enemy.

CHAPTER 1

OUR SHAM
DEMOCRACY

Why We Aren't a Proper Democracy
Where is Our Constitution?
The British System
The Prime Minister
Ministers of State
Political Parties
Politicians
The Establishment
The Electorate
Law
Patronage
Corruption
Power is the Drug
Fake News?

Why We Aren't a Proper Democracy.

Perhaps little needs to be explained about the idea of democracy, because it is believed to be widely understood. The term seems to be one much bandied about with the implied assumption that it is a good thing. Democracy is of course government by the people. Since this is usually impractical, and thus inherently weakening of the principles, actual democratic countries arrange for representatives of the people to govern on their behalf. Methods are very variable and doubtless affect actual outcomes. I have something to say about this later, but my initial observation is to argue that the voting franchise should be as wide as practicable, ruling out only a small proportion in society such as the very young, the very mentally ill, and the seriously criminal.

If you are going to be led by politicians they have to be ultimately accountable to your community, so that if they underperform they can be booted out. Since it is unwise to trust any politician for long, and most not at all, citizens need, enshrined by law, voting power to give either tentative support or the sanction of removal from office.

The arguments in favour of democracy are usually taken as read, but they are worth stating and they are not so slight. We do need some coercive authority structures in the modern complex world to get things done, granted.

But without democratic control we have no say over who exercises the power and no ability to monitor their performance, or get rid of them for poor attainment. Providing everyone within reason a vote helps to build in the notion by implication of equal esteem. But there remains the unanswered question of how to prevent the persecution of minorities by action or omission. Note that elements of a democracy include not just a vote in general elections but equality before the law, the rule of law, separation of powers, free speech and a free press, freedom of movement, a written constitution, a bill of rights. These elements of themselves will not prevent the persecution of minorities, but they are necessary pre-conditions nevertheless.

A major flaw with democracy in principle (often seen as the least bad of all political systems, but bad nevertheless, as Churchill famously claimed) is that the public probably vote out of self-interest and lack of knowledge in the main, so frequently producing a mess. This criticism I worry about and agree with, whilst believing that a higher status for politics and universal unbiased education on the subject will only partly ameliorate the situation.

Gordon Graham's critique of the democratic state starts with the claim that the votes of 'the ignorant and prejudiced' are given equal weight with those of the 'informed and impartial'. The system also empowers what could be an irrational majority over the wishes of a minority. If we selected who could vote on some principle and test of competence we should not only have practical difficulties, but we would also be moving away from the democratic ideal towards some kind of élitism. There is nothing here to stop tyrannies, be they of State or people, yet the myth is perpetrated that democracy does just that. In the era of the Cameron government, for example, we effectively saw the rise of a one-party state owing to public failure to endorse the main opposition party. This disenfranchised those who were not its followers. Resigned apathy was one natural reaction, indifference another. Some of the cures to me are simple, but unlikely, starting with making it illegal not to vote, and introducing proportional representation. This is a main concern of mine, that democracy is compatible with thoroughly rotten politicians and outcomes, so much of my actual critique will come in the form of comment on particular detailed aspects later in the body of the text.

I used to think that democracy was everything in a political system, the more thoroughgoing and participative the better. I paralleled democracy with the means to scientific progress, where open-minded researchers tested theories empirically to find the best fit with reality and changed their tentatively held views accordingly. This latter, of course, is a construct, an ideal. And the parallel is based on a conveniently unexamined analogy, one which might fit better here, somewhat imperfectly there.

I have moderated my view to the lesser claim that suitably self-improving and humane political systems should be fundamentally democratic, whilst at the same time incorporating key elements of authority nevertheless. Most of us in the West have recent historical reasons to be very well aware of the dangers of too much power being placed in too few hands. Yet it is time to emphasize a balancing truth, that power widely disseminated can be considerably diluted to a point of ineffectuality. We shall learn more of this later.

There are other strong reasons to advocate a degree of authority too. There can sometimes be a pressing need for quick decisions, so the right to make these on the basis of limited consultation is a necessity, so long as we can somehow build in appropriate safeguards of competence and accountability. Precisely where the balance between democracy and authority lies is a grave weakness of the desirable model, for there is probably no general answer; circumstances will alter cases. However, we need not worry overmuch within the present system, for it is really very authoritarian, with many-tiered institutional hierarchies, and not especially democratic (a surprise to brain-washed citizens who thought otherwise because the press told them so).

There is another enormous flaw at the heart of democracy as a system, which is a moral one. To make social progress we sometimes need to experiment, as the scientists do. But this can adversely affect people's lives where we get it wrong, such as with the endless mucking about of the Education system, where life chances of children are at stake. In general the populace is not very trusting or forgiving of failed policies, so this will have to change within limits. In order to do so it will need in my estimation a much better scientifically literate public and a political class far more willing to share the details of their good intent in advance with those affected.

It would be a grave mistake to see democracy as a static model, or a related collection of such. It is continually developing, at least in its theoretical dimensions, whilst ironically the performance of actual democratic states over the longer haul begins to look decidedly ropey.

One major matter that has yet to be satisfactorily resolved, for all but the benefitting small minority, is the control of a capitalist economy, now rendered more complex and difficult by the globalization dimension. It is not yet clear even how compatible democracy and capitalism are. The issues will be considered later, in chapter 5.

Another question is the extent to which what might be termed 'social democracy', as a programme of citizens' wellbeing across a wide-range of issues, is both desirable and realizable within a democratic framework. That citizens in various democracies are increasingly unhappy with their lot, and are showing it in various ways including the ballot box, is now a commonplace.

It is also true that whatever lip-service the law pays to safeguarding the rights of whistle-blowers, the reality is that they are almost invariably persecuted one way or another, and with impunity. The reputations of organizations and the top people in them are considered more important than the improvements that might stem from inconvenient home truths.

I offer one final example of our democracy being a sham, although they are numerous. It is enshrined in Tory legislation which lays down a code of practice on what local government can publish and how, even when elections are not in the offing. In the case of Wirral Borough Council a row broke out when the ruling Labour group proposed in 2016 to publish its own bi-monthly newspaper. The minister intervened to stop it, mainly on the declared ground that it could be in competition with local commercial newspapers and so bad for trade. But these consisted almost entirely of advertising material with little public information or journalism included, whereas the Council wished to inform its residents about their services and help on offer, surveys having demonstrated a widespread ignorance. What the regulations were really about in the main was making sure that local government could not openly criticize central government, the sort of thing we see suppressed in communist regimes and deplore there.

So what we have in Britain is a mainly authoritarian country and institutions with a few democratic and pseudo-democratic elements to placate the masses. Among the pretend aspects I include our voting system, which distorts representation and disenfranchises. Its ideal among the political classes is either a one-party State or a Parliamentary dictatorship. Nowhere in the world is there a fully developed and thoroughgoing democracy; the concept is an ideal to which some regimes allegedly aspire. It is a matter of degrees. And those that make the loudest claims to being democratic, often including the noble word in their title, such as North Korea, which calls itself 'the Democratic People's Republic of Korea', can be among the most repressive and totalitarian of all.

The ringing words of Beatriz Garcia, though referring to Spain, are an aptly succinct description of the United Kingdom too as a country where democracy is falling into disrepute because of its deficits and shortcomings. I can do no better than to quote and commend her words to you.

'Yes, we question this democracy because it fails to support popular sovereignty: the markets impose decisions for their own benefit and the parties in Parliament are not standing up to this global fact. Neither in our country nor in the European Parliament are they fighting to put an end to financial speculation, whether in currency or in sovereign debt.

Yes, we question this democracy because the parties in power do not look out for the collective good, but for the good of the rich. Because they understand growth as the growth of businessmen's profits, not the growth of social justice, redistribution, public services, access to housing and other necessities. Because the parties in power are concerned only for their continuation in office…Because no politician has to live with what they legislate for their 'subjects': insecurity, mortgage debt, uncertainty. We question this democracy because it colludes with corruption, allowing politicians to hold a private post at the same time as public office, to profit from privileged information, to step into jobs as business advisers after leaving office, making it very profitable to be a politician.

Yes, we question this democracy because it consists in an absolute delegation of decision-making into the hands of politicians that are nominated in closed lists and to whom we have no access of any kind. Nor is there proportionality between votes and seats. We question this democracy because it is absurd that the only way to 'punish' a party is to vote for another one with which one does not agree.

We question this democracy because the parties in power do not even comply with the social provisions of the Constitution: justice is not applied equally, there are no decent jobs or housing for all, foreign-born workers are not treated as citizens. Excuses are not good enough for us. We do not want to choose actually existing democracy. We want a different life. Real democracy now!'

Where is our Constitution?

Anthony King's majestic book 'Who Governs Britain' is a very detailed account which considers all the players – politicians and others – in turn. Highly involved with issues of constitution, it offers nuggets of suggested reform, including adopting elements of the so-called Nordic model. Very critical, it puts its finger on many of the current weaknesses. Accordingly, it will be necessary to try and do it justice in my comments here.

King's assessments of the limitations are pessimistic (born of realism).

'It is not within any British government's power either to fashion 'a country with drive, purpose and energy,' or to transform Britain's complex existing social structure into any sort of 'Big Society' (a one-time dream of David Cameron). Modern British governments can nudge, goad, incentivize and encourage, but they can seldom, if ever, bring about radical economic and social change.'

He goes on:

'Who, then, governs Britain today? The short answer is: no one institution and certainly no one individual. Governments of the United Kingdom, like the governments of other liberal democracies, are multiply hobbled and constrained, by global market forces, by international institutions, by the courts, and by the press'.

The philosopher, A. C. Grayling has written a somewhat despairing book entitled 'Democracy and Its Crisis', in which he points out some more flaws, without necessarily giving practical suggestions for their remediation. He is spot on in saying that special interests have subverted the system for their own ends, these being notably commercial. He correctly shows how easily Party interests and political expediency can hold sway above the benefits to the country at large. Perhaps his leading insight is the realization that democracies teeter between mob rule and that of an elite.

The British System

King characterizes the British system of government as highly centralized, power-keeping not sharing, 'establishmentarian' not particularly democratic, loosely representative rather than strictly mandated, with an adversarial essentially two-party system of government and opposition, and an accountability broadly expressed by an otherwise passive and uninvolved electorate voting roughly once every five years. I might add that its complex history is manifested in vestiges of residual power relations between the continuing Monarchy and the official Government.

Our first-past-the–post voting system virtually ensures the Conservative Party will remain in power for the vast majority of the time . It needs far less than half the votes cast and consigns most votes as wasted and their casters disenfranchised. You either vote for somebody with no chance, or provide surplus votes for an elected candidate. Electoral boundaries have steadily been gerrymandered to reduce Labour's chances. Minority parties can poll huge numbers of votes without gaining representation in Parliament. A current example of distortion is that Labour needs to dominate seats in Scotland to have any chance of an overall majority in the UK Parliament, yet the SNP rules there, elected on a tide of desire for Scotland to stay in the EU. This is fundamentally why Labour's official platform was to remain and it strikes me quite wrong that our system should dictate a Party's views.

What I want to see, in the general terms outlined above, is highly devolved power-sharing, a breakup of the old cosy ruling classes and professional politicos, democratic decision-making by coalitions of proportionately-represented groups, sharper and more regular accountability through mandated delegates of the people, and frequent binding referenda on key issues of principle and direction. We need powerful regional assemblies and local councils with significant powers represented on them.

Let me say a few words about referenda in general. Widely disparaged by the British press and ruling party politicians, and conveniently blamed for the Brexit mess, they are on the contrary legitimate tools whereby the views of the electorate may be canvassed. In practice they have not been utilized a lot here, but in principle they could be used as great deal more, and often, to take soundings on the national mood over a whole range of issues. Nor do they need to remain in the crude and simplistic form they were for Brexit. They could be advisory or a mandate and they lend themselves to an emerging digital world where voting could be as elementary as changing channels with the TV remote. So I say to dissenters everywhere-promote referenda wherever you can-locally, regionally, and nationally. Establishments do not like them and most people are not yet used to them, so results can be refreshingly destabilizing for the powers that be...

I believe these things because government and politicians have been mostly neither transparent nor accountable much of the time, have been put up with stoically by an increasingly disenchanted population, have ruled largely in the interests of the powerful, the moneyed, and the high-born, with authoritarian methods. Above all, the systems have become worn-out, failed us repeatedly, led the nation nowhere in particular, left a country broke, sold off, in debt, at each other's throats, segregated, wasteful of resources, deteriorating in its social capital and values, unethical, frankly plain dirty and disgusting.

Brexit gave the country some semblance of a chance for independence, a fresh new start where foreign influence would be reduced and we could have a bigger say over our own destiny. King wisely counsels caution over believing that the extent of our new-found freedoms will be anything like total. The rough distribution of power was that, whilst we retained within the European Union control over defence and foreign policy, taxation, pensions, social security, health, much of education, transport, local government, and energy, we were subject to free migration of people between the nations, shared agricultural and fisheries policies, redistribution of resources to stimulate the economies of weaker nations, restrictions on our state aid to industry, various environmental standards and requirements. But larger factors outside our control are to do with the operations of markets and multinational firms. As King put it:

'successive UK governments have struggled, sometimes unsuccessfully, to prevent multinational companies from taking over British firms and then closing down a substantial portion of their UK operations or transferring them overseas'.

Then again, as a nation permanently in debt, we are at the mercy of international money lenders. Our banks are too large as a proportion of national wealth, rendering us 'highly vulnerable to external shocks'. And foreign-exchange markets largely dictate the value of the pound, thereby strongly influencing the conditions under which we can trade with other nations. These, and other constraints apart, such as those arising from foreign alliances and memberships of international organizations, we do need to possess sovereign power to make our own laws where we can.

The Prime Minister

Then there are unfortunate, unaddressed constitutional problems surrounding the office of prime minister. One glaring one is that he or she is the media magnet for the whole government. Lazy journalism goes to town and simplifies everything down to a personification. It diminishes the perception of government and gives a disproportionate say to one person. Better is required.

The second scandal is that the prime minister is not chosen by the people; the very tenuous democratic connection is that the people may have elected a political party to govern, among whose ranks a prime minister will be chosen by its MPs, sometimes, as with Teresa May, without even a contest between rival candidates! This has got to stop. We saw that it led in the case of Mrs. May to a leader soon thereafter exposed as too lightweight for the job. There are serious limitations on even the prime minister's powers, it is true, but the position is far too important to be outside public control. Conveniently, nobody has bothered to write into laws fair and just constitutional rules over this, as with so many constitutional matters that an involved electorate would repeatedly turn into the issues they actually are.

A third scandal is that the prime minister's job is not really laid down in sufficient detail. There are certain things he/she has to do, of course, like appoint (and fire) ministers, see the Queen, speak in Parliament (sometimes), hold cabinet meetings, fete foreign dignitaries, but this still allows considerable scope for doing (or not doing) what he wishes. It has been said that both Cameron and Brown wanted the office, but had little clue what to do with it when it came their way. This also has to stop. The most influential political figure in the land must be not only a credible figure to 'represent' the nation, but someone capable and motivated to fulfil an exacting job description. There is too much attempting to equate party interest or personal predilection with national interest. The temptations of the office are an obvious lure – celebrity, travel, luxury living, money-making, and leisure can all, and do, divert incumbents from their huge weight of responsibilities.

Ministers of State

Ministers are a serious problem as well. To quote Anthony King again, talking of the (smallish) pool of MPs from which they are chosen:

> 'Some are old and frail, some are ill, some are lazy, some drink too much, some have skeletons in the closet, some are wildly unpredictable…some are too nervous, some are too dim, some are impossible personally.'

A lot are also career politicians with little or no experience of working life in the 'real world'. Add to that their likely short tenure, their lack of interest and experience in administrative affairs, the fact that they are frequently shuffled from one office where they have little knowledge or competence to another, their need to make their mark urgently in the here and now, their tendency to throw up ill-conceived laws which they expect to be drafted in a hurry – all this and more usually adds up to indifferent, if not downright disastrous performances. So what is to be done? Well, I expect little will be, but many of the solutions are actually embedded in the criticisms.

Alongside reform of Minister quality, and intimately bound up with it, is the need to improve the civil service. Time was that they would serve all their careers within one department of state, where they could become very knowledgeable about the particular problems it confronted. Nowadays, civil servants are likely to be whisked between departments, thus ensuring a deterioration in the quality of advice they offer to Ministers. Another trend, also in need of reversal, is the increasing appointment of political advisers, to provide help with communications and policy formulation. Apart from the unfortunate conflicts of interest and status with career civil servants, what is instead lacking from the outside is formal specialist expertise from the walks of life affected by the Department's remit and potential scope. Internal skill deficits, such as their notorious ineptitude with information technology projects, should be rectified without delay. The old 'mandarins' (former managerial giants in the civil service) ought to return to prevent the bureaucracy getting a permanent run around.

Political Parties

I have dealt with the corrupting tendencies of financial sponsorship of political parties elsewhere. Here I want to comment on other unfortunate aspects of the party system in need of significant reform. The first glaring point that strikes me is that official paid-up party membership of even the 'large' parties, Tories and Labour, is very small – only a few hundred thousand – compared with the voting electorate – probably over forty million. And yet these parties totally dominate in terms of elections and rule of the country. What is more, the MPs whom we are gullible enough to vote into Parliament are in effect selected by a small activist cadre within the party machine behind closed doors. These seem to me serious democratic deficits. It's a bit like contests on television, such as the endless cookery shows. We are gripped by the rivalry and will have our preferred winner. But few seem to question whether these were the most worthy contestants in the first place, or by whom and how they were chosen.

If you join the local branch of a political party you will soon be reminded of where the balance of importance lies: they will expect you to distribute leaflets, knock on doors, and make financial donations. They won't be a bit interested in your political views or policy ideas. But we the members should contribute these and be selecting the candidates who stand for local government and national offices.

Of course, all this is on the assumption that we want political parties to continue. I don't. I think there are powerful arguments against. Take ideology. It tends to drive a party like Labour and it will be something that very many people will never be able to stomach. Those, on the other hand, who are pragmatic politicians, like many a modern Conservative, can and will be accused of blowing with the wind, courting popularity above principle, standing for nothing much beyond self-preservation.

If you look at most issues it may be difficult to see how they could relate to just one ideology. What can happen is that, partly for historical reasons, a party gets saddled with an incoherent rag-bag of policy stances across the range of issues, which all loyal and faithful members are expected to sign up to and defend. Internal disagreements are always perceived as a definite weakness, eagerly seized on by our irresponsible media and magnified to emphasize a rift. Again, if they were scientific about it, differences would be tested by evidence, not the struggle of the fittest.

Regarding the financing of political parties it is worth adding a footnote arising from conduct in the 2015 general election by the Tory party. On the intervention of the Electoral Commission, which acts as independent watchdog, the party was fined £70,000 following investigations by twelve police forces in different parts of the country. Essentially, creative accounting was used to mask the fact that their local candidates in about twenty constituencies incurred expenses well over the permitted maxima. State funding, if carefully designed and policed, would reduce the unfairness.

Political parties are a big part of what is wrong with our democracy, because their rule oscillates the country between contrary ideologies. Since the Tories and Labour are numerically quite similar in support, roughly half the country at any one time is disenchanted with what is being done in their name. A lot of the political programme is about undoing what their rivals did before, which is hugely wasteful of time and money. We need to move away from such adversarial politics to reasoned, scientific discourse which brings evidence to bear.

Politicians

Turning next to look at our politicians as a species, times have changed. A lot used to quite successfully combine an outside career with their duties at Westminster. This is much more difficult nowadays owing to pressures of time. A so-called 'political class' has emerged, whereby they graduate in an area such as Politics, Philosophy, and Economics (PPE) at Oxford, take jobs as Parliamentary aides and researchers, then emerge through a party machine as candidates for election as MPs. Thus they never leave the circle, or require the kind of background experience of the outside world of work that might properly qualify them to pontificate and make national decisions about it on behalf of the hapless rest of us.

There are elements in the House of Commons demonstrating, according to Nick Clegg, 'a political culture of insufferable vanity and irresponsibility' (the **i,** July 2017). He is distanced from the debating style which traditionally comes from the public schools, where 'wit, entertainment and flamboyance often win the day above seriousness, substance or content.' He cites Anthony Grayling, whose book 'Democracy and its Crisis' asserts that British democracy 'has become flabby, corrupt and hollowed out by narrow vested interests, big money and unrepresentative elites.' Significantly, not one of the emergent democracies in Central and Eastern Europe after the collapse of the Berlin Wall copied our own democratic model. Perhaps, then, its parochial guardians are blind to its many faults and too complacent about its virtues?

Immersion for long periods in the 'Westminster bubble' is, thank goodness, now increasingly regarded as an unhealthy development. But doing something constructive about it is quite another matter. Cut out their second jobs and make them concentrate their efforts might be one way. In my world you would look first at the strange lifestyle of MPs and drastically reform it. For example, they would be given a job description and become accountable for its discharge just like the ordinary employee is. Currently they do what they like – a national scandal. Secondly, hours would become, say, weekday nine- to- five like normal office workers put in, not being whipped at times of crucial votes into attending late night debates. Thirdly, duties would be rather different. Roughly half their time would be in Parliament, as the executive arm of Government, the rest working in the constituency. Gone would be their roles of debating and passing laws, now hived off to a standing organization of publicly elected experts advising the government of the day directly. Their involvement in scrutiny policy and practice, however, would be expanded, through an enhanced system of select committees covering every major aspect of national life, but with real legal teeth, not the mere ability to make loud noises of disapproval which are then ignored.

The Establishment

Owen Jones has provided a solid and weighty polemic regarding the activities of the Establishment in his book of the same name. I am anxious to derive benefit from his curative prescriptions rather than his, so far as I am concerned unexceptionable, analysis and account of its operation and its (considerably negative) effects on the public interest. Establishment ideology he finds easy to expose, regards it as a definite threat to democracy, but what does he offer by way of proposals for reform?

In line with his critique of democracy the Social Mobility and Child Poverty Commission published a report in 2014 indicting the 'cosy club' rule of the country through its public school products. This by no means new revelation was backed up by a depressing array of statistics showing the stranglehold these people have on our key institutions. Given that only seven percent of children in Britain attend private schools, how is it that only twelve percent of peers in the House of Lords went to comprehensives, over half the top media professionals were privately educated, as were a third of MPs, seventy percent of judges, and more than half of the most senior civil servants? Doubly aggravating is the assertion that we have been trying to open up opportunity for decades. Does anyone really believe it?

Jones starts by claiming that 'a democratic revolution' is 'long overdue' 'to reclaim by peaceful means the democratic rights and power annexed by the Establishment'. He admits this will be very difficult to bring about, because:

> 'in some awful way, people are beginning to give up. The Establishment has left many people resigned, devoid of hope, without a feeling that it is possible to resist.'

So as to try and build a popular movement of opposition, we first need 'a compelling intellectual case that can resonate with people's experiences and aspirations'. Secondly, the opponents of the Establishment should harness their efforts collectively instead of behaving in a fragmented manner. But apart from these practical observations, Jones retreats into providing a pen picture map of the kind of developments he would like to see happen, rather than arguing as to how they might be achieved.

Anyway, for the record his utopian vision would include the following. The unions ought to be strengthened in order to provide democratic bargaining in the workplace and a reduction in the power of bosses. This he feels is essential to restore the living standards of workers. Rail companies should be renationalized: we cannot accept their private monopoly profiteering on the back of heavy public subsidies in a false market. By positive intervention the Government could revolutionize and pump prime the green industry movement. This would form one strand of a wider strategic plan to broaden our manufacturing base and remove overdependence on the City's financial sector. At the same time we would restrict foreign ownership, establish state control over strategically vital fundamental activities like the nuclear industry, steel, shipbuilding, defence, energy, agriculture and fisheries. Taxation would be progressive and powerfully gather from the rich, backed by draconian sanctions. There would be a politically balanced press, police corruption would be combatted through a genuinely independent and external complaints body. Politicians would be barred from 'revolving doors' with business and denied second jobs. Patronage would be illegal, be it via donations or honours.

Nick Clegg, the former Deputy Prime Minister in the Coalition Government, both liberal and atheist, has called for the disestablishment of the Anglican Church of England, an event long overdue in my belief. This cosy connection goes back to the reign of Henry the Eighth, whose violent schism from the Roman Catholic Church in 1534 set up the monarch as head of the Church of England and led to much religious butchery before modern times. Conservatives, true to form, can see little wrong with these arrangements and have always opposed reform, but they seem increasingly out of touch with present day realities. We have rather a predominantly secular society in which there are many different religions, reflecting the varied origins of immigrants over the years, but the bulk of the populace do not practice any. In such a place it seems democratically inappropriate for one church among them to hold representation by right, through no less than twenty-six bishops in the House of Lords. To people like me the formal opportunity for any church to hold influence over government policy on non-church matters is anathema. Church-going and membership, though in my opinion sadly misguided, should be left as a private hobby and its organs treated by the State accordingly.

A few words ought to be said about two more Establishment institutions, although these are more extensively treated in my book 'Radical Bureaucracy'. The first is The House of Lords, the second largest governmental body in the world, with over 800 members. Many a legislature gets along quite nicely without a second chamber, but here it sticks in spite of prolonged opposition from democrats. Parliament is woefully incapable of even cutting it down to size. The Fowler report, for instance, thinks they might scrape by with just 600 members! The trouble is the entrenched vested interests and the fact that MPs like the idea of being 'kicked upstairs' to retain a cosy club membership and influence in their declining years, long after most of us have retired. So it is sustained by a kind of corrupt patronage these days in place of the positions formerly secured by inheritance.

The second institution, which might take even more shifting, is the Monarchy, because this, quaintly, enjoys the affection of large numbers of the British public, perhaps especially among women. Attitudes to celebrity seem to me mostly a malaise, and this is true par excellence of royalty. Their popularity differs according to which ones they are and it varies quite a lot over time. Nevertheless, scandal after scandal, and layabout upon layabout never strike the decisive blow against their continued opulent and publically funded lifestyle. The masses continue to swoon and genuflect.

The Electorate

The way the public at large behave is an undeniable factor in the quality of the government we receive. At the time of writing they were very disenchanted with politics and politicians in general. They had a profound feeling of being let down. Politicians have been dishonest, inept, or have otherwise failed, as it seems to them. And so, convinced that one bad lot is just like another, very many have switched off altogether. They do not vote, or attempt to keep up with political affairs, which admittedly change with great speed and complexity these days. This is very dangerous for any democracy, as extremist elements tend to fill voids.

I think there is a communication crisis too, in that what the public think at any time is mostly very imperfectly known or understood, whereas the media and the opinion poll firms think they get it. Consequently, politicians are wired into responding to what they believe, frequently erroneously, that people are thinking. Brexit is a classic case with endless unwarranted pseudo-interpretation of a collective one-day vote on a simple-sounding question.

There is a growing problem for individuals in trying two-way communication with institutions, public and private, political or otherwise. You write letters or email them and they do not reply, or send just an acknowledgement, or refer you to the internet, or deliberately evade any questions you ask, or take an age to respond at all. The internet is the ultimate cop-out. If you ask for any information in person or by telephone these days it is not long before they point you to it, thus absolving themselves as they see it of any further responsibility to help you. The onus is put right back on you to research things as best you can, assuming you have the computer resources and skills, and that the relevant sites are adequately designed and not inaccurate or commercially distorted. The sense of disconnect, the suspicion that the forces are ranged against you, the sheer frustrated feeling of impotence-these are likely reactions which become ingrained.

Regarding politics, though, part of the trouble just has to lie within the electorate itself, I regret to say. In my world something like the old subject of British Constitution and Government would be a compulsory examination subject at secondary school, not some watered down module on 'citizenship', designed to ennoble the status quo, our 'glorious' history and traditions, and to indoctrinate compliant citizens of the future with xenophobic zeal. As matters stand, we have by and large a politically ignorant and uninformed population, one where adult education classes are not offered or asked for in subjects like politics, economics, or sociology, unless for the tiny minority who are pursuing them as qualifications for their future careers.

I make a plea that the nation does not conclude from all the furore over Brexit that referenda, worthwhile democratic tools we could usefully use and develop more, are not worth the candle. That could unfortunately be an effect of the media coverage, which has been endless, speculative, misleading, and boring. What the public would do better to realize is that Brexit has surfaced a power struggle in which elected MPs through Parliament have sought to assert their will irrespective of the people's democratic majority vote and against the government of the day.

Another worry is that a sizeable portion of the electorate will switch off almost altogether from the news, the very stuff of politics, because of the endless negativity and disagreeable argumentation, as well as downright disasters, they see and hear portrayed in the media on a daily basis. Their lives are hard and miserable enough without taking on the extra burden of the mayhem seemingly going on all around them.

This is going to sound offensive to somebody, but the public en masse to an extent make it easy for politicians because of the very basic lives they lead, their simple wants and needs. Most rise little above the large mammals apart from their emotional range in that they are dominated by the nuclear family, preoccupied by food, children, and home. It is higher education which provides the threat and challenge: the more people learn how to think and acquire knowledge, the more they are liable to ask awkward and searching questions, to demand more complex things, a less material lifestyle.

A relatively recent development, in America and now here, is that Governments are being advised by generational studies from psychology. The population is divided up into age groups and the main general characteristics of each age group are profiled. So, for example, we have the 'Baby Boomers', people born in the period from 1945 to 1964, and the 'Millennials', those born between 1977 and 2000. Individuals can naturally be quite different, in views and behaviour, from the stereotype they come up with, but it is the latter that characterizes the age group as a whole, because statistically the vast majority are broadly like that. It is then but a short step to the political parties aiming to design policy options that will appeal to the particular age group of concern, like the Tories did at their October 2017 conference in trying to woo the youngest voters.

Law

What can one say about law, when the country has no written constitution to moderate the conduct of its government, no bill of rights to safeguard its people, a totally inadequate system of legal aid, so that most people cannot afford to seek justice in the courts, a judiciary unrepresentative of wider society, a whole lot of bad laws enacted by self-serving politicians, an irrational system of sentencing, clapped out prisons, and much illegitimate activity, such as raiding the firm's pension funds for private gain, not even defined as criminal.

Judges have got more influential, though it is healthy that they are also receiving closer media scrutiny and are not generally accorded public respect by virtue of office anymore. Sanctions are needed though: it should be easier to remove them. And it might help if their ranks were more representative of the public at large. Another nonsense is that their rulings do not have to pay any regard whatsoever to the likely consequences. Enslavement to the letter of the law can impede a rounded view of an issue.

The legal profession needs a bomb under it in so many ways, from its administrative slowness to its fat fees, from its remoteness from the public to its antiquated rituals and court dress codes. Our adversarial system pits one set of lawyers against another, so relative competence, rather than guilt or innocence, can be a big factor in the verdict. Clever barristers can suppress the truth and fool juries. In practice there is a presumption of guilt before trial, the very opposite of what is claimed, with salacious media and bent coppers ensuring that the innocent can rarely clear their name. Leaving Europe should eventually have a favourable spin-off in that rather few UK lawyers ever got to understand European Law, though so-called human rights are likely to suffer relatively under UK sovereignty. And too many financial and fraud cases collapse because the Crown Prosecution Service is incompetent: it does not have the money to employ top lawyers. The law allows itself to be used for political ends, such as denying new members of the Labour Party the right to vote for their leader, as happened when Jeremy Corbyn was opposed by MPs.

Law-making is perhaps the largest and most fundamentally flawed aspect. Anthony King says:

> 'the cumulative outcome is a bloated statute book and innumerable volumes of secondary legislation replete with laws, rules and regulations that are – by common consent – ill-drafted, over-complicated, totally incomprehensible, internally inconsistent, only loosely related to one another and in imminent danger of resulting in wholly unintended consequences. Provisions relating to the same matter are often scattered over a number of separate statutes.'

Clearly, we need to start again and we would have to have appropriately designed and staffed new institutions to do so. They need to be expert in law and whatever topic the law is being made about. They require independence from the judiciary, from Government, from Parliament. An elected national people's body would vet and comment on proposals for change.

Patronage

One reason for public contempt towards politics is the value system exposed by patronage. We already know, from such as the Committee on Standards in Public Life, the sort of things to do to help clean matters up. But politicians and public alike have so far lacked the necessary resolve over a period going back a generation or more. I am not going to provide here an exhaustive list of needed reforms, but will mention a few just to give the flavour of what I would hope for.

Parties, if they must be retained, have to be put on a reliable and stable financial footing so that they can be released to compete over policy and other political issues. Their monies should be equitable, limited, and state-financed from taxation to eliminate sponsorship by industry, unions, and rich donors.

Since in my world the House of Lords would not exist anymore the temptation for a prime minister like Cameron to pack it with sympathetic peers for services rendered would no longer arise.

What we do about lobbying, cash for questions, privileged access to enable undue influence on policy generally, is less clear. Except that we must outlaw them beyond formal, managed and transparent conduits, at the same time setting up quite draconian legal penalties for transgression, including future disbarment, obviously. One major reason for advocating a participative democracy in which the great bulk of the population get to use mechanisms that ensure their views are heard and heeded is to drown out, or at least cut down to size, 'lobbying' interest groups, which would otherwise and do now skew influence in favour of the already rich and powerful. So the avenues of involvement between interest group representatives (frequently private companies and charities) and government need to be codified in law, effectively monitored in action, and transparently reported on with objectivity. There are certain obvious dangers which have not yet been addressed; notably, the revolving door between appointments on either side, which lead to corrupt practices like contract preferment.

Honours are in some ways the easiest to condemn and the hardest to reform. Patronage from Premiers should clearly become a thing of the past. Under my system Royalty would have been abolished, but whilst it remains it should be removed from having any truck with, let alone being used for, formal endorsement of recipients. People rightly get cross, too, when honours are awarded to people who are simply doing the job for which they are paid. In my world we would not even have such rewards going to local long-suffering worthies, such as the elderly lollypop lady of many years standing. It strikes me there is something unpleasantly patronising about them, as if they could in any way make up for the blatant exploitation via the pittance the servile are paid. Those who toil and are claimed to be worthy of their hire should be paid a decent living wage. And while we're at it let's get rid of quaint, pathetic anachronisms like 'Order of the British Empire' (OBE). We no long have an Empire and a good thing too! The whole edifice of hierarchical awards, I regret to conclude, is riddled with deep-seated traditions of class prejudice and social division. And so it attracts my contempt not respect.

Corruption

Most countries in the world, one suspects, are politically 'corrupt' to some degree, and their people know it. But 'How corrupt is Britain?' is the title of a book and a question posed by David Whyte as its editor. He shares with me a belief that United Kingdom citizens tend to regard corruption as something that happens in other countries rather than our own. Like me he finds that Britain is nevertheless a very corrupt regime, but to argue and evidence this he first addresses the meaning of what turns out to be quite a slippery term.

He starts with the World Bank definition of corruption as 'the abuse of public office for private gain', the glaring omission being that 'the private sector is conveniently distanced from the definitional terrain of corruption'. David Beetham in the same book moves beyond this 'narrow definition' to include in addition the following concerns:

- corporate sector subversion of public officials;
- two-way appointment interchanges between business and government;
- preferential lobbying access to the ruling party by the rich and powerful;
- corporate funding of political parties in return for favours like honours;
- off-shore tax haven usage to reduce taxation in the home country;
- cover-ups of wrongdoing by politicians and officials;
- persecution of whistle-blowers;
- police collusion with journalists over gathering personal information by illegal means.

So, weighing all these elements in the equation, Beetham broadens the definition of corruption to: 'the distortion and subversion of the public realm in the service of private interests'. By this yardstick its institutional and individual scope is comprehensive, covering government, especially at national level, public bodies, the police, the banking and accounting sectors, insurance, law, media, industry and commerce.

An interesting feature is that the public seem much more tolerant of what they see instead as 'unfairness' in society, such as where top executives receive multi-million pound pay packages, when such activity, though sadly perfectly legal, could reasonably enough be deemed 'corrupt'.

All sorts of other behaviours could conceivably fall within a reasonably extended definition of 'corruption', such as wherever we fail to attain transparency from organizations, public or private, when excessive profit is pursued, prices are hiked, statistics doctored, reports are spun, partial arguments put, opponents personally rubbished, or pseudo-markets are formed with bogus competition.

I stand by this analysis in the possibly naïve hope that the public will open their eyes to what under these yardsticks should now be seen as very widespread corruption indeed in our society. I do not, however, intend to produce a full catalogue of misdemeanours, nor dwell on a cause celebré or two; examples are unfortunately all too easy to spot on any day by casual perusal of a 'quality' newspaper. What I will do, though, is to provide a few modest pointers as to where to look. So here goes.

The first place if you could shine a spotlight would doubtless be in the heart of government itself – say in 10 Downing Street between the prime minister and his political advisers. To quote the memorable book cover remark of Hilary Wainwright, it would be 'like a hand grenade blowing apart the accumulated myths of Britain as the squeaky clean 'mother of democracy'. Then you might be a fly on the wall at high level discussions within the large national and international companies. Shockingly, you would have to turn a beam or two onto the police force, since case after case has highlighted lying, cover-ups, institutional racism, false accusation. Visit the City to watch noses in the trough. Look at the fine print protecting insurance companies from pay-outs to legitimate claimants. Try to uncover systematic mass child abuse scandals within the Catholic and Anglican Churches, or in the children's homes run by, or on behalf of Social Services.

Wherever you have monopolies the lack of accountability is likely to provide too much of a temptation for somebody there – be it chronic overcharging by the 'Big Six' energy companies, or within the international cartel that constitutes the main four accountancy (and auditing) firms, or private rail companies declaring massive 'profits' whilst publicly subsidized by the taxpayer.

They are easy to find, frequently difficult to prove, of course, and liable to continue, in spite of exposure, as society signally fails, again and again, to hold these people to account in any meaningful way. That we need changes in the law to render sharp practices illegal and to make the penalties on conviction draconian seems unexceptionable. And then you realize, of course, that the most corrupt aspect of all will remain, namely the power of the Establishment to sustain it in their own interests. And you have a public culture with low expectations and its own dishonest streak never far below the surface.

One inevitable consequence of having a one-ruling party state like ours is that the powerful within it are tempted to misbehave. Since the supreme Tory value is money, it is not therefore surprising that in March 2017, George Osborne, the sacked former Chancellor of the Exchequer, announced he had been appointed editor of the London Evening Standard. He declared this was fully consistent with his discharge of duties as an MP in the Cheshire constituency of Tatton, and with the other four jobs he presently held, some extremely lucrative. Gentleman George was estimated to be receiving over one million pounds a year, as against his MP's salary of £72,000. He had no intention of standing down, declaring that it added value for MPs to bring their experiences of other walks of life to the House of Commons. To their credit the Commons Committee on Standards in Public Life reacted by announcing a review of their criteria for MPs holding second jobs whilst in office. The issues were how these other calls on time impinged on an MPs ability to represent their constituents and also whether the nature of the job was compatible with this primary role, or in conflict with it. The outcome was unresolved until a snap general election was called and Osborne at last realized, or was told, that he could not stand again…

Power is the Drug

'Power' as a philosophical concept will have to abstract from the fact that it is much and mostly discussed in life without any such reference, although scientific usage analogies abound. For instance, power is often regarded as causative in a vague sense: we talk of powerful people and imagine their influence as somehow down to their position or status without bothering to try and quantify how much might be a result of, let's say, force of personality. Then again, power is commonly said to reside in coordinated groupings of people, or institutions. Power tends to be associated with purposive acts, such as economic contract exchanges. And according to some political theorists both 'coordination power' and 'exchange power' are needed, but not all admixtures will work in a particular social context. We therefore see that the concept of power is somewhat more elusive than at first sight, especially in its origins, although it may be obvious that power (of variable situational extent) resides in heads of state, the law makers, those who dispense rulings of a court, owners and controllers of private companies, and so forth…

An important corrective to any attempt to provide salvation through politics is projected by Naim's book 'The End of Power'. The title is eye-catching, and presumably a publisher's device for selling copy, for it is not, and could never be, literally true. What it actually means is that the traditional sources of political power

– namely governments and the political establishment classes more widely – are weakening quite substantially. Naim discusses the many reasons for this and mounts a convincing argument that the trend is set to continue some way yet in the grip of a variety of forces.

He starts by characterizing power as 'the ability to direct or prevent the current or future actions of other groups and individuals'. Power is channelled typically by force, by codes of action, by advertising influence, and through rewards, though these methods mix in practice.

The book explores the decay of power – alleged to be becoming 'more feeble, transient, and constrained' – in its 'causes, manifestations, and consequences'.

Naim's analysis is entirely across the world and within all aspects of individual societies. He indicates barriers, to include monopolies, military dictatorships, single-party systems, domination by race or faith.

The cause of power decay among the powerful is said to be 'the rise of micro power', manifested by minor countries, 'non-state entities', small companies, innovators and new entrants, unfortunately including 'pirates, terrorists, hackers, traffickers, and cyber-criminals'. The fields are disparate and there are grave dangers of power becoming 'radically scattered and diffuse', to no desirable social end perhaps.

What happened, of course, is that some countries and some companies grew very big, rich and powerful. And the power of multinationals appears to have been considerably strengthened by the rise of globalization, allowing them much freedom of action to operate beyond local laws and considerably reduce their tax bills. And, not to misunderstand Naim, these 'mega players' will continue to be weighty and very influential. He does not predict their demise, certainly nothing like the 'end' of power highlighted by the book's catchy title.

Naim sees three major dynamic levers weakening big power play though; there are more people with greater mobility and a better education. Increasingly they are brassed off with the limitations imposed on their lives, as we have discussed. Non-conformity is stimulated by greater cynicism over the gap between political promises and actual attainment. There is greater awareness through media of alternatives, more selfishness and an assertive desire for self-determination and fulfilment in a rapidly changing world, which holds fragmented values and shows declining community spirit.

Within the nation we are experiencing tentative movement towards more participation in democracy, louder demands by minorities, factions, and single interest groups displacing belief in parties, clamour for more devolution from capitals to regions, from leaders to laypeople.

The analysis may be messy and too generalized, given the enormous disparate complexity of the fields of action, but as far as it goes it has much to be said in its favour. Sadly, I suspect none of us knows what to do about it. Naim's own solutions are hardly adequate, focusing as they do mainly on his perceived requirement for 'strengthening' political parties. He wants people to trust government and political leaders again, but says parties need reorganization, transparency, accountability, less hierarchy, more grass roots empowerment and young persons' involvement. This sounds naïve to me and I think he will have a job and a half to carry through a programme of such reforms. The work is a timely reminder that life is not getting any easier for politicians, but it will be dangerous if used as a defeatist excuse for our not standing up to the big battalions.

The main philosophical questions about power are ethical – who should have it, in what forms, and how much? And since there is a coercive element to power, which sometimes will need to be exercised, not merely threatened, the concept of violence is interlinked.

It has to be conceded that there remains a deal of scope in a 'free' society for strong and energetic individuals to seize 'power' in areas of life that interest them, maybe to the advantage of those close to them, but with adverse consequences for some others. It seems to me likely that the public do not tend to see anything wrong in principle here. It is probably inevitable in practice anyway.

Yet a democracy needs to set out the official repositories of political and managerial power and its limits, the open criteria and methods for choosing those in power and their removal for specified shortcomings. Especially critical are the constitutional arrangements for ensuring a clear-cut division of responsibility between those who rule (the Executive), those who make the laws, and those who punish the transgressors (the Judiciary). You will notice that this so-called separation of powers is not thoroughgoing in the United Kingdom, which for the avoidance of corruption and far more effective government urgently requires some credible elected body of experts other than the Executive to make its laws.

On the other hand I am happy with the 'split personality' of MPs whereby they have both to represent their constituency and consider national policy (from a Parliament in Central England), especially as I argue for MPs to be locally mandated.

A gaping hole, however, comes in the fact that we do not have proper constitutional principles underscoring and limiting the relative powers of government and private sector firms. This is one area that requires a great deal of attention to redress the erosion of powers from government. Companies should have to operate within a legal framework that is rather more than that relating to contract law, and which goes much further than is currently possible, so as to outlaw and punish those who exploit people and planet for socially undesirable ends.

Then there is the aphrodisiac of power. Far too many people, it seems, lust after it. They grasp it then frequently do not know what to do with it. In all walks of life, of course, there are people occupying positions of power that are beyond them, and lots more denied the better fist they could make of it. That's life, I suppose, with flawed preferment using inappropriate criteria or judgements.

However, in the political arena in particular this is a very serious matter indeed, because it is par excellence where people can succeed through the ballot box to positions in which the gulf between what is required and what they have to offer is truly staggering. Show me a person who desperately wants political office and I will probably be looking at someone quite unsuitable. This is another potential weakness of democracy oft realized. And it is hard to know what to do to remedy the tendency. Clearly, we have somehow to encourage people of quality selflessly to offer themselves to the collective cause. We are therefore probably not looking at sinecures, but at fixed-term contracts, with suitable secondments from their previous jobs, or otherwise safeguarded future employment. Entry qualifications should be a good deal tighter – they are running the country for all our sake's

– so surely we don't want every Tom, Dick or Harriet eligible to let us down.

One matter that surprises me is that the lust for power is not regarded as a mental illness to be studied and treated. It is a question of degree, perhaps, but there could be clinical judgements in effect ruling out certain people from applying for, or carrying out, a wide variety of jobs from the political to industrial management. The motivations, probably concealed, of those who put themselves forward are deserving of much closer scrutiny. After all, appropriate psychological profiles are prerequisites for candidates applying for many lesser jobs.

Mary Dejevsky, writing for the Independent in October 2012, argued, somewhat disturbingly, that 'top jobs' today might be too big for anyone. That is another dimension to the debate over the diffusion of power, though this might be more about roles being excessively demanding through their design dimensions of scale and complexity. To which she added media scrutiny and the concomitant need for incumbents to present themselves well in the face of hostile questioning. That perceived deficiency has undermined such notables as party Leaders, BBC Director-Generals and Metropolitan Police Commissioners, because instant judgements are made by the unaccountable media oiks in their lust for a scoop, even if it has to be artificially induced and dishonestly spun. Naturally, it behoves the authorities to design jobs properly. And that should never just stop at the top, by the way, as I know from bitter personal experience.

There is something else, quite profound and hugely significant, that I want to say about power. In her ground-breaking book 'Followership', Barbara Kellerman explodes the myth that we can give an accurate account by concentrating on leaders to the virtual exclusion of everyone else. Such an approach has dominated what has been written in history, current affairs, and in the textbooks on management. But this is not always an approximation to the truth. If subordinates play a part the dynamic is distorted from what is conventionally and simplistically understood to be the relationship.

Kellerman first categorizes followers into five self-explanatory types – 'isolates bystanders, participants, activists and diehards – grouped by level of engagement'. At one end of the spectrum we have the utterly withdrawn; at the other those fully active and committed. In each case they will support or oppose the leader.

She says it is difficult to apply ethics to such behaviour, as situations will dictate relevant considerations, but it is generally good to support a good leader or oppose a bad one, and conversely for what is bad conduct. It is also bad usually to do nothing, as isolates and bystanders will.

The Kellerman hypothesis is truly radical, for it shows that 'people with no apparent power, authority, or influence have an impact on those far better positioned than they'. Backing it up by insights from various subjects such as psychology, sociology, and history, Kellerman spotlights something of the importance of followers and shows it is no new phenomenon either. There is also evidence that all types of institution, even command organizations like the military with rigid formal hierarchies, are potentially affected, and that 'followers the world over are getting bolder and more strategic'. She goes on: 'They are less likely now to know their place, to do as they are told, and to keep their opinions to themselves'. Perhaps there is hope for whistle-blowers after all.

Blurring can also occur in the line between leaders and followers, superiors and subordinates. It tends to shift, with leaders sometimes following. And the growing influence of followers is aided by the new technologies, using the internet to spread ideas and opinions across vast numbers of people almost instantly. Then there are the informal networks of the workplace, which can involve the lower ranks. Crucial, therefore, can be the relationships between subordinates and other subordinates.

So, all in all, the analysis points to a democratization of power, certainly, but also, as Naim realized, to its weakening by diffusion. I think this must be the price we pay, for staff usually know these days whether their boss is up to the job, whether he wants to be there, whether he got the post on merit, by luck, or as a result of some unjust preferment, and whether he is treating his staff fairly.

Fake News?

In this brief account of power and influence, Curran and Seaton's classic textbook entitled 'Power Without Responsibility' is mentioned here owing to my conviction that the media need to be considered as a powerful influence on the public and political classes alike. I found the book disappointingly repetitive, too bound up with the (extremely complex) history of the media, and very light on newer technological developments and their consequences. It, and its ilk, are notwithstanding, important reminders, and not only for media studies students and employees either. It behoves all of us, I believe, as responsible citizens, to think long and hard as to how we achieve the optimum balance between their freedom of expression, individual rights of privacy, and the needs for security in and of the realm. That the media require major reforms, within an appropriate framework of regulatory law, is not, in the author's view, open to serious denial, unless you are a self-interested member of the media industry yourself. They know not the damage they do and seem to care rather less.

It is hardly a revelation to point out that the United Kingdom media are biased in party political terms, the newspapers hopelessly skewed in favour of the Tories and opposed to the Labour Party. Add to this the fact that the BBC, as the national television and radio broadcaster, is perennially subject to Government interference in what has effectively become a country with a single governing political party and it ought to be acknowledged by the fair-minded that the people are not properly served. Then factor in the very poor general quality of information coverage and debate, and the low-life preoccupations of the popular tabloid press generally. In my ideal world these failings would somehow disappear, yet it is very difficult to see how so long as there are journalists. The main trend in the industry currently is for newspapers to collapse financially and close. Whilst news content is increasingly available on-line it is not resolved whether enough of the public are willing to pay to keep them going.

There is also a major problem with local news. Wirral may not be a typical area when it comes to local media coverage, but it is illustrative of some of the issues. There is 'pop' music radio for teenagers, there are a couple of weekly trade newspapers full of advertisements, with a skeleton staff and journalistic reporting confined to the parochial and trivial. Television is based regionally, in Liverpool and Manchester and outside the Wirral area. Naturally it is preoccupied with the cities' concerns and individual crime or health scandals. It is likely that other parts of the country outside the large conurbations are similarly let down by lack of coverage. So it does not look as though private enterprise can be relied upon, but neither can the BBC on its track record to date. Like all public bodies it needs proper control from the outside as to its objects and performance.

Vexed questions concern conduct of the media, not least because the mass public have shown themselves incapable of maturity of attitude towards people who appear on television, or radio, or write cheap articles for the popular (gutter) press. On the one hand we need to uphold the principle of freedom of the press, for to do otherwise is to risk government not called to due censure for its actions. On the other hand, we surely require a sufficient degree of regulation to prevent abuses of that privilege. In this country the balance has not been struck. In a nutshell, politicians are too scared of the consequences of perceived repression with the backlash damage to their reputations. And so the little people in particular continue to suffer. Media in effect organize public courts, provide ready-made opinions, and condemn the innocent with impunity and without trial. Livelihoods are lost, marriages ruined, the sensitive driven to suicide, whilst the heartless media see and accept no responsibility for their own actions and are rarely called to meaningful account.

We have come to a pass now where when journalists stand trial with political aides, or police or whistle-blowers in companies, over the exchange and release of private documents, the other groups regularly receive prison terms, whereas the journalists are exonerated.

As we have seen from the foul abuses on so-called social media, the law and practice in relation to communications by computer and internet are way behind technological capabilities. People verbally abuse and threaten others with almost total impunity.

Matters should have come to a head in the aftermath of the famous Levison inquiry and report, whose proposals were largely rubbished by the press in their own self-interest argued as noble defence of our liberties. No law to enshrine privacy rights of citizens emerged in the aftermath; no stronger machinery of regulation was imposed. Though cosmetic changes came about, the new scrutiny machinery was ignored by those newspapers who so decided.

Government attempts so far to reign the media in have been spineless, indicative of a timidity born of fear rather than a principled defence of the values of free speech. Illustrative is the weak-kneed response to Levison which ducked meaningful implementation of his recommendations in the face of howls of self-interested protest. We see it time and again on television: politicians being reasonable and self-restrained (though too often evasive) in the face of nasty questions, the interviewers regularly displaying hostility, impatience, rudeness, lack of knowledge of the subject-matter and the like. What I think is needed here is for a systematic fight-back, perhaps not quite with the ferocity of President Trump. Let's see if somehow by concerted campaigns we can get news reporters and political correspondents to encounter opposition, attacks on their ignorance, destructive analysis of their questions, damage to their reputations by probing into their own personal lives, and the establishment of genuine accountability and tough sanctions for their inappropriate actions. Wouldn't it make for fun viewing if journalists could actually lose their jobs!

It is not merely journalists and unscrupulous citizens who are culpable, naturally. There was a lot of fuss, rightly, in 2015 about Prince Charles abusing his position as heir to the throne by writing clandestine letters to ministers seeking to influence government policy. One laughable example from his so-called black spider memoranda, subsequently exposed by public pressure, was his passionate defence of funding for the notorious quack 'remedies' of homeopathy. Admittedly Charles' advocacy appears to be restricted to a number of rather idiosyncratic causes dear to his heart, relatively trivial in the overall scheme of things. But it is a point of principle nevertheless and what if they had been politically charged? Where is our Constitution when it is needed?

Tony Blair used to bemoan his decision to bring onto the statute books a Freedom of Information Act, on the grounds that it had caused untold trouble to politicians ever since. Yet why, you may ask, should voters and investigative journalists not be able to find out what governments and institutions are doing ostensibly in our name? It is entirely predictable that as Prime Minister himself, David Cameron sought cross-party support for new legislative measures to veto publication of a wide set of documents. Critics, such as myself, worry that such action would render the Government less accountable and responsive. It may be worth recalling that under the Act former Labour Foreign Secretary, Jack Straw in 2009 successfully vetoed airing the contents of legal advice given to the Government when it was contemplating the subsequently ill-fated military conflict against Iraq. The matter is also important because of low morals in journalism, where some, denied access to the truth, may simply make it up, as the 2017 debates about so-called 'fake news' attest.

So what does the term 'fake news' really signify? Regrettably, in its Trump-like manifestation it is a weapon to provide an instant emotional riposte. It can be overlaid with political purpose, such as attempts to discredit the purveyors of unpalatable views or truths. Literally, of course, fake news is just made up, for whatever reason, including smoke-screening. But it becomes complicated in usage and leaves a deal of unanswered questions, notably in its relation to opinion. Media today are too long on opinions – those of their owners, editors and journalists – but they mostly do not, economically cannot, investigate stories thoroughly to separate truth from fiction, even should they be objectively disposed to try and attain balanced judgements around the facts. In this world where spin and appearance regularly take the place of reality we should all try to be watchful. Complexity and accelerating change are unfortunately making discrimination a difficult set of skills.

The Conservatives' campaign in their snap election of 2017 was a scandalous affront to the democratic process and fake in almost every way. It was breath-taking in its estimation of the gullibility and limited intelligence of the voters. Masterminded by a public relations machine behind the scene, it focused simplistically on the image and constructed personality of the Prime Minister, Teresa May. Out went the Tory policies, absent and unavailable for comment were the government ministers by and large. Obvious and superficial attempts were made using clever wording to steal the opposition ground. Teresa May fronted almost everything, in carefully choreographed and controlled televised appearances which put her among 'friends' and kept the public at bay. She refused to debate and resorted instead to repetitive and elementary claims in fed mantras such as 'strong and stable leadership'. Jeremy Corbyn, as her main opponent, was personally vilified at every opportunity, branded a Marxist throwback and an incompetent leader of a 'chaotic' Labour party. Labour's humane policies – broadly aimed at giving millions of ordinary people a better life in terms of health, housing, education, security, income, and welfare – were described either as unaffordable, or not properly costed, sometimes both. And as though to show her dependability for the nationalist Brexit cause before we started negotiations, she took sideswipes at the European Union, using tough and bellicose language sometimes personal and calculated to offend. The politically skewed media lapped it up and helped to reinforce her message.

This is a very good example of what the psychologist Stanley Cohen terms 'moral panic', by the way. It is a widespread feeling that an evil of some kind threatens society, in this case Brexit. The mass media are responsible for generating it, whether accidentally or by design. And when it happens politicians react in various predictable ways. What interests me about the phenomenon is the extent to which the problem comes to be properly discussed and then solved by active policy implementation. A useful study might take a raft of instances and try to establish the truth about what has changed after a reasonable period of time. The fact is that people tend to be fickle and therefore the media are too.

So typical punters today, or at least the busy intelligent ones among them, are switching off. Fed up to the back-eyed teeth with daily negatives from the doom and gloom merchants in the media they lack the patience to engage with it. Tired and dispirited they avoid it in favour of entertainment. Disgruntled over not being listened to by those in power they see the dangers in commentators making snap judgements based on scant information. They want information not opinion, facts not emotional outpourings, patience to await events rather than speculate in advance about them.

CHAPTER 2

THE TROUBLE
WITH POLITICS

INTRODUCTION
ENDS
Obligation
Equality
Justice
Freedom
Human Rights
Tolerance
Violence

ISMS
Conservatism
Liberalism
Socialism
Communitarianism
Marxism
Situationism
Populism
Anarchism

ACTIONS
Policy Wonks
The Art of the Possible
Can We Do It Better?

Introduction

Jeremy Paxman spent a professional lifetime interviewing politicians and their ilk, so his characterization of them in the book 'the Political Animal' must surely count for something. He claims politics by its nature attracts a lot of loners and people keen to try their luck for attention and accelerated elevation. Politics has always provided amazing possibilities for the advancement of people with very modest ability. There are also villains, in hopefully smaller numbers, as well as the psychologically disturbed. Unhappy childhoods can be a spur to seeking recognition, he thinks. We have spoken already about those who wish to change society, but opinions differ as to how many of the genuinely altruistic would–be servers of society there are. At any rate, all in all, they seem to Paxman a peculiar bunch, certainly not in any way typical of the public at large. They include a lot of hard workers, but mavericks a plenty too. Most seem to like, and be relatively good at, talking. But some use it to deceive, to plot, to climb the greasy pole by false loyalty and backbiting. Results, on the other hand, suggest that ability to actually get things done is rarer. In the end the critics liked Paxman's book, but thought that sadly he had failed to solve the mysteries of this strange breed that dares to speak for us all, whether we like it or not. I regret I cannot do so either, but hope to throw at least some light in other ways as my own book unfolds. We have identified an overall weakness in the fact that the results of our selection processes are so variable in suitability.

Speaking of which there is the perennial problem of sex, both actual and in terms of our very varied attitudes and tolerances to the practices associated with it. Parliament has traditionally had the taint of old-fashioned men's clubs, with a copious sprinkling of public school characters and chauvinistic ways. Ever since female MPs started to increase in number and display feminist ambitions for gender equality Parliament's practices have come under increasing attack. During that time social attitudes may well have changed too, although in ways not quite clear, and certainly unhelpful in their tendency to believe without deliberation what the gutter press exposes. Claims were almost all historical, alleged incidents unwitnessed, and varying from the quite legal to the quite opposite by grey degrees. As the book was being finalised the media frenzy was at a high level, the Defence Minister having resigned for unspecified conduct unbecoming, and with expectations of many more accusations, involving particularly the abuse of power by such as MPs over their staff. In this day and age it is faintly ridiculous to give over 600 MPs allowances so they can employ their own staff, no questions asked. If in place of the arrangement we had a separately administered staffing agency it could provide the central human resources safeguards so sadly lacking.

Quite frankly the situation is a mess, and one moreover that I do not see being resolved to anyone's satisfaction by internal inquiries and personal witch-hunts. As I pointed out in my Memoirs, public sector employees have been bound for years by legislation and codes of practice meted out by central Government, despite the fact that its own standards were low, its monitoring lax, and its complaints procedures for victims virtually non-existent. Like sex in the wider world, perhaps, it is only fun for long if you do things that are not generally approved of with new partners of similar taste and are not found out. Otherwise it brings misery, denies or ruins lives. I realize that this statement is itself controversial, especially for serried ranks of women, but I am, as they say, past caring what others might think on the subject, having suffered myself so much over the years by it. It seems to me we are hopelessly damaged.

I do not intend 'Manifesto' to be a work of political philosophy, with rigorously argued positions. Rather, I incline to what most other commentators now do, namely to assert my views and preferences. Nevertheless, interest in philosophy does not allow me to say nothing at all on the matter, despite widespread professional disappointment with the philosophical impact on politics to date.

The Oxford Companion to Philosophy lists no fewer than thirty-six concepts which are said to be central to any political philosophy, whatever its conclusions! Unfortunately, I have neither the ability nor the space to give a systematic and comprehensive treatment of them all. At the risk of gross distortion I will therefore just pick out a few controversial ones, which I believe to be of key importance, and give modest consideration to them in order to try and establish a coherence and consistency to my work overall. The concepts I have chosen are obligation, equality, justice, freedom, human rights, toleration, and violence.

They come with the warning preface that a merely analytical approach to political concepts is inadequate to deal with the many value issues and ends that crop up in practical politics, or with empirical questions to do with means and procedures. And further, that demarcation lines between these kinds of problem are often blurred. For instance, political concepts may not themselves be value-neutral. And the issues in any case can spill out into sociology, economics, psychology, law, history, and beyond, and are in turn partly fashioned by them.

Philosophy within its other main strands, such as theory of knowledge and metaphysics, has never escaped from its great traditions, wherein famous practitioners wrote works which raised main questions and provided definite answers and are still taken seriously and actively considered to this day. Political philosophy is no exception, so we are stuck, rightly or wrongly, with the surviving influence of even ancient philosophers who lived more than two thousand years ago. I am one of those who wished it were otherwise and that progress in the subject had decisively relegated the old masters to the history books.

Analytical philosophy often proceeds via conceptual analysis, but the method does not seem especially promising when you have something of the order of thirty such concepts, some overlapping or otherwise interconnecting. We may be able to clarify the use of terms, but the gains might be marginal given that probably no common political agreement may ever be established as to their precise practical usage.

Anyway, I shall start on my list of concepts first, before trying to link them to brief comment on the main influential ideologies, to none of which do I personally owe much allegiance, I have to admit.

ENDS
Obligation

The first concept, obligation, namely 'political obligation' is frequently taken for granted, because we are born into a society which conditions and constrains us within various boundaries of freedom to act. All societies express, imply, and behave in ways that claim we have an obligation to obey the laws, and they will exercise various modes of coercion to ensure that we do.

If we can be proven to have a political obligation to the State in which we reside it might provide a justification for the existence and authority of the State, beyond matters of pragmatic practicability, such as its uniquely placed ability to protect person and property (or, unfortunately, do the opposite). Because the State seems so pervasive and familiar we should not assume at the outset its inevitability or legitimacy.

The basis for this obligation is far from obvious. One line of thought is that as citizens we have an implied contract with the State (which invariably claims to act in our interest). But the thought can scarcely deal with the obvious attack that most of us did not actively agree to this 'contract', having little practicable option not to abide by it, since we cannot escape and have little power to oppose what we don't like about it. Most of us were born into it, after all. Similar arguments, such as Rousseau's elusive 'general will' fail by obscurity, and 'national interest' mostly by deceit.

The fairness argument, that we must have an obligation to the State if we accept benefits from it, fails the test of universality, because there will be more than a few citizens unwilling to accept the benefits, or failing to be given any, perhaps. Utilitarianism – which claims that political obligation on all is a requirement for us to receive the best possible overall outcome – fails morally because it is prepared to sacrifice individuals to the greater good. And because in practice we cannot always calculate where the balance of advantage lies. I think obligation to the State is strongly questionable at the extremes, where war has been declared, say, and citizens are therefore coerced into fighting, whether the war is just or not and regardless of whether they approved of it. In a democracy, of course, if a majority is in favour of having a State with such powers over us, that, I suppose, is that. Except we would hope powerful reasons backed it, and moral grounds as well.

For some reason early political philosophers such as Hobbes, Locke, and Rousseau tried to envisage man in a theoretical state of nature and use their assumptions about human nature to work out how we would behave. They then proceeded to argue for various political and socio-economic rules that would put right any defects. The whole project was hopelessly flawed, partly because we cannot agree on the fundamental characteristics of a state of nature. Even if we could it would be too far removed from our present situations to inform us over requisite actions. Moreover, our psychological knowledge of the human condition is still inadequate to give clear pointers to how we would probably behave. So it is not a worthwhile starting point or especially useful concept.

The talk of moral laws, and whether human beings are intrinsically good or bad, and what would follow, just cannot gain a purchase here.

The idea of political obligation gets very much murkier when we examine the nature of our dealings with friends, family, and working colleagues. Here we have very variable relationships and commitments, of course, some freely entered into, others merely tolerated, perhaps resented. Does this lead to a conclusion that different individuals may have different State obligations in different degrees, as we seem to in our personal dealings?

And what of the argument that there is no such thing as political obligation after all?If this is true, a citizen is released from any general moral duty to the State. He then has to exercise his own judgement in the situations where he finds himself, now obeying, then defying the requirements placed at his door.

So where, dear readers do I stand? Well, you may have noticed the slide in my preceding paragraph from the term 'political obligation' to 'moral duty'. Coercion is not enough. Fear may ensure compliance, but does not generate an obligation. Such would have to have a moral component, though other drivers like affection, or community-mindedness could be just as significant factors, or more so in reality.

Only one of these, namely morality (or ethics, if you will conflate the two as I do) has an elusive source of grounding beyond simple reciprocity. I conclude, tentatively, that we develop and discharge obligations to our social circle based on such human factors which occur in the way we conduct our lives, but that it is very much non-proven that there is any generalized 'political obligation' to the State beyond the limited legal obligations arising for individuals who voluntarily enter into contracts of a temporary or permanent nature with it or its organs. They will have to try a lot harder to convince me, anyhow.

R. M. Hare, the moral philosopher, says that there are sound moral reasons to obey the laws. These are that breaches will harm people's interests, that there will be higher social costs of enforcement, and that such breaches may encourage others to break the same law, and perhaps others too. All three boil down to seeing or predicting the proliferation of practices reducing the public good. They are about consequences. However, he concedes that some of these reasons 'are weakened or disappear if a law is unenforced…, or if it is observed only because people have motives independent of the law for doing what it enjoins'. And so 'reasons for obeying the law in general can be defeated by reasons for breaking it in particular cases – the exceptional cases in which there is a moral justification for crimes or acts of rebellion'.

Equality

Equality is the subject addressed by LSE Professor, Anthony Atkinson in his book. Encouragingly he does not regard rising inequality as inevitable and wishes there to be more equality than there is:

> 'It is not solely the product of forces outside our control. There are steps that can be taken by governments, by firms, by trade unions, and by us as individuals to reduce the present levels of inequality'.

He outlines a whole plan of proposals to do so, with some of the major ones as follows.

There should be a national pay policy to provide 'a statutory minimum wage set at a living wage, and a code of practice for pay above the minimum'. 'The government should adopt an explicit target for preventing and reducing unemployment', underpinned by 'guaranteed public employment at the minimum wage'. There would be 'a more progressive rate structure for personal income tax', as I argue elsewhere in the section on tax reform in the next chapter, 'with marginal rates of tax increasing by ranges of taxable income, up to a top rate of 65% (I might put it higher.) Council tax would be reformed too, making it a well-banded 'progressive property tax based on up-to-date', regularly reviewed and adjusted cost assessments, instead of the present reliance on house prices around 1993, when it was last systematically addressed. 'Child benefit should be paid for all children at a substantial rate but brought within income tax'. Atkinson acknowledges that Education reforms will also be needed to promote greater equality of opportunity.

So Atkinson's programme is about placing redistributive measures at the centre of government policy. He believes we can learn from the action taken historically at those periods when inequality came down. (Yes, there have actually been such). And it is important to prepare the ground and the electorate before embarking on what has to be very determined and sustained action. Individuals can help also 'by their own actions as consumers, as savers, as investors, as workers, or as employers'. He accepts that 'market forces may limit the range of outcomes', but is optimistic owing to our generally much better standards of living these days, and the perceived narrowing economic gap between nations in the developed and developing world.

My own concerns are that, laudable as I find Atkinson's analysis, and in awe as I am over his expertise, I fear his prescriptions, taken as an overall plan, are far too radical to be seriously entertained by a United Kingdom government in power, much less a sustained long-term programme which would need all-party support. Because alongside social security, employment and redistributive taxation, he also wants to do the same with capital and technology. Every citizen would be given some capital at adulthood and the returns on small savings guaranteed to beat inflation. He is right in his urgent call for poverty to be tackled and right also in noting the extent to which the rapidly changing economy is an egalitarian threat. But unless laws are passed making the private sector subject to the same constraints as the public sector, we will proceed, as we usually do, in the twin directions of private affluence and public squalor. The plan is much dependent on the state accumulating a massive fund via its taxation mechanisms to enable it properly to fund (without international borrowing) its social redistribution of finance. It would in the process have to take significant stakes in private companies and property, something conservative state-minimalists would be certain to oppose.

Justice

'Justice' philosophically speaking is a concept of ethics concerned with who should receive benefits and burdens, and to what extent. In my darker moments I tend to equate it with a noble, yet unachieved social ideal, one which I also regard as unattainable. We frequently see celebrated causes on the news, such as the Hillsborough Football Disaster, or historical child abuse cases, in which relatives typically campaign over many years at great personal cost in their quest for 'justice'.

My cynical reaction is to say that the major organs of the state, administrators of the law included, conspire to cover up, to counter allege, to fail to prosecute, to fail to compensate, in short generally to lie and cheat and delay so that what the victims and their relatives are able to extract in the way of so-called 'justice', if anything at all, is but a pale imitation of the ideal. There remain, too, the serried ranks of the complicit whom the law does not touch. The reforms necessary to obviate case after case coming forward are largely obvious and almost invariably ducked or diluted, for the established forces of evil are just too entrenched and our culture as a whole not sufficiently activated, its selfish values mostly lying elsewhere.

The theorists differentiate types of justice. Typically, these are 'retributive' and 'distributive' justice. The former is concerned with moral arguments for punishment of wrong doing. Distributive justice is about the moral suitability of apportionment of benefits and burdens to recipients. A branch of this later is sometimes called 'corrective justice', as the ethics of compensation are applied.

But what is crucial here to characterizing an 'injustice' is where people are treated unequally without adequate reason for the discrimination. What is not always clear, or agreed, is adequacy of reason. Moreover, the justice principle sometimes has to be weighed against other ethical and non-ethical factors of relevance.

A perennial problem with value ethics is that values impinge.

John Rawls' twentieth century book 'A Theory of Justice' has been very influential with political philosophers, for and against. He sets out two principles. The first, and prior in hierarchy, asserts rights for all, to be equal over a large range of basic freedoms. That is why equality is maybe logically prior to justice, since deviations from it are seen as a mainstay of unjust treatment claims. The second principle attempts to give a basis for legitimate deviations from equality. This would give greater benefits to the most disadvantaged, but the justification Rawls gives is the highly dubious, hardly moral one, in which he claims everyone would chose this outcome out of self-interest if placed behind 'a veil of ignorance' before they knew their relative positions in society. I have hinted in the above account at some obvious points of attack on this left-leaning work (apart from the fact that it is left-leaning which some would sadly find obnoxious enough). The scenario is an artificial construct which, if true, would surely brook little opposition if introduced and enshrined in law? Except that we know very well it would.

While the Rawls position is undoubtedly prominent, it is far from the only criterion attempting to justify differential rewards. Other better known ones we use ourselves when it suits an argument are effort, need, ability, historical tradition even. So this is one point at which the theory lets us down. We would hopefully aim to be consistent, but there seems no bedrock position to be found.

Given the plethora of sometimes mutually incompatible values behind these arguments about what constitutes justice in given contexts, it is easy to become attracted to pluralist solutions. One such is by Michael Walzer. He claims, as his book title has it, that there are 'Spheres of Justice'. These are complex departures from equal treatment legitimated by the nature of their own individual social sphere. Multifarious 'goods' are produced and distributed in ways peculiar to the given sphere and its traditions, but subject to social change, over domains such as finance, health, education, family, political constitutions, law, and so forth. We are up against incommensurables and rapidly altering complexities, viewed through the filters of human ideology and value preferences. They cannot be unravelled to everyone's satisfaction. Which is nevertheless not to say that we should give up on heroic striving to create a better society in this regard.

Freedom

Freedom is one of the supreme virtues, they say, of living in a democracy. We are at liberty and can decide our own destiny. Thus, subject to minimal constraints, we can say and do what we like, go where we wish. This is obviously supposed to include choosing our jobs, friends, and marriage partners. There is a very big proviso – we are only morally free to act in ways that do no harm to others, a more difficult outcome to be certain of than it might at first sight seem. So the question arises as to whether people, left to their own devices, will generally behave morally or no. And if the answer is not, some kind and degree of restraint by the State is presumably legitimized in the interests of society at large. Justifications will thereby tend to vagueness. Which is what political manipulators love. When politicians are stuck for slogans, 'freedom' is one of those noble-sounding and rousing terms that can be bandied about to positive effect without much risk of a fuller examination. Nowhere will you find such ideas as existentialist doubt – that agony of indecision when you are at liberty to do what you like, but also have the burden of responsibility for your choices.

It is therefore straightforward after all this time to work out that freedom of action will not deal with the problems of inequitable distributions of wealth and property. How could it, when we can all feather our own nests within the confines of very liberal laws?

Human Rights

Ruth Putnam considers human rights and the liberal tradition. She carefully distinguishes human rights from those provided by law, those by virtue of exercising some office or work, those of individuals arising from contracts and wills. Human rights proper, also called natural rights, are those said to belong to all persons by virtue of their common humanity. Historically, the list of such rights will include 'life, liberty, property'. Their claimed justifications are either religious (they are supposedly God-given), utilitarian (for the maximizing of public good), or merely that they are self-evident (which is an intellectual cop-out).

Liberal politicians have traditionally supported three human rights in particular – 'property, equality before the law, and equal participation in the political process'. Of these, the last was perhaps the most contested. Putnam's survey concludes that 'the moral issues which advocates of rights of persons seek to deal with are complex'. She then looks at the right to life, which she says is the most basic right you could claim. If not that, then nothing would qualify. Yet this right, if right it is, is far from being universally observed. In our own culture for instance many agree with the death penalty for murders and see no objection in principle to the notion of sending its soldiers to war. Even the moral primacy of the right to life has been denied among human rights advocates. We are left with the realization that rights-claims are heavily context-dependent, which was not part of the original meaning of universal entitlements.

As time goes on, human rights claims are elaborated, leading to the risk of conflicts between them and to less commonality of agreement among supporters. Moreover, the liberal assumption of equality is false. It is always equality in some respect only and the individualism fostered by liberals leads inevitably to the capitalist society with it vast inequalities. Admittedly, liberals would claim social progress has been achieved in such areas as outlawing slavery (not unfortunately the same as eradicating it) and allowing votes for women, but since liberalism rests on false assumptions it cannot serve us for the future, according to Honderich, a sentiment I share. To me human rights do not exist in any natural way, but are social constructs variously enshrined in actual laws.

We are getting close to freedoms here, so it is to the topic of civil liberties, regarded as a very important branch of the human rights movement, that we now must turn. Thomas Jefferson's excellent definition of freedom will be our working principle: 'Rightful liberty is unobstructed action according to our will within limits drawn around the equal rights of others'. It can therefore be seen that laws and deterrents are needed to ensure that as individuals we do not transgress the boundaries such a creed would obviously impose for the greater good. So far so reasonable. But, as we know, in all societies there are restrictions on civil liberties enshrined in law that may be greater than those that would strictly be necessary to safeguard Jefferson's principle in practice. How are they justified? Tom Head explains there are three main ways the attempt is made:firstly, to protect us from harming each other, actually or potentially; secondly, to act as caretaker for society; thirdly, to produce a certain kind of society.

Now in my estimation we would be foolish to accept without fuss anything brought in beyond the needs of the first argument, that of our protection. Once we get into the second and third reasons we find politicians, who usually represent a minority view, trying to shape society in ways and into forms that the democratic majority do not want. We have to be watchful that our liberties encompass both (negative) freedom from various constraints and (positive) freedoms to act in certain ways. Anarchy at one end and State repression at the other are the extreme and obviously dystopian results of negative and positive freedoms respectively, so it is at least clear that we need to be somewhere between if we are to live in a just and balanced society. The tragedy is that theory runs out without giving us exactitude on where we should be. There is sadly much scope for political argument and a wearisome ebb and flow of actual liberty based on endless tinkering with the law in accordance with the power, fads and fashions of the moment.

Civil Liberties pose questions of achieving a happy balance between individual freedoms on the one hand

and community security on the other. A key problem with this in Britain is that the main political parties believe in civil liberties to quite different extents, the Liberal Democrats perhaps being the keenest, the Tories the most willing to sacrifice the 'sacred' principles. Another difficulty for the civil rights movement comes at times when the country feels especially threatened, such as in the aftermath of a major terrorist atrocity.

I have long favoured a Bill of Rights and Responsibilities, to be written as a main plank of a national Constitution. This would obviously have to rehearse values, but would emphasize both individual rights and our civic duties. The latter are rarely dwelt on, but it is worth reminding ourselves, following our opening concept of 'obligation', that there are responsibilities like the payment of taxes, a general obedience to the law, willing participation in voting, jury service, looking after the well-being of any children, disabled, and elderly in our care, respect for the environment, fair and equable treatment of our fellow citizens, and so forth.

By the same token we should be entitled to justice under the law, no imprisonment without trial, no false arrest or long detention, trial by jury, private communications (subject to certain judge-directed exceptions for particular persons) and a general presumption of innocence unless and until proven guilty. We should be entitled to expect that, by and large, the national forces of law and order will keep us safe from property crime and personal violence.

Some would say that we can take all these conditions for granted in Britain, but that is regrettably not the case. In fact the loss of our rights and freedoms are only too easy without the constant vigilance of the relevant campaigning voluntary groups, as policy ebbs and flows, as government reacts to ever changing events. Civil rights are constantly under attack. They are fragile and may need to be won again and again.

I shall talk a little about 'human' rights next. It is somewhat ironical after the Brexit vote that we ought to be looking to Europe for this. As I said before, I do not believe in natural law, so there is a sense in which none of us have any rights, but the trick is to enshrine in law the ones we find most beneficial. Now the European Social Charter, ESC, is not fully incorporated into United Kingdom law, but should be regarded as a civilized starting point, because it gives us among other virtues the rights to protection of health, family, social, legal and economic entitlements, housing, no poverty or social exclusion, free state primary and secondary education, affordable, quality child care, finance for carers, safe, secure and healthy working conditions, fair pay.

Obviously there are other elements of similar ilk and not all the ones listed above are absolutes, some being (disputable) matters of degree, such as what constitutes a living wage, or the extent to which legal aid should be free. Other noble principles take the form of aims which might be difficult to bring about and enforce, like the protection of personal reputation under unfounded allegation, which would require considerable fettering of the much-vaunted free press.

So freedom of expression will now be dealt with under this concept as a final issue. For speech and the written word, Stephen Norris makes a distinction between 'equal speech' and 'freedom of opinion'. As Honderich explains it, 'the first has to do with who expresses an opinion, the second with the opinion itself'. What may seem at first not especially significant Norris claims otherwise: 'the accelerating degeneration in the quality of political discourse in 'free' societies is motivation enough'.

Regarding the first freedom of opinion, Norris finds in favour of the arguments in its defence that:

> 'in suppressing an opinion we run the risk of suppressing something true… (and) …it is undesirable that the truth be suppressed'.

Although he admits:

> 'it is far from clear that with respect to every conceivable truth, general knowledge of it would be more desirable or beneficial than ignorance'.

On the other hand Norris considers that the concept of equal speech 'needs to be re-evaluated, and perhaps rejected'. He cites the danger of abstraction, which can make matters seem reasonable when they are not. Norris remarks on the obvious fact that the speech of an expert is of superior worth (on a topic on which he has expertise) than that of an ignoramus, or just somebody whose own expertise lies in another domain. As he so aptly puts it:

> 'What rights should we suppose generated in the multitude of cases where it is in no one's interest, or in the interest of only a few, that decision be left to the haphazard divinations of incompetence?'

He looks at types of speech in relation to 'kinds of subject, circumstance and function'. We should not treat 'putting forward an idea, without argument or evidence', on the same footing as 'advocating a policy which is likely to affect the lives of millions'. He proposes that:

> 'the general category of speech…must give way to the results of a more refined analysis if we are to enable ourselves to adopt the frame of mind necessary for considering the possible benefits of abandoning the principle of equal speech'.

He asks 'where do we draw the line?' and concludes, unhelpfully at the last, 'that there are many lines to be drawn'. And so, as I hope my commentary demonstrates, we are in a semantic fog and likely to remain so.

Tolerance

This is a live-and-let-live philosophy which sees peaceful co-existence amongst people with profoundly different values and beliefs. It now extends way beyond religious and political issues to encompass moral disputes quite generally. Some of its main arguments of justification are the fact that we can ourselves be wrong, there is a richness in variety, we are respecting individual entitlements to be different, and thirdly the price of conflict in society is too high to pay.

Such toleration or tolerance is frequently a matter for discussion in the United Kingdom over sex, religion, and race, given the multicultural nature of our population following periods of large-scale immigration from contrasting parts of the world. It is quite possible, both in principle and practice, for disputes to occur over the requirements of toleration in these different areas of life.

My particular concern relates to where to draw the line. We may usefully start here with John Stuart Mill, who provided the harm criterion for legitimating intolerance. Of course, we need to agree on what is harmful first before we can use it, but we may question the assumption of tolerance being the usual appropriate mode of conduct even where no harm can be demonstrated and precisely for that reason. Feminists probably do just that when they attack pornography, for example. Clearly, dispute will be hottest on those topics where there is deep moral disagreement. Harm is at its trickiest when we weigh in the balance alleged mental harm, especially as people's sensitivity and resilience differ so widely and there is an extent to which you can choose how something affects you.

Tolerance is one thing, relatively easily conceded sometimes where it is merely a matter of one opinion being in opposition to another in a world of ideas. But when that opinion is then subject to political enactment into actual practice, tolerance can become a deal harder as people believe that harm is being done, that we are retreating from whatever vision they have of a desirable society. You have only one life: you don't want to have to live it in a country whose practices and values you despise. Take it from me: the lot of outsider is rarely a happy one.

Violence

This is the odd concept out in our list in that it constitutes means not ends. In general there ought to be a powerful (amoral) predisposition against violence as a way to secure ends, however noble, because it offends against humanity. There are many practical arguments against it too. It rarely wins hearts or minds, it can be time-consuming, costly, have unpredictable outcomes, cause physical and mental agonies, and it is a waste of lives.

At the level of nation states war is appealed to as a way to attain political purposes. My almost invariable preference is for peaceful settlements of conflicts instead, and where these cannot be achieved, that the problems be dropped as intractable. The sole exception I would brook is when it is a matter of stark choice between survival and death – this could be seen as the 'just war'. My analysis is admittedly not underpinned by universal natural law or human rights, neither of which has successfully been morally grounded.

If I say this of the interstate behaviour of countries, so much more so is it appropriate to oppose terrorist groups and individuals in all their forms. Since terrorism is completely intolerant, so it must be opposed and overcome by violence without the tolerance earlier discussed. This is the second kind of 'just war' perhaps. Put bluntly, if we are faced with an ideology that says we should be killed (because we are not true believers, or for any other reason) then self-preservation requires an intolerant response. We do not therefore seek to prosecute such people by due process of law. We do not seek to convert them from their indoctrinated beliefs. We summarily kill them before they kill us.

'Coercion' will here be dealt with alongside 'violence'. We do not usually call it violence when the State acts against individuals, but it is either violence or the threat of it nevertheless. Obviously, for there to be coercion potential action or other adverse consequence must be held over the person coerced and there must exist the power to bring it about in the absence of compliance. In practice it will be almost impossible to keep a moral element out of the equation. Even if the coercion is entirely sanctioned by law there will be those who morally disapprove of it. Typically, the coercion is considered inappropriate in kind or degree. Finally, I leave out of discussion coercive situations in which the cause is not of human agency; someone may be ill, for example, or unable to travel because of bad weather.

Ted Honderich has famously written on violence, with partial defences of it by individuals in particular situations. A key argument against violence, of course, is the idea we have already discussed that we all have a social contract with the State which includes an obligation on us to obey the laws. Honderich disputes the reality of a social contract, saying, as I do, that we never willingly signed up to anything, but were thrown into a society with very little choice or powers of resistance. The law-abiding requirement stems from the practical need for us to behave in peaceable ways, so we can mostly all rub along together. He cited another argument against violence, moral necessity, which covers prohibitions on all sorts of behaviours that society could not properly function with. The trouble with this, is that if moral necessities existed (and it would have to be demonstrated), they could and sometimes would conflict. It is frequently held, therefore, that violence may be justified to avoid a larger evil, say the reduction of 'great misery and great injustice'. So civil disobedience has its uses, methinks.

ISMS

If the sort of political theory discussed above were adequate to the task we should be able to take its findings as unambiguous pointers to political practice. Unfortunately, it falls short, as we have seen. Most certainly, it has not prevented a variety of political ideologies springing up and being influential. We shall therefore now turn to their brief characterization before evaluating them in the light of what lessons from theory we may have derived. Each has a vision of society its proponents wish to see realized, so that will be one obvious place to look for clues. The ideologies often mix in ends and means, adding to confusion.

Conservatism

I want to deal with Conservatism and its underlying philosophical ideas before I continue with this book because the Conservative Party is now so powerful and politically entrenched in the United Kingdom that, in effect, we have a one-party State with it in charge for most of the time. And yet the Conservative Party has a broad range of opinion within it – we saw that over their Brexit divisions – so it is important that we come to understand what is going on here for that reason also.

In its literal meaning you might think that Conservatives are all about resisting change. They like the status quo, have a reverence for our traditions and institutions. However, that is not the experience of any of us who have lived under the drastically reformist Thatcher or later Tory leaders, like Cameron and May. Which prompts a suggestion that the name of the party does not constitute one of its bedrock principles after all. One that does echo its thoughts is their respect for a kind of established order that has developed historically over many years, honed on the trials and errors arising in previous generations. They will use a (probably bogus) appeal to a shared identity and culture, of ways of doing things. They usually abhor constitutional change. It is perhaps an oversimplification to equate this group with the Establishment, but there is much in common, including a protection of existing hierarchies in the private sector.

On the other hand many Conservatives are also reformers. They distrust planners, however, fearing the unintended adverse consequence. Especially where things can seem to be running well, they may be reluctant to embrace major change. They can appear complacent over what seem to others obvious faults in society.

A lot of them want to reduce the scope of involvement of government, being content to set up a framework of law and policy within which private firms can operate very loosely regulated free markets, seen by them (erroneously) as the most effective model for the economy. They castigate public bureaucracies (other than their own) as sapping of energy and initiative.

Naturally they are only human: some are not above being opportunist, adopting positions and policies that they think will have widespread popular appeal. This is always likely with any ruling party when it does not enjoy a safe voting majority in the Commons.

The philosopher Ted Honderich has written a coruscating critique of Conservatism in his eponymous book. He saw their ideology as:

> 'the defence of the particular kind of property-rights most useful to entrepreneurial and efficiently acquisitive persons, and to persons already owners of large things, and to others whom these two categories of personnel choose to benefit, above all their children. There is opposition to the principle of equality – that we must

make well-off those who are badly off by effective policies, including transferring goods from the well-off to the badly off and also reducing demands for rewards or incentives by those who do contribute more to the means of well-being'.

With the Conservatives it is especially important not to consider so much what they say as rather observe what they do. All parties, and all people, are selfish in some degree: it is human nature. But, according to Honderich, the Conservatives are nothing else. 'Conservatism is based on no moral principle'. To serious critics like Honderich Conservatism is immoral self-interest, influenced by superstition about the wisdom of the ages rather than the application of a modern scientific rationalism. It has led to obscene inequalities and a cruel desire to crush the welfare state. I would concur, having personally suffered all my life from the anti-aspirational effects of their policies, especially in the public sector workplace. They say they are the party of aspiration. My advice would be to avoid working in the public sector if you aspire, as they do not cater for it there.

Liberalism

Liberalism needs to be characterized and considered, given its standing as a major political ideology, albeit one that has not held numerically strong national voting power in the United Kingdom since the days of Lloyd George early in the twentieth century. Their advocates press for civil and political rights for the individual, which necessitates a substantial range of personal freedoms over areas like expression, occupation, association, and sexuality. In other words, it neutrally accepts pluralism and demands a framework of toleration of competing opinions. Notoriously, though, this much-vaunted freedom is said by critics to be mainly about creating an unfettered capitalism, where property rights are strongly protected by law, albeit there is supposedly equality of opportunity (not enough to make the difference.)

So freedom would need a philosophical underpinning, and one which explained why it is valued as trumping community values. It is also far from clear that a pluralist society, with its myriad individual views, would be stable. How could it find sufficient common ground to meld its citizens into a sort of purposive collective enterprise, involving some obligations to the State? If nationalism is out, could the shared commitment to individualism be enough of itself? Not all liberals think so and neither do I.

Nick Clegg, the former Deputy Prime Minister in the Coalition Government, wrote of his experiences in the book 'Politics Between the Extremes', a characteristically candid account of his successes and failures. First of interest to me were his notions of liberalism as a former Liberal Democrat Party leader. He conceded that it is 'out of step with the populist mood of our times', but defended it as 'a rational, reasoned political creed'. He saw liberalism as 'a philosophy of enlightenment, of head not heart'. He went on to say that 'liberals believe in evidence, reason and logic', admitting that these were 'hardly the best tools to pack an emotional punch'. On the practical side 'liberals seek to reform our lopsided electoral system, spread competition, devolve power'. But many of the outcomes of liberalism in practice cannot presumably be anticipated, because he explained an approach based on what I see as scientific principles:

> 'the politics of reason rests on a belief in the value of scrutiny and debate. It therefore requires an open state of mind, not a closed mantra of certainties. It requires a continuous acceptance that one's opinion could be wrong'.

The values liberalism seeks to promulgate are: 'liberty, tolerance, equality before the law, compassion, internationalism'. He sees it as hopeful (and I see it as ironical and ridiculous) that British Society has become more 'liberal' in outlook, on such matters as race, gender, lifestyle choices, respect for other faiths, whilst simultaneously reducing the Liberal Democratic Party to near oblivion at the polls.

Socialism

'Socialism' is these days so often a term used in a derogatory manner. This is unfortunate, for it has at least the following noble elements:

- justice founded on egalitarianism,
- the use of rationalism and empiricism,
- the aim to free people,
- community spirit and cooperation,
- public participation.

It is moot where a description of socialism should start, but I will do so with R. H. Tawney, who was a left-leaning Oxford University academic who split opinion during the first half of the twentieth century. His brand of socialism was driven by Anglican Christian beliefs and experiences in the trenches during the First World War. Teaching at the newly formed Workers' Educational Association, WEA, he wrote books across broad, but connected fields such as economic history, social welfare, and religious ethics, as well as education. Some of his ideas radical then are commonplace now. For instance, in his famous book 'Religion and the Rise of Capitalism' he looked at the economic developments of the 16th and 17th centuries, concluding that the pursuit of materialism had reduced the impact of morality. He had an uneasy relationship with the established church, though, coming to believe that they pulled their punches in the defence of 'goodness'. He thought it always needed nurturing and defending; charity he supported, but realized it was not enough of itself to provide social justice for the poor. That would require the right kind of structural changes for the making of a democratic society.

Perhaps needless to say nowadays, he opposed selfish individualism and inequality. His works were foundation stones for the Welfare State that Atlee's government created after the Second World War, albeit that took place within the acquisitive materialist framework that Tawney despised. He was weaker on the methods by which society should be changed, vacillating between guild socialism, gradualism, and revisionism. Nevertheless, and somewhat depressingly, his analysis remains accurate for the present day, the many adverse and destructive elements of capitalism still holding sway despite their devastating cost to the underclasses. On the other hand, any move towards a more socially responsible society is unlikely to be underpinned by Christian beliefs as such in our increasingly secular age.

Some people say that Anthony Crosland's 1956 book 'The Future of Socialism' was the bible of the left wing in Britain. Unfortunately, it probably still is, its agenda largely unaddressed in the intervening years, its thinking never definitively updated, although attempts have been made, notably by Peter Hain. The book was informed, as in my view it must be, by a range of disciplines across the social sciences, but interestingly, and in a way like Habermas, he claimed that sociology:

> 'rather than the traditional fields of politics and economics (is where) the significant issues for socialism and welfare will increasingly be found'.

He then looked at a good range of policy areas, such as education (he was the Minister under the Wilson Government), social welfare, industrial relations, and the economy.

Crosland's time came after the post-war Attlee Government had established the Welfare State. Living standards were rising and the owners in business were no longer running industry. It was the period when professional managers really began to take over and productivity was doing well. So in that context he concluded that Marx's prediction that capitalism would collapse had been disproved. He was inclined correspondingly to believe that the actual ownership of the means of production was not especially significant after all, probably a fatal error in our later age of foreign ownership of essential industries.

Crosland made the distinction between ends and means a bedrock principle. 'Ends' were non-negotiable because they represented outcomes underpinned by core values. 'Means' on the other hand were the methods required, be they policies or institutions. He came to conclude that means were much more subject to pragmatism, so that, for example, nationalization and public ownership might or might not be appropriate; it would depend on the conditions at the time rather than be the ideological commitment most associated with the left wing. (This is my view too, although tempered with a moral lens).

What was important was to reduce inequality 'enough to minimise social resentment'. The agenda was about improving welfare, ensuring a fair distribution of rewards, equality of opportunity, and reductions in 'class stratification' as well as reducing barriers to, and improving channels for, social mobility. All very laudable, say I, except that too benign readings of the status quo at any particular time lead to a complacency about current norms being the desirable ones and make it all too easy to rule out wealth redistributions. The weakness, essentially, is that people's evaluations of what is reasonable and just will differ so much.

Whilst generally lauded as impressive, and certainly relevant for a generation thereafter, Crosland's analysis was in some ways limited and in others flawed, as hindsight easily shows us. In the latter camp sadly has to be his underestimation of Conservative opposition and his over-optimism about economic prosperity; among limitations the fact that he did not apply his principles to the international dimension.

My treatment here is largely due to the perceptive expertise of Giles Radice, formerly Labour MP for Durham North. 'Revisionism' is the word used to describe Crosland's approach to Socialism. We always need to look behind the dogma and its message to observe what is actually happening. Applying this frame of mind, it can be seen that our stance at any given moment must be a provisional one, subject to frequent adjustments of method in accordance with change, but always consistent with our guiding system of values. This is a useful and timely lesson, but it takes us only so far. It does not begin to solve the problems of the age.

When we jump forward to contemporary times we can see what is claimed to be a much more radical and left wing agenda, as broadly outlined in Jeremy Corbyn's Ten Pledges. Set out as slogans to comprise an agenda for social change, they state as follows:

1. full employment and an economy that works for all;
2. a secure homes guarantee;
3. security at work;
4. secure NHS and Social Care Service;
5. a national education service, open to all;
6. a secure environment;
7. the public put back into our economy and services;
8. income and wealth inequality cut;
9. an equal society;
10. peace and justice at the heart of foreign policy.

The subsequent Labour Manifesto for the 2017 surprise general election is a much more comprehensive treatment of society's ills and how to overcome them. Entitled 'For the Many, not the Few' it sets out a plan for reform, using progressive taxation, which would renationalize rail and mail, as well as the energy companies and the water boards.

Now I treat these Labour themes at more length in the relevant parts of my present book, for what we have above is far too vague. But what I want to emphasize here is that this is not a 'radical' programme, where 'radical' is a word to be disparaged. It is not a matter of being extreme, it is not 'reds under the bed', nor is it complete either. It is clear, for example, that key elements of society are untouched by the ten pledges. To name but a few such, a comprehensive plan would also have to include major constitutional reform and an adequate and integrated multi-mode transport infrastructure proposal. Nationalization could also be extended, for example to the basic industries of steel and shipbuilding. Perhaps all these are intended to come later.

The agenda is nevertheless ambitious, being such a long way away from present realities. It is easy to sense the hopelessness of it all for those like me of a pessimistic inclination. It seems to reinforce what I have long suspected: that, apart from left-inclined theorists and the genuinely altruistic, Socialism is not our natural home, but something we may come to from extreme conditions of oppression, when we temporally decide to align our forces. In divided, fragmented, and antisocial Britain I can see the sentiments working piecemeal, small-scale, temporary, driven by issues, in small social enclaves. And only there.

There is something else. My partner is good at making up words and she coined the verb 'squalidifying', whose meaning is fairly obvious. Its applications to our society are patently legion, ranging from the muddy fields at pop concerts and other summer events to the drug culture, and the littering commented on in the chapter on Saving the Planet. But my partner was specifically referring to the unfortunate and seemingly endlessly repeated phenomenon of trashing our dwelling places. Typically a problem family lives in straightened circumstances. The residence becomes squalid. Nobody lifts a finger to improve it. There are thousands like it across the country. Eventually, even by our abysmally low national standards, it is deemed unfit for human habitation. The family is rehoused by the Council. The cycle of tearing down begins again. So it seems to me that Socialism fails by another yardstick, even though it is more geared to helping such people than the other parties are. It has no answer to the problem. So ultimately this is one of the big excuse arguments the Tories will use for not providing help – the resources tend to be wasted because there is not enough mending of ways.

Communitarianism

Communitarians believe in building strong and moral communities with a higher emphasis on group rather than individual needs. As Michael Walzer does in his 'Spheres of Justice', Communitarians are thus inclined to attack orthodox liberalism: individualism tended to crowd out the 'common good' (an elusive set of conditions, I have found, incidentally). Liberalism is also universalistic, whereas Communitarians tend to focus on small and local communities with their own traditions and practices. 'No man is an island', say the Communitarians, meaning that part of the liberal's individual 'identity' is in fact partly a function of his social roles. Carried forward it is not clear what precisely would emerge other than a diversity of communities. And without a clear moral force, presumably grounded in other principles, where is their critical evaluation of those communities that are dysfunctional or otherwise undesirable? A related weakness is that some people can suffer oppression in multicultural groups. It is telling to note that there is no political party in the United Kingdom specifically devoted to a thoroughgoing Communitarianism, which is more likely to be found among opposition parties in totalitarian East European States.

Marxism

We will start with Karl Marx, whose work has variously been classified as a phase called 'Scientific Socialism' (wrongly, for it is not scientific) and Communism, which describes a (utopian) classless State, whereas many Marxists do not believe society will evolve that way.

There are a lot of problems with Marx, which is to make a massive understatement. Fundamental is that he is regarded as the original source of the left-wing thinking which provided an intellectual 'foundation' for Communism. So to the extent that he was wrong they have a problem. Secondly, whatever his good points – and they may be considerable – he was an historical figure living at a time quite different from our own. Thirdly, the British media have shamelessly rubbished him for years; so much so, in fact, that it is well-nigh impossible to consider him objectively. They usually make no distinction at all between Communism and Socialism, for instance. Fourthly, we are used to pigeon-hole ideas, whereas Marx's thought covers ground now 'belonging' to a variety of separate academic subjects, notably economics, history, and sociology, as well as the politics most people associate with him (much of which was in any case contributed by his collaborator Engels).

Marx does us a service in emphasizing the history of societies as that of class struggle, even though contemporary

British politicians like to play down the concept for their own purposes. The trouble is that Marxism has been abused by unscrupulous tyrants to design disastrous economies and repressive Communist States, so there is more than a danger that it will be dismissed, irrespective of its merits, on that account alone.

Nevertheless, we should not turn away from his critique of Capitalism so readily, for it contains a withering indictment of many features that beset us today, and could therefore be used in any serious plan for remediation. Some of the elements will now be set out below.

Marx pointed to the capitalist tendency to generate specialized jobs for economic efficiency, so alienating workers, who felt disconnected because their own contribution was unseen or largely unrewarded. Jobs are insecure because firms are unstable in a changing and competitive environment, so people are treated as expendable, regarded more like commodities.

His polarized contrast is, of course, between rich capitalists owning the means of production, and poor workers, who have nothing to sell but their labour. This leads to extremes of inequality, and a profound sense of resentment among the workers. Their lives are governed by these economic forces outside their control and they are uncaringly exploited.

Moreover, Capitalism faces an endless serious of crises, says Marx. For example, whenever we have consumer surpluses, some workers are no longer needed in production, so unemployment rises.

According to this bleak assessment, adverse social effects are also inevitable. Marriage, for instance, becomes an economic contract, overlaying affection with dependence. And feminism is no remedy, as it merely gives women the same kind of economic problems as faced by men.

A lot of this characterization of Capitalism should strike a chord of familiarity if we are honest, whereas it is also easy to see that much of Marxism is just plain wrong, of course. For a start it is unworldly, utopian in its claim that history will automatically follow an economically determined path to a classless society, where the wealth is collectively owned (and the problems of a life of toil solved). In that regard it seems naïve, the 'end of history' by another route than laissez-faire liberalism, the more so perhaps since Marx also claimed his thinking constituted a science. Whereas we now know that there are no major laws of historical development of any kind, and that in consequence Marxism has little predictive value with regard to the nature of future societies after all.

It is to some a pity. His claim that Capitalism is doomed can be mocked and resisted with ease by those with a vested interest in its survival, and in much its present form. His adoption of the Hegelian doctrine of the 'dialectic' – that progress is the consequence of internal conflict – may well be partly true in that politics is never free from dispute and dissent, except that it begs the important question as to whether progress (in a socio-economic and political sense) is actually possible, never mind being systematically pursued.

If in the dialectic, 'thesis' and its opposite 'antithesis' must invariably be present, and come together to fight it out, leading inevitably to a new 'synthesis', can we really swallow the mechanics as <u>the</u> universal way? Can we then accept that Capitalism must be doomed because it embodies its own antithesis? Would that not then be true by the same argument of any thesis whatsoever?

Where it might be more constructive to dwell could be in examining the concept of 'alienation'. Marx contends that the capitalist system alienates us from bosses, from other workers, even from ourselves, since work is a depersonalized activity for most, instead of being creative and life-enhancing. This should be a grave concern to capitalist bosses and owners, because a discontented workforce has the potential to be less productive, more troublesome. And where the quality of life is poor, or merely not worth the effort needed to acquire it, social problems and pathologies are inclined to manifest themselves well short of political opposition or mobilization of resistance. (Marx famously predicted revolution, but so far Britain has avoided it, though others have succumbed as close by as within the continent of Europe).

Whilst it is well-known that the concept of alienation arose out of Marx's analysis of the severance between capitalist ownership of the means of production and the workers whose labour generates that production, Adam Schaff has valuable things to say about alienation as a generalized social and philosophical problem – in fact a social evil. He points out that alienation canbreak out anywhere as a dispirited or active opposition to some social fact, but that it can in principle be eliminated in specific cases, whilst remaining a 'permanent danger'. As he has it with Conservatives firmly in his sights: 'it is culpable to renounce that possibility because of one's own particular interest, or to place group interests above the interest of society as a whole'. He accuses the Establishment of veiling facts and helping 'people to fail to notice those things which they find inconvenient. The veil often takes the form of a myth of 'orthodoxy".

Despite the popular press disparaging Marxism on a daily basis, it sees fit by gross simplification to ignore subsequent developments in Marxist thinking. Which is more than a pity given their rich diversity and the attempts to reapply what is relevant to current societies.

Gramsci, for instance, produced the important concept of 'hegemony' – the way in which the ruling class directs and organizes society using its cultural power. This Italian revolutionary saw ideology as a key tool for this purpose; not all is achieved by force alone or the threat of it. The idea has of course been widely taken up by rulers since whatever their political allegiances. Then there was Adorno in 'The Dialectic of Enlightenment'. His study of totalitarianism shows how repressive States often concoct myths to create the appearance of reasonableness, whilst removing genuine freedoms. Decent looking Tories in smart suits and with nice accents have been doing this to us for years.

Marx declared that a purpose of philosophy is to change the world, and this aspect in particular has been worked on by the Critical Theorists, who, in my view, offer the most practical and appropriate approaches within the Marxist tradition. Their very ambitious and long-term project is to integrate all the major social sciences, including politics, economics, sociology, psychology, and history, the better to critique and crucially change what is happening now across Western societies. I applaud this, not least because we need cross-cultural thinkers to communicate by holding interdisciplinary dialogues together, and because we have obviously lost our way.

The leading contemporary social thinker from Critical Theory (which originated in Germany as the Frankfurt

School) is Jürgen Habermas. Part of his strategy is to develop the 'public sphere', a 'third space' between the private space of the family and that occupied by the State. Unlike the other two spaces, the public sphere is not controlled. Being more democratic, hopefully, it allows an exchange of communication that can address common interests. These could then be mobilised to lobby the State for appropriate provision. So tradition would be under criticism from the grass roots leading to a consensus for change. But Habermas in his old age is less optimistic now owing to corporate control of the media, as well as the fact of fragmented popular opposition strengthening the hand of the Establishment. In the British context today he would certainly be seeing the need for us to establish the likes of a reformed written constitution, the formulation and legal enshrinement of a people's bill of rights, continued pressure to ensure independence of the Judiciary, free from influence by the Executive, all things I argue for elsewhere in the text.

Situationism

Situationism is a lesser-known political creed, perhaps, one exemplified by the 1967 book, 'The Revolution of Everyday Life' by Raoul Vaneigem. It pointed out a key failing in Marxism that the masses have not responded to their oppressed situation by rising up against Capitalism as the Communists predicted they would. Quite the contrary, in fact, workers have enjoyed accumulating material possessions, some borrowing way beyond their means to do so. The Situationists, as do I, clearly despised such passive acceptance and rued workers' apparent acquiescence in forms of social control, from legal erosions of human rights to manipulation of our thoughts and wants by media and advertising. One depressing consequence would appear to be our preoccupation with increasingly trivial everyday lives.

Populism

Not a new concept in origin, Populism has been much talked about recently in connection with the growing disillusionment of electorates in Western democratic states. Brexit and the Trump election were especially cited as examples. It is rather unlike the older 'isms' discussed here in not so much having an agenda of its own, but being a vague feeling that the ordinary people are being exploited by the political elite that runs the country. 'Isms' usually find themselves firmly at one place or other within the political spectrum, but Populism can be left, right or centre. Neither is it associated with any given class. It is, however, a feature, perhaps an inevitably inherent one, of democracy itself. It plays an uncertain role in focusing on the problems of how to obtain and maintain adequate representation, given that most countries are too big for direct democracy to obtain.

What populists are looking for is whether the 'will of the people' can be put into practice without damaging distortion.

It is difficult to see how these movements can be successful. For one thing they are invariably opposed by the ruling elite. Secondly, general disgruntlement does not readily lead to a coherent reformist programme. And even if it did, where would the organization come from? Opinions differ, but populist 'parties' are often seen as dangerously extreme, tending to destabilize the party structure. We also have the media with their own, not always overt, agenda, which play a role, whether we like it or not, in deciding what is going on before considered views can be established. For example, the Brexit referendum result suddenly had the media claiming the leave voters comprised a populist movement themselves. Speculation then continued unabated to build up a picture of a dichotomized nation within which a small majority supposedly had a raft of scores to settle with the Establishment. Many of these had little or nothing to do with the European Union, though much was admittedly linked to issues of economics and immigration. Then there was the puzzling French election of 2017 in which the mainstream political parties' candidates for President were rejected overwhelmingly in favour of a man with no previous background in politics leading a one-year-old party with no elected MPs.

I fully expect the political class to reassert itself and gradually reclaim the ground. Populism will flounder without the revolution it advocates, cannot afford and could never organize or achieve. Hopefully, its warning messages will nevertheless be heeded and lead to worthwhile democratic reforms. The worry is, though, that a measure of public disaffection will probably continue, undermining the legitimacy of government.

Mishra's characterization in 'Age of Anger' is apt:

'...this improvised programme of belief and action cannot be neatly mapped onto the classifications of ideas and movements (fascism, imperialism, liberalism, Islamism, bolshevism), or the broad sectarian categories of 'left' and 'right', 'liberal' and 'conservative', that commonly mediate our understanding of history and current affairs. Closer attention to beliefs, mind-sets and outlooks releases us from ideological and often moralizing categories; it reveals some shared aspirations, hopes, bitterness and dread between left and right, West and East, and apparently clashing 'isms''.

He goes on:

'Instead of making history, individuals find themselves entangled in histories they are barely aware of, and their most conscientiously planned action often produces wholly unintended consequences, generating more perplexing histories...many dreams of individual and collective greatness can never turn into realistic projects... There is plainly much more longing than can be realized legitimately in the age of freedom and entrepreneurship; more desires for objects of consumption than can be fulfilled by actual income; more dreams than can be fused with stable society by redistribution and greater opportunity; more discontents than can be allayed by politics or traditional therapies; more demand for status symbols than can be met by non-criminal means; more claims on celebrity than can be met by increasingly divided attention spans; more stimuli from the news media than can be converted into action; and more outrage than can be expressed by social media.

Simply defined, the energy and ambition released by the individual will to power far exceed the capacity of existing political, social, and economic institutions.' We may 'lurch between feelings of impotence and fantasies of violent revenge. In an economically stagnant world that offers a dream of individual empowerment to all but no realizable dreams of political change, the lure of active nihilism can only grow.'

This analysis is very powerful and I incline to nihilism myself in response to its veracity. To be defeated by the prospects for Populism, however, emphatically is not to act as apologist in favour of the status quo, whose systems are irretrievably broken.

111

Anarchism

This is the belief that not only do we not need State government, but neither is it even legitimate. The most famous modern text covering this ground is Robert Nozick's book 'Anarchy, State, and Utopia', wherein he reasons from the usual mythical state of nature in which there would be no such thing as political authority. To avoid the obvious consequences of lawlessness people would seek security by banding together for protection of persons and property. 'Protective associations' would slowly emerge wielding the power and extracting the dues to guard, deter, and punish offenders. Eventually a larger, more dominant 'protective association' might develop. With sufficient geographical coverage it could form a sort of minimal State. But whilst justice is thereby seen as protecting entitlements and freely entered exchanges, there is nothing to show how any starting point on the division of property could be justified. Moreover, how could a minimal State be any more than minimally effective, given its very restricted raison d'etre?

It is very important to understand the moral and conceptual implications of what Rawls (quite radically) says in opposition to anarchistic tendencies. He claims that 'society is a cooperative venture for mutual advantage', but if people are to volunteer to be constrained (in a quasi-contract) under moral rules and thereby mutually cooperate, they must surely all be able to benefit from the arrangement. So the ultimate foundation is self-interest, a rational stance for people to take. This is why he argues that if we were all behind a 'veil of ignorance', not knowing our life chances, we would opt for a welfare state in case we needed it ourselves. (This does not seem psychologically sound to me . There are always chancers.) David Gauthier takes the argument further in his book 'Morals by Agreement', saying that the adopted moral rules must also have a (non-moral) rational justification. Rawls disagrees, because under our pluralistic societies there is a surfeit of (conflicting) moralities. Alternatively we just need agreement on how to live together (as though our moralities would not influence and get in the way of such debates). So on this reading any concept at all could fly out of the window, even justice!

ACTIONS

Policy Wonks

I need to say something now about 'policy' – those plans for change that politicians are so fond of. In dealing with policy politicians would do better to heed the warnings laid down by sociologists and psychologists about the dangers of their plans. For example, in 'Liquid Times', Professor Bauman, a sociologist, considers our lives in Britain characterized by an 'age of uncertainty'. This is an example of what Badiou was saying. The fluid nature of change implied by the title he claims is too fast for us properly to adjust to. This will be exacerbated in a period when social welfare support is being stripped away, as under the Cameron and May governments. The undue strain on individuals and families is importantly, but not only, financial; it arises also from the 'episodic' and 'unstable' elements in such a life.

Multifold problems exist at the policy level, in theory and in practice. Fundamental is how to frame a policy so that it has (desirable) objects to attain. Implementation requires a nurtured environment within which parameters like level and type of resources, time-frames, as well as implementation teams, are set, monitored, and kept under constant review, with the ability to adapt appropriately as progress is made or not. Ideally, there should be properly controlled experimental pilots designed to test the feasibility of the policy. Ongoing review also needs to be alive to unintended consequences, desirable or otherwise, so that corrective actions can be applied.

And what about the barriers to successful policy implementation? They are legion is the short reply, for multifold reasons like inertia, cost, lack of vision, vested interest, power that is too diffuse and thus weaker than required, ignorance, the failure of the community as a whole to have a coherent set of core beliefs in common. Rafts of laws are rotten; some are obsolete, other (new) areas will have yet to be addressed.

One of the fatal elements in political programmes is their presumption of the possibility of sustained progress. I neither believe in the likelihood of programmes producing progress in general well-being, nor even in the underlying principle. Without wishing to rehearse all the reasons set out in the relevant chapter of my book 'Radical Bureaucracy', it can perhaps briefly be said that social progress is not demonstrably evidenced in the way that scientific progress is so obviously an established fact. We have insurmountable difficulty even with the concept: there is not going to be agreement across the nation as to what constitutes such a thing as social progress. This is partly because of selfishness and partly owing to the prejudices of ideology. Clearly, it then follows that we would also hopelessly differ on the means of pursuit. In any event we are always overwhelmed by the inescapable elements of nature and the human condition.

Amazingly, there may be a case for relativism in the political world in that, as Foucault claimed, 'solutions' work only in specific places at particular periods of time. That could be a source of defeatism for those who, like me, would wish for a universal end-point of desirability for each and every society, one fully commensurate with scope for human expression, development, and happiness, and which continued to change in optimal ways thereafter as conditions warranted.

Whilst we have established some anchor points for the beliefs of the political parties, there is scope for differences of emphasis and priority among members. There is also the need to address current problems across the whole range of activities in a complex modern society. So the temptation is there for pragmatic and quite temporary adoption of opportunist policies aimed at playing to public opinion, or what the media and sampling polls perceive it to be. Not only may these policies stray a long way from the party's supposed bedrock principles at times, but they sometimes fail to cohere among themselves, looking like a collection of inconsistent initiatives. These are ideational dilemmas at the heart of systems of party politics. It then becomes quite difficult for voters to identify with a party; they will agree with party A on one matter, party B on another, party C about a third. When it comes to an election a lot of the people feel disenfranchised. They may look to what seems to them the least invidious choice.

Why every UK Government gets things wrong via its policies is the subject of an important book called 'Conundrum', by Richard Bacon and Christopher Hope. To quote from their introduction:

> 'They often spend precious taxpayers' money wastefully and even stupidly. They hire as civil servants some of the brightest people in the country and then employ them in ways that stifle their creativity and inhibit them from

taking personal responsibility. And they often change the ministers who are the temporary political heads of government departments with such bewildering speed that it is all but impossible for those ministers, even the highly talented ones, to obtain a sufficient grasp of what they are doing before being moved on'.

Bacon and Hope explain that 'most of the conversation in politics is about how things should be rather than the mechanics of getting there'. And 'in large areas of public administration, especially…on anything new, it is quite normal for things not to turn out as planned'. But they also 'seem to be very bad at learning from mistakes'. Researchers on policy implementation have concluded that 'to make the ordinary happen is far from easy'. But 'implementation is as important as ideology in politics'.

Sometimes a policy objective is badly thought out, or there are not:

'enough people with the right experience, computer system failings, sudden changes in 'priorities or plans for legislation', irrelevant or distorting targets'.

So whilst it is true that politicians as a class need to be better able to formulate policy, notably to anticipate its unintended consequences, they have to become more interested in monitoring its implementation, intervening with connective action where necessary. Likewise civil

117

servants have to be up to their onerous modern roles as accumulators of relevant knowledge, transmitting decisions to those responsible for implementing them, providing Ministers with timely and appropriate advice, and acting (this is more controversial) as guardians of the public purse. There are clearly grave faults on both sides. The authors conclude their book, after exploring many a failed case history from the heart of government, with a plea for psychological exploration to develop insights into why, within this political framework, people behave the way they do. We need more emphasis, in other words, on the human resources that go with the physical and financial ones.

The Art of the Possible

Can we have progress in political philosophy? The question echoes what has been asked of every other branch of philosophy, so politics is surely not exempt. Certainly when you look at how seriously, still, some people take political ideas forged centuries ago as relevant to the present day you may beg leave to doubt it. On the other hand, novel approaches do sometimes crop up, such as Rawls' treatment of justice, which led to frenzied academic activity over their analysis and development. Insights are doubtless generated, but whether decisive solutions appear is moot. Philosophers themselves are apt to bemoan the relative absence of 'progress' in political philosophy during the whole of the twentieth century, quite a state of affairs if true given the numerous radical departures during that time in other areas of philosophy. What view of this you take somewhat depends on the role you allow for ethics and its connections to politics in general. Nevertheless, there could be progress of a kind in more humble ways in that specific new problems do emerge with which political philosophy then engages. These are mostly examples of seeking justice in varied contexts. Such as internationally on a global scale and our responsibility towards future generations. Justice is an important underlying theme of my book and discussions of many aspects will be found in the text.

The scope of political theory is very wide, because the issues facing society are legion. Among the key topics covered by conventional treatments are government, the state, constitutions, sovereignty, power, authority, legitimacy, democracy, representation, law and order, justice, rights, equality, welfare, property, the market, planning, security, and green issues.

Political science, so-called, is, I fear, not really science in the ways expected of the physical and biological sciences. We are far from having a scientific political model, for this should have predictive as well as explanatory power. So the works I am commenting on, and the views I express, are more in the camp of political theory than political science, which is a pity, but we are where we are.

In her book 'The Political is Political', an erudite work of considerable subtlety, the Cambridge writer, Lorna Finlayson contributes an academic polemic of critical analysis, which takes as target the apparent stranglehold on contemporary United Kingdom politics of liberal philosophy, broadly and conventionally conceived as a programme underpinned by laissez-faire, capitalist economics. As a political scientist herself, she attacks political philosophy for having suffered a process of 'de-politicization'. By which she means that debates are characteristically set up in such a way as to impose strict limits on the kind of dissent possible. It is as though we talk only within the confines of a general political outlook, or paradigm, in which the underlying assumptions and boundaries of possibility remain unspoken and unquestioned. I think there is a good deal of truth in this, whilst it is also probably a failure of our imaginations. The present book tries to keep these strictures in mind and to transcend them.

Lois McNay, in her book 'The Misguided Search for the Political' brings to bear a contemporary critique of political theory, the sentiment that if we are to develop an effective political agency of life enhancement we need a rather better understanding of (and doubtless empathy for) prevailing social conditions, especially the adverse.

She admonishes contemporary political theory for a perceived, relative neglect of social suffering, calling this an academic tendency towards 'social weightlessness'. Although it is radical democratic theory we are talking about, it nevertheless fails properly to press the social justice claims of those groups where social pathology has taken hold, so that for them their social suffering has become politically invisible.

McNay critiques Mouffe's idea of 'democratic agonism', which drastically opposes the ideas of political decision-making based on deliberation and consensus, because it obscures the power struggles in social life. What we need is a 'stable institutional framework' within which disagreement and conflict can be conducted, says Mouffe. But even where the dialogue is always required to prioritize the interests of the oppressed (and when would we do that?), social weightlessness is still the outcome, claims McNay. The political bottom-up ideas of radical pluralism proposed by such as Connolly and Tully do not meet the bill either, albeit they start with everyday struggles and build towards a more generalized political theory. McNay thinks all these theorists ultimately fail to come to terms with, let alone transcend:

'the lived reality of deprivation and marginality that may lead to dispositional reluctances on the part of disempowered individuals to participate in political activity'.

She concludes by averring that 'challenging oppression and exploring pathways to empowerment' is far more important as an aim of radical, democratic political theory than refining a model, that its 'fundamentally negative nature' is fully consistent with a constructive approach, one which naturally enough contains a normative element. We should come down from our ivory towers and work instead in the gutter.

So, whilst we have probably established that it is unsafe to leave politics to the professional politicians, what are we to make of the uses of political theory in solving our numerous serious political problems? Although my sources have been wide-ranging, I cannot in all honesty claim to have made a comprehensive study of the contemporary literature, and I very much doubt it would be possible for a whole team of specialist commentators to cover the ground either. But what we have, I think, are enough indications for a tentative conclusion that political theory falls considerably short and probably always would. In its descriptive mode it might well provide useful factual insights into practice, here and there. Yet where it points in the direction of suggested behaviours its underpinning becomes prone to ideology. The further it is removed from its historical context the more doctrinaire it is in danger of becoming. And so my initial gut feeling about political theory has been reinforced in the writing.

This is a big disappointment to me; I am used, as a natural scientist, to the value of theory in predicting results which we can subject to experimental test. So a given theory should get a hard time soon enough if it is wrong or flawed. But in politics 'theory' is a term not subject usually to such killer blows. Thus political theories tend to live on irrespective of their applicability or usefulness because their social science tests are so nebulous – contested, factually and normatively – but rarely decisively. The path for a true 'political science' to follow will therefore have to include a genuinely scientific and thereby rigorously defined use of the concept of theory, but discoveries are to date somewhat limited, albeit important, such as in the predictive field of opinion polls with their statistical basis. And they have had their own spectacular failures, like the Brexit vote. Life seems too complex, messy and unpredictable to be neatly encapsulated by a modest construct like mere social theory.

Finally, we come now to a succinct evaluation of where the various mainstream ideologies fit in the context of the political theory concepts discussed earlier. Conservatism has to be rejected altogether because, although strong on obligation and coercion in style, it does not believe in, or produce justice for the many, reductions of inequality, or high regard for civil liberties. Liberalism has to go because unfettered individualism has led to rampant capitalist exploitation and an atomized, undisciplined society. Socialism, though scoring better on justice and inequality, fails to convince also owing to its demonstrable lack of headway against those majorities that reject thoroughgoing community spirit and action. As I have also shown, Marxism, too is founded on flawed predictions of social development and historical drivers of change, though both it and Socialism are the best places to look for insights into what the good life might consist in for the vast majority. Since Populism is against rather than for, and as yet to show longevity, I discount it also.

Which leaves what exactly? Say that the parties are clapped out, irrelevant. Fortunately for them, although few of the public will join them as members, we cannot yet look beyond and they will not go away voluntarily. We urgently need to side-line them and somehow generate informed and thoroughgoing neutral and independent debate to develop in detail ideas and plans for just where this country wants to be going as a whole. If it does…

Can We Do It Better?

It is not part of my project to talk at length about how politics should be effected, though palpably the way it is done provides a major irritant for a lot of people. I would hope that politicians will become more able, learn in time to be more sophisticated and avoid the kind of pitfalls the public berate them for, such as simplistic sloganizing, failure to answer the question, concealing their plans and motives, lying and dissembling generally.

But behind the scenes front-line politicians do need advisers with intelligence, training and expertise to lick their ideas into shape, and even to provide most of them, one suspects. There seems to be no shortage of such practitioners. In fact, the trend of political advisers to formulate programmes and package their presentation seems to be growing. General elections see them increasingly calling the shots, coaching the politicians on how to look and what to say. Having said that, Mrs. May relied almost entirely on such an approach in the 2017 general election and it was a disaster.

Since so many of the ideas forthcoming look wretched to large swathes of the populace, it might be worth musing over whether philosophy, and especially ethics, could help improve their quality. According to Bernard Williams, the moral philosopher, they should start with the very practical-oriented question: 'what is the best form of society we can get to, starting from here?' But can we just lift philosophical ideas as ready-made solutions for the problems we face?

Jonathan Wolff, a contemporary political philosopher, does not think so, because they tend to be 'ideal theories', visions of how things should be, but without worrying about implementation difficulties. Such a 'top-down' approach could incorporate a moral stance, but the strength of our convictions is no guide to whether the morality is soundly based. It is much better, he says, and a deal more likely to be acceptable, to take a 'problem-driven' approach, building up from the bottom with any abstract principles, lines of reasoning, and empirical evidence that may be relevant.

Thinkers from other disciplines or none will frequently and unconsciously have moral theories at the back of their minds, however. They may be 'absolutists', believing some things to be absolutely right or wrong, whether through religious or secular convictions. Or they may be 'consequentialists', thinking that events consequent on a policy causing them would be good or bad and that this should morally decide the matter. In practice, though, people tend to be swayed by both kinds of stance, whilst the philosophical theory books sometimes portray them as incompatible. The thought is that we are probably not going to get consistency here, but accommodations might at times be feasible issue by issue.

Neither need we be much exercised by considerations of whether moral values are objectively true or merely subjective, emotionally laden preferences or imperatives, if you like.

Fortunately, not all public policy areas are philosophical questions thus needing a philosophical input to answer them. And when they are, ethical considerations can still be some way down the queue in terms of importance. Ultimately, and it may be an unpalatable truth, 'there are no knock-down arguments in public policy'.

Fortunately, progressive thinkers in other parts of the world have come up with some interesting ideas to improve our practice. These will be discussed in the next chapter.

DREAMS AND DIRECTIONS

Today and Tomorrow

The French socio-philosopher Alain Badiou has written a book entitled 'The Century' which aims to characterize the present (or at least the recent past in the shape of the 20th century itself). What he comes up with is that there are many such characterizations, not just one only, that we take a view from some given standpoint – say warfare – and see a tiny facet of the prodigiously complex whole. Quite commonly our standpoints are partial and judgemental – we may for instance look at terror, criminality, democratic movements, artistic schools, literary trends, scientific advances, technological effects, culture and so on. Badiou is rightly suspicious that we colour and cloud our accounts through our own distorting prisms.

This must therefore mean that a politician wishing at a particular moment of history to be an influential social actor on events and outcomes has to have a factual understanding of the present based on these kinds of perception. And that is far from a neutral, objective starting point for the prescription of policy.

If we are considering possible utopias and ways forward towards them, we had better first look at likely future developments. This is so as to get a handle on our changing context of operation, its opportunities and constraints. One visionary with a somewhat unexpected take is Yuval Harari in his book 'A Brief History of Tomorrow'. His thought-provoking contentions include the staggering claims that mankind's hitherto perennial dominant preoccupations – famine, pestilence, and war – are well on the way to being conquered. We have, he says, the knowledge and the means to transcend them. But, even if that is not unduly optimistic, have we the sense and constancy of human nature, say I?

Anyway, if we indulge Harari for a little, what may come to replace these problems and, by implication, constitute a positive and worthwhile human agenda? Always assuming, of course, that we do not instead continue to make false and self-destructive choices. And snatch at glittering goblets before evaluating their likely worth.

Well, a first prudent move would be somehow to secure 'ecological stability'. We do not just rape each other currently, we rape the planet. Beyond this, Harari's suggestions seem to be highly contentious. For example, he would go for greatly increased life expectancy, whereas I would be much more concerned to reduce the vast existing inequalities between us in life expectancy that depend on origins, environment, and life experiences. He wants to search for the key to happiness, both material and psychological. Well, good luck with that, beyond ensuring our physical comfort, which though obviously desirable is neither a necessary nor sufficient condition.

What is possibly sinister, however, is Harari's belief in the rise of new 'religions' to replace such as radical Islam and Christian fundamentalism, be it Catholic or otherwise. I am all for these going, of course, but I am not prepared to swallow the alternative notion of 'data religions' that obsess about computers changing us by genetic engineering (not just eliminating disease) and with brain-technology interfaces. Imagine a world where data algorithms decided our future and started to reproduce themselves...

Zizek has analysed the present international political malaise in his controversial book 'Living in the End Times', which predicts that capitalism is fast approaching its terminal crisis. He identifies four worldwide key factors as the ecological crisis, economic system imbalances, rapid development in biogenetics, and major social divisions. He has, needless to say, taken a lot of flak. Apart from deniers, many do not like his Marxism, consider Lacan's psychoanalytic theories which he espouses as unhinged, and are impatient with his polymath tendencies to wander off piste into artistic and cultural subjects and the like.

My own critique is rather different, though I take the point about Lacan, who, as far as I can understand him, claims that the unconscious is structured like a language, which seduces and controls our reason. In a nutshell those who claim rumours of capitalism's death, just as with the alleged demise of physics or the end of history, are likely to be surprised at the capacity for originality in change. But the main thrust relates to the key factors. Why stop at four only? And how can we be sure each on its own, or perhaps in concert, can do for capitalism? Where is the evidence? All we can surely claim is that capitalism will probably undergo big changes. But that is too trite.

Humane Politics

Steve Hilton, former special adviser to Prime Minister Cameron, in his book 'More Human' sets out a blueprint for politics with a human face. But he asks us to believe that we can take back power from the mighty Establishment, all the vested interests, simply by becoming personally and persistently involved – developing a fully participative democracy from the grass roots upwards. He plays down the people's profound disillusionment with party politics, their distrust and revulsion over politicians, in the sense that he assumes our defeatism and lack of interest are easily overturned. Well are they? And if not, would it work? A rational calculus of probabilities says highly unlikely.

I have mentioned some of Steve Hilton's ideas in lukewarm terms, but his 'Big Society' 'was just a dream' in the opinion of **i** writer Chris Blackhurst in 2015. He sold it to Cameron, but Cameron could not convince his Cabinet. And really it is at bottom a pretty cynical idea. Get all those have-nots to volunteer to help others, for nothing, then we can cut down on paid civil servants and local authority staff and save ourselves a fortune. That way, public services will deteriorate, but we shall all be much more socially minded and involved in hand-to-mouth community projects.

Balance

I state a preference for a balanced society, by which I mean all sorts of things, such as capitalism with a human face and welfare system, only modest inequalities of income and wealth, thriving public and private sectors, no region favoured over any other, absorbable levels of immigration with the kind of skills we need, full and gainful employment for those who wish to partake in it, no discrimination on inappropriate grounds like race, gender, age, disability, a progressive system of taxation based on ability to pay, an economy with a full range of properly developed sectors, a fully integrated modern transport system, the denial of institutional buying privilege; hence the abolition of private health care and private education.

On this question of balance we need to mature as a society to recognize that both private and public sectors have vital roles to carry out, as was indicated in the section in chapter 3 on the Entrepreneurial State. The trick would be to allow, indeed encourage, each sector to do what they are best at, whilst ensuring regulations and penalties to provide essential controls over their less desirable activities and tendencies. It should be recognised that both sectors can spawn individuals who are fundamentally corrupt. Stereotypes mislead. Private operators, for instance, can defraud, abuse staff, cream off excessively large sums for personal gain, incompetently reduce companies to receivership, rape the environment, cut corners over health and safety, and so forth. Public sector personnel can be lazy, and/or of low quality, their organizations employing top heavy staffing with silly job descriptions, and being financially inefficient, as well as operationally ineffective. But their social conscience is usually more developed on the other hand.

Wellbeing

The supreme political goal, according to Edward Kent, ought to be the identification of and 'securing the wellbeing of persons'. Obviously he feels that, whatever the rhetoric of politicians, it often isn't. He quotes a paper written by Margaret MacDonald, entitled 'The Language of Political Theory', which:

'directed an attack against the whole enterprise of

political theory, its upshots, and its irrelevancy to the way governments actually perform'.

She was equally scathing of the political philosophers from both left and right, all 'likely as not to distort the political reality which they are designed to clarify, and subject to exploitation by unscrupulous political leadership'. And as 'they attempt to identify constants presumed to give universal validity' they end up in fact with 'time-bound speculations' locked within their own historical cultures. Unfortunately:

> 'despite their conceptual weaknesses traditional political theories nevertheless live on in the public consciousness as low-grade ideologies and slogans which all too frequently take the place of reasoned persuasion in the formation of public policies'.

Since the Cold War, 'which pitted ideological blocs against each other' there has been 'the phenomenon of dissent arising within systems'. Traditional political theories cannot really handle this development. Analysis tends to be one-dimensional and there is little interdisciplinary understanding. Indeed:

> 'the very complexity of the social, economic, and political problems confronting theoretical analysis comes close to making the enterprise itself a doubtful one'.

Kent proceeds to champion democratic ideals – notably popular participation, equality, communication, persuasion by evidence and argument, and cooperation. But he says:

> 'despite the existence of democratic ideals, the practical exigencies of decision-making processes in liberal as well as socialist regimes betray authoritarian strains which threaten respect for persons'.

These include the very opposite of democratic ideals – 'managerial decision, élitism, propaganda, manipulation, and coercion', throwing into relief the age-old balance between desirable ends and acceptable means. And so 'petty tyranny of public and private organizations strikes virtually every household'.

Therefore, increasingly, people have begun to realize that the incomplete democracy as presently practiced 'is not the universal social panacea'.

> 'It patently cannot survive periods of crisis in national systems'. 'Tyranny of the majority threatens weaker interest groups. Election to political office and the distribution of resources are constantly subject to manipulation by power groups'. 'There is a widening credibility gap between national leadership and the voting populace'.

Kent sees violence as almost invariably futile against the might of the State, but approvingly points to 'methods of resistance short of full-scale revolution' that have been 'pioneered and tested'. Groups with common concerns can be assembled and mobilized 'into effective protest communities on short notice and with relatively limited resources'. 'Small groups can bring to bear power greatly out of proportion to their size'. Which was what Moses Naim was partly saying earlier in the section on power in the first chapter.

Among the techniques he advocates, old and with new variants, there is publicity, but with care taken over choice of an 'attention-getting tactic', which is of great importance 'in the shaping of public opinion or the curbing of excesses of authorities'. 'Ridicule, official embarrassment' have their uses too.

'Large groups can disrupt vital social functions by blocking modes of transport, refusing to pay taxes'. Selective boycotts may help, along with exposures of sensitive documents or unrevealed policy plans. 'Specific legal remedies may be discovered in the existing body of law'. Then there is civil disobedience, also addressed elsewhere in the present book.

Self-Determination

Mihailo Markovic explores the idea of whether what he defines as 'self-determination' is really possible in modern societies, or merely a 'utopian dream'. The definition is as follows:

> 'Self-determination is a process in which conscious practical activity of human individuals becomes one of the necessary and sufficient conditions of individual and group life'. He accepts in setting this out that 'self-determination' is always conditioned by a given social situation, by the level of technology, the given structure of production, the nature of political institutions, the level of culture, the existing tradition and habits of human behaviour'. But despite these realities, he sees self-determination as still feasible provided they 'constitute only the framework of possibilities of a certain course of events...and that (people's) subjective choice is autonomous, genuinely free and not compulsory'.

He then lays out four basic conditions for self-determination as so conceived to be realized. The first is that the direction of social processes must 'no longer be in the hands of any institution which enjoys a monopoly of economic and political power', but that 'people themselves must decide on all matters of common interest'. Secondly, people must have 'reliable knowledge of the Society's situation, of its scarcities and limitations, of the existing trends, of the conflicts to be resolved, of the alternative possibilities of further development'. The third condition requires there to be a very powerful public opinion democratically arrived at, but lastly this needs to be based on a full sense of the identity of the society and the people's 'real general needs'. It would seem to me that we fail miserably as a society on all four tests.

Markovic is a Marxist and so sees his model working only in a:

> 'society organized as a federation of councils composed of non-professional, non-alienated representatives of the people…at all levels of social structure: in enterprises and local communities, in regions and in whole branches of activity, and finally at the level of the society as a whole'.

Now there are all sorts of problems with this planned structure, as must be evident. The vision for society he outlines would not be an attractive one for most members of society and it is totally unclear, even if it were, just how we might proceed from here to there. People could be attracted to the notion of self-determination in principle – they like the idea of deciding things which are in the hands of the big battalions. But, very sad to say, most folk are not sufficiently interested, able, or determined enough to see such a project through, even on a small scale. Society is replete with examples of how even very committed people in order to attain a small piece of justice for themselves had to campaign for years in a climate of high risk, uncertainty, strong unbending opposition and cost. The general will might be easier to find (probably only at times of national crisis) than the general interest, so lack of clear direction or purpose is likely to characterize most popular decision-making. People will not be able to handle complexity, be it of organization or technology, nor is it clear how self-determination can point to a legion of individuals all agreeing to waive their own personal beef for the common good. The model appears to disparage expert or professional inputs and it is not clear to me quite why.

Nevertheless, there is a nugget to be mined here. It is an attempt, sorely needed, to seek a solution to the ever more pressing problem of how to run a democratic society in a way that achieves agreed worthwhile socio-political and economic objects in a broadly acceptable way without their imposition by a ruling class which holds most of the power and shows contempt for the populace. We have a long way to go.

Collective Action

Very importantly Pierre Bourdieu points to the oft forgotten significance of the unexamined. The prevailing paradigm comes to seem natural to most who live within its period, so that some issues remain untreated, perhaps even forgotten, certainly not generally recognized. He does not accept that we are free to change all of this, though we do have some powers of self-determination as well as influence, despite our inherent politico-social programming.

Bourdieu considered our thought patterns and classification systems. Once these are created they tend to arrange our subsequent thinking within them. Secondly, those cultured maps which become dominant tend to be in the interests of the ruling class, which therefore seeks to reinforce them to preserve the status quo.

Gillian Tett is a high-powered economist, an anthropologist by academic background, and a student of Bourdieu. In her book 'The Silo Effect' she applies both her backgrounds to the working life of organizations, private and public, to provide 'lessons of amelioration'. The nub is that we too often work in 'silos', which is to say, largely cut-off from other silos, unaware of their thinking, so unable to benefit from their ideas, and in turn unable to influence them with our own.

So what are Tett's prescriptions? Firstly, it pays to keep teams flexible, with membership changes possible and structured contact with other teams utilized. What comes to mind here as an example is the long-standing tradition in the civil service for officers to spend all their career in one department of State. This has its merits, of course, in terms of a build-up of continuous expertise, and will be appropriate for some staff and levels, but it inevitably leads to a narrow understanding of government. Secondly, we need 'translators', key staff who are well versed in getting groups successfully to communicate with each other across academic divides. Imagination is a periodic requirement to challenge the prevailing classifications and assumptions.

The imperatives of the analysis, and Tett's developments of it in institutional contexts, can hardly be overstated. Self-determination, it seems, cannot be achieved without the right kind of collective action. We classify and categorize in order to control our grasp of external and internal reality. But we also over-specialize, so risking a loss in communication capacity that can be disastrous. We develop 'tribalism', 'tunnel vision', leading to inappropriate ways of behaving which have even been known to destabilize financial markets and bring down companies.

Zoe Williams is a contemporary left-wing journalist and author. In her clever and amusing book 'Get it Together', for instance, she provides a now increasingly echoed and familiar depiction of our 'primitive, failing' State, 'in which people cannot afford necessities', such as 'shelter, food and warmth'. Her book is at root a plea for us to have the better politics she thinks we are entitled to.

Her chapters discuss many of the faults with British Society today, notably the continuation (and indeed expansion) of poverty, the struggle of the NHS to meet demand within budget, the unaffordability of houses for the masses, tax evasion among the rich, the perceived problems of uncontrolled immigration, the failings of education and its unequal availability, the lowering status and politically enforced decline of the public sector, the inadequate measures taken to avert environmental disasters, our social fragmentation into family silos cut off from community, the lack of accountability to the State of multinational corporations.

My interest in this kind of analysis, which I largely take as accurate, is to assess the prescriptions for change for the better. Ms Williams' views are somewhat incomplete, but she does see potential in collective action, and the rise of protest organizations – a predictable enough response as far as it stretches.

But, as with all commentators, terrific as the descriptive analysis is, her ideas for improvement are much less so. She starts pessimistically:

> 'the very bit that's meant to brim with optimism and possibility is the bit that depresses the hell out of me'.

She quotes Robert Unger, a Brazilian political philosopher and former government minister:

'we have lost faith in any of the large available understandings of how structural change takes place in history, and as a result, we fall back on a bastardised conception of political realism, namely that a proposal is realistic to the extent that it approaches what already exists. This false view then aggravates (our) paralysis.'

Whilst the statement is probably too sweeping, we do tend to think within fairly narrow parameters when contemplating change, so it can be a useful corrective to the self-imposed limitations on our horizons.

Zoe Williams understands only too clearly that 'meaningful change is not going to start with a manifesto shopping list of policy suggestions' (we have seen right through enough of this from the political parties over the years to know that it rarely has satisfactory results). But, she says, 'it will start when we create a new normal', instead of 'waiting for mainstream politicians to give us the answers', and again 'leadership will not come from the centre'. She chides us for feeling powerless and claims the remedy lies in her book title, with us all pulling in the same direction, (except that we never do).

Grassroots Resistance

You may be forgiven for thinking that what goes on in the Eastern bloc of countries under the Russian yoke, or at least contemporary influence, is little to do with us. And, most certainly, it is something of a relief that what we suffer is by many magnitudes milder. Nevertheless, there is the commonality of view that our people and those of, say, Vaclav Havel's Czechoslovakia, share a feeling of helplessness in the face of the sort of vast problems and shortcomings of our society outlined by Zoe Williams under an undemocratic and unresponsive ruling élite. That is, sadly, the condition of Britain at the time of writing, though possibly without the overt oppression, except in the underclass. Havel, a humble academic and poet, who by popular acclaim later became his country's prime minister, wrote an inspirational book for the people entitled 'The Power of the Powerless'. In it he considered a seemingly hopeless project, namely the prospects for democratic change driven by people living in totalitarian circumstances. In effect that is our plight too: we live under a de facto one-party state whose first past-the-post voting system denies effective representation to the clamouring alternative voices.

And so the practical mechanisms by which opposition can effectively be mounted, as explained and discussed in Havel's tract, are relevant to all of us who are yearning for a civilized alternative to the self-serving and heartless Establishment we seem to be stuck with. So what did Havel propose we could do about it?

He notes first that attempts to resist democratically

the totalitarian (authoritarian) State tend to start in civil society in areas not closely reached by the State. There is an issue, very relevant to contemporary Britain, about the necessary and sufficient conditions for a morally healthy society. We palpably do not have one, since 'deceit, manipulation and opportunism', as Steven Lukes says in his introduction, are commonplace, where politicians are expected by the public automatically to have 'dirty hands' and to be generally motivated by self-interest, unless they can individually prove otherwise (as some in fairness can).

Havel emphatically rejects the conventional kind of opposition to the regime:

> 'Merely by establishing a different political line and then striving for a change of government would not only be unrealistic, it would be utterly inadequate, for it would never come near to touching the root of the matter'.

I rather concur. And he then goes on to describe British citizens, though he is actually talking about his own countrymen, as 'soporific, submerged in a consumer rat-race'…and who 'would simply find anything like revolt unacceptable'. Havel's 'dissident movements', by contrast:

> 'turn away from abstract political visions of the future towards concrete human beings and ways of defending them'.

In chiding those who would crudely apply Marxism (or any other ideology) outside its origins in time and place, he also turns his scepticism on those for whom appeal to legality functions as an excuse:

> 'It wraps the base exercise of power in the noble apparel of the letter of the law:it creates the pleasing illusion that justice is done, society protected and the exercise of power objectively regulated'… 'The legal code is a façade, an aspect of the world of appearances'.

And again:

> 'the most important thing is always the quality of life and whether the laws enhance or repress it, not whether they are upheld or not'.

The seeds of Havel's proposals for action lie in what Vaclav Benda calls 'the development of parallel structures', although he is by no means optimistic himself. He shies away from having formal organizations in this civil society; their principles should be diverse and minimally regulated. What he wants to see is 'the rehabilitation of values like trust, openness, responsibility, solidarity, love…held together by a commonly shared feeling of the importance of certain communities'. 'Self-management' would be the order of the day. Ideally:

'these informal non-bureaucratic, dynamic and open communities that comprise the parallel polity' are a 'kind of rudimentary prefiguration, a symbolic model of those more meaningful political structures that might become the foundation of a better society'.

So it is to culture we need look for embryonic new structures, which presumably in time would somehow have to widen from information networks to engage in the other spheres of life as well. That is the harder part and I do not see the mechanisms.

The right Left

Now there is an understandable desire among political thinkers of independent mind to reach beyond the twin poles of socialism and liberal capitalism, both widely considered seriously flawed, perhaps to have failed altogether. One such attempt was supposedly Blair's 'third way', by which he sought to make the Labour Party palatable to the country, in effect by friendly overtures and financial and regulatory concessions to industry and commerce. For a time he appeared to have succeeded, at least in voting terms, but he was pragmatic rather than principled, resorted to spin, and was ultimately discredited, mostly for reasons to do with duplicity over warmongering in Iraq along with the Americans. And the 2017 general election seemed to spell the demise of the Blair project, at least in the sense that a substantial minority were prepared to vote for Corbyn's much more left-wing agenda.

In something of this vein, although himself a Corbyn critic, the left of centre thinker, Owen Jones has produced a nine-point manifesto for a fairer society with the following elements. He wants democratic public ownership for services such as the NHS, railways, and energy, a charter strengthening workers' rights, ending all zero-hour contracts and no doubt internships where you work for nothing but the experience, a universal system of childcare substantial enough to free-up parents to join the workforce, re-empowering local authorities so they can build houses, regulating private rents where there is extortion, a statutory living wage phased in and progressively removing the public subsidies from businesses, a strong and determined campaign to recover the tax non-legitimately withheld by companies and the rich, publicly run banks with elected taxpayers on boards and with a mandate for regional investment, lending to small businesses and green industries, as well as higher tax rates on those earning more than £100,000 per annum to fund jobs for unemployed youth.

Jones claims much public support for his ideas, whilst conceding they will be howled down by the Establishment and its media. He does not regard his programme as particularly to the left of the mainstream and neither do I. These plans, and others like them, are all worth a try and he says they constitute an 'agenda of hope', where otherwise we have little. My moderating comments are to do with the fact that all such reforms would be rigorously opposed in practice and could have some unexpected adverse effects. For instance, merely nationalizing a failing service is not automatically going to put it right of itself, giving workers more rights will discourage some employers from recruitment, and monitoring what constitutes a reasonable rent is not an easy option in practice. Nevertheless, the underlying sentiments and broad thrust have to be sound if we truly value such principles as equity and justice.

I agree with Jones that 'a democratic revolution is long overdue' 'to reclaim by peaceful means the democratic rights and power annexed by the Establishment', except that I do not recall we ever had them. He admits this will be very difficult to bring about, because:

> 'in some awful way, people are beginning to give up. The Establishment has left many people resigned, devoid of hope, without a feeling that it is possible to resist'.

So as to try and build a popular movement of opposition, we first need 'a compelling intellectual case that can resonate with people's experiences and aspirations'. Secondly, the opponents of the Establishment should harness their effects collectively instead of behaving in a fragmented manner. Remember that the Establishment consists of powerful economic institutions, so is very hard to take on. But apart from these practical observations, Jones retreats into providing a pen-picture map of the kind of developments he would like to see happen, rather than arguing as to how they might be achieved.

Yasmin Alibhai-Brown, who won a journalist of the year award in 2016, wants 'an open and mature democracy, not controlled by vested interests'. I do too. She points out the hopeless right-wing bias of our major institutions:

> 'This Government, the Royal Family, the leaders of the Armed Forces, newspaper proprietors and most editors, the Institute of Directors, the Confederation of British Industry…peers, those appointed to public sector service boards share core beliefs about wealth, privilege, capitalism, militarism, individualism and self-interest… the police, government and secret services have spied on, infiltrated and tried to discredit or criminalize those fighting economic injustice and environmental devastation. Most Britons passively accept these illegal State activities and do not challenge the status quo. (So) the established order remains firmly in charge'.

This Establishment cadre is maintained by appointing its own, the elite being drawn from a narrow private school-educated and affluent middle class. The dominance has been criticized by none other than the ex-Prime Minister, Conservative John Major, who was uncharacteristically educated at a state school and left with modest 'O' level qualifications.

An altogether more profound thinker, someone very little known as yet in the West, is Roberto Unger, previously referred to, who, though Brazilian, nevertheless has very relevant things to say applicable to our situation. In his major tome 'Politics – the Central Texts', Unger presents both an explanatory theory of society and a programme for social reconstruction which is neither Marxist nor social democrat. He (correctly) rejects Marx's historicism, denying there are any such things as laws of a science of society. On the contrary, he regards existing social arrangements as haphazard and replaceable. This has the effect of considerably broadening our sense of what is possible. Grounds for optimism can then flow from viewing with fresh eyes programmes for rebuilding our economic, political, and social institutions. Instead of a tendency to view present arrangements as sacrosanct, or at least bedrock, we can align them instead with the experimental nature of democracy and think outside the box. So far so good.

Unger's views start from the uplifting premise that 'humanity is greater than the contexts in which it is placed', or putting it another way:

> 'no *natural* social, political, or economic arrangements underlie individual or social activity'. (Wikipedia).

This obviously leaves the field open in principle for change and experiment with our institutions and rules with a view to our betterment by it.

He criticizes conventional social theory since, as we have mentioned, while it acknowledges that society is constructed, again it nevertheless fails to see that there are many more possible modes of social organization than those few that we live under, albeit that all are inevitably influenced by their starting points. It hinges on an imaginative failing in most of us; we are hidebound by our conditioning and the familiar contexts we experience.

Unger's arguably utopian vision is of an 'empowered democracy' where individuals and groups can interact. There would be 'freedom of commerce and governance at the local level'; meanwhile central government would 'promote radical social experiments' with institutions.

Unger is critical of the current legal system and wants to unpack the ideologies behind the laws. He is worried that historically an individual's legal rights are 'inseparably locked together with property rights'. He then proceeds to argue in the book that private rights as legally enshrined are undesirable. What he wants to see is a regime in which no part of society can easily take control, and he regards the disintegration of property rights only as the prelude to a new order. Property would be split up into a number of powers to be vested in different rights holders. Individuals would have immunity protection against the public and private powers, rights to have institutions changed to avoid personal oppression, and rights of equality in claims by others against them.

In truth it is very difficult for me to grasp how all this might work in practice, especially as Unger claims the methodology is quite compatible with existing institutional structures. Such a radical reformulation of rights into discrete facets looks to be a mammoth undertaking, one which would be anathema to rulers and ruled alike here. You can just imagine the screams and rages from those with vested interests for a start. It would all take an age, with endless scope for legal obfuscation and opposition at all stages.

One crucial question which Unger tries to address relates to what the left wing can offer in these days of neo-liberal capitalism crisis (for that is what it is). He starts by criticizing the Left as lacking a proper agenda. One branch he says are short of ideas, but mostly just point out shortcomings in markets. This would broadly apply to the Corbyn faction. The other branch largely accepts the present model, working to reform it at the margins via limited redistributive taxation measures and the retention of a modicum of humanity to gloss over welfare cuts. This would be the stance of the Labour mainstream – Miliband and the other Blairites.

According to a review of Unger's 'The Left Alternative' by Michael Mathias, Unger proposes a third Left and gives it five main ideas. Firstly, countries should start approaching markets and globalization on their own terms, not those of business. Second, he has various plans for shaking up education and moving towards meritocracy. Thirdly, markets need to be democratized, to enable other players to be included, such as the small-scale, those with social property, private agents. Banks would be supplemented by other lenders and there would be a capital fund for the players to use. A fourth proposal would require each able-bodied adult (and this I like also) to provide an element of hands-on social care – for the old and young, the poor and the sick. Finally, he wants to extend the frequent use of direct democratic tools, like referenda, political campaigns to be publicly funded, and active institutions to destabilize 'entrenched hierarchies' legally. Again I approve in principle, whilst being doubtful whether the means can be developed and opposition overcome.

His challenge to the Left is at heart a rebuke for the cautious Conservatism they have adopted, and their failure to embrace the ambition truly to transform society. But it is sobering to reflect on the slow and painful performance in practice of Unger's pupil President Obama, admittedly facing structural opposition throughout his service. Perhaps Unger's zeal outstrips his grasp of political realism, albeit he was a Brazilian government minister, or maybe the soil will be more fertile elsewhere than in the

United States, somewhere, I suspect, quite undeveloped, where monolithic institutions do not yet exist that would have to be stripped down or plain eradicated in the processes he advocates.

Becoming a Democracy

Manuel Arriaga, a research professor at New York University, has done us all a great service by writing his book 'Rebooting Democracy'. It starts with the premise that rising populism is the result of electorates realizing that politicians rarely serve their interests. It then seeks possible practical remedies by looking at various initiatives that are occurring in different parts of the world.

He depressingly outlines ten reasons why politicians fail to represent us. He argues that they always will. First there is corruption in its many forms. Secondly, when elected politicians tend to react to people's emotions not reason. Career politics, thirdly, attracts people who are ambitious, self-serving, and not necessarily talented enough to obtain commensurate fame and fortune any other way. Our system of representation can fourthly give them the feeling of being immune to public control, able to pursue what we may find objectionable policies. His fifth reason is that the party machines are undemocratic too, and lead to unscrupulous behaviour to get on.

A sixth problem is that politicians work within a cultural norm, a bubble of abnormality compared with ordinary life. Power can go to their heads, so they tend to seek out and identify with other elites and are correspondingly unsympathetic to their electorates. The sense of belonging to a group affects their behaviour and beliefs. As I have said elsewhere many times, ideology distorts opinion: they have it in spades. And, as a political class, they are very untypical of the general population as a whole. Finally, as though this was not yet enough to make a damning case, politicians are nothing like as powerful as we expect and think they are. (Moses Naim again). Many factors connive to make it so, of which the large multinational company is but one very obvious exemplar, financial limitations and international communities being others.

As citizens we let ourselves down by not properly supervising the politicians we have delegated decision-making to. And we compound the error by sloppy thinking over our electoral choices in the first place. For example, we tend to identify simplistically with a particular party, so favouring its candidates without much reflection. Many of us are too lazy or irresponsible to vote at all (should it be made compulsory?), though defeatism is understandable given the difficulties of making any headway over reforming the political system and its constitutional tenets.

Arriaga describes several interventionist measures taken by various democracies, of which 'citizen deliberation', 'electoral reform', and 'abrogative referenda' are the main ones. The first has a citizen's group, randomly selected for a single term, deciding a policy issue together. It sits as a panel, taking evidence and expert opinion, considers interest factions, and has the enabling support of lawyers and administrators. This happens in British Columbia and after a vote the panel publishes a public statement. The policy is then enacted and implemented, an obvious virtue being responsible participation by citizens. Another merit is that the selection has more chance than conventional methods of being truly representative of the community.

A bolder approach on similar lines would see the random selection from all over the country of a large 'citizens chamber', in effect an upper house of Parliament (instead of a largely hereditary House of Lords like in Britain). This would be able to oppose and block government measures passed by the lower house. Government would not necessarily be weaker, but reforms would be more considered by society.

Elections are in urgent need of reforming in order to make them fairer and allow voters properly to express their true preferences. As matters stand in England the electoral system is shamelessly rigged in favour of the ruling Conservative Party, and the first-past-the-post principle ensures that many votes cast for the unelected are simply wasted, no matter how many there are. Obviously, over time any ruling party that does not fear being unseated by its electorate is more and more likely to discount their views. Corruption will also set in.

One tool Arriaga says that will help 'break the stranglehold' of the 'large, established parties' is 'rank voting'. Voters no longer express a preference for just one candidate, but place them all in order of preference. Now there are various different versions. The method favoured in the book is a form of proportional representation known as the 'single transferable vote', STV. This operates mathematically so that what happens to your vote will vary according to relevant circumstances. If you vote for somebody who has arithmetically no chance of election, your vote is allocated to your next favourite candidate. Likewise, if you vote for somebody who already has enough votes to be elected, your vote will be transferred to your next choice instead.

This will not be enough on its own without safeguarding reforms to ensure the main parties do not undermine it by redefining constituency areas. For example, if the constituencies are made small, they will produce few seats, so reducing smaller parties' chances of obtaining representation. The ruling party can also alter constituency boundaries in its favour against a main rival by splitting their vote across a lot of constituencies, so weakening their opposition in each.

A further necessary reform is to wipe out private funding for political parties because it gives such differential resources to run election campaigns and fund membership operations. Public funding is therefore required, many countries awarding differential amounts based on the number of votes (not seats) won by the party at the previous general election.

The third method advocated by Arriaga in his quest for politically participative and democratic nations is the referendum. This can be used between general elections as a way to inform the decisions of the political class. Now the United Kingdom referendum on European Union membership suffered from deep flaws. Firstly, the public were not used to referenda and not all believed in them. Secondly, the question was crudely framed on the ballot paper. Thirdly, hopelessly dishonest and self-serving campaigns of disinformation were run on both sides of the argument by the political class and the media. To mention but one more glaring weakness, the constitutional standing of a referendum in respect of making binding decisions, and in its relation to Parliamentary decision-making, was not first considered and cemented, thus leading to a plethora of legal and administrative challenges.

So, if referenda are to be satisfactorily used in future, as I said in the first chapter I would hope to see, they need a proper constitutional context within which to operate, one that addresses the above problems for a start. Suggestions made by Arriaga include its combination with a Citizen's Panel, to evaluate the publicly proposed referendum via its expert representatives and to feedback genuine information, not propaganda, ahead of the vote. The scope of a referendum would have to be laid down in advance, and might begin quite modestly to build public confidence, perhaps with powers to endorse or revoke political decisions, but falling short of being able to overturn laws or refer politicians back for a bye-election, or even oust them for serious misdemeanours.

In conclusion, what is being said here is that developing democracy is not merely about filling in deficit gaps, but actually seeking to empower and involve voters in decision-making from a basis of better information and a more just frame-work. Gradually, a population could be encouraged to accept an ongoing rather than intermittent process, one in which their influence could be real and actually felt.

Hence one of the features I would wish to see in a properly civilized society would be a removal of all the major barriers to its democratization, as well as eliminating the large existing democratic deficits. This sounds both noble and vague in the abstract, so I will simply list a few of the vast number of examples by way of illustration:

- abolish the Monarchy and proclaim a republic,
- replace the unwritten and uncodified constitution,
- add a Bill of Citizen's Rights and Responsibilities,
- introduce the best system of proportional representation,
- prevent unequal treatment before the law,
- abolish regressive taxation,
- develop use of referenda as a major democratic tool,
- abolish the House of Lords,
- disestablish the Church of England

I conclude with a still relevant quotation from an old champion of the left:

'Many of our existing institutions can be adapted from their present role as props of the status quo… (to) …. become agents of the profound changes necessary if we are to avert the serious economic and political problems which now confront us…a diffusion of power through greater democracy…bears no resemblance to the structures of an East European state. On the contrary, the corporation now consolidating itself in Britain…has far more in common (with them). There is no reason why the great institutions of the British state should remain at the disposal of any one social system, one class of people, one set of values. In a democracy we need institutions that work for the benefit of us all'.

Tony Benn 'Arguments for Democracy' 1981.

CHAPTER 4

OTHER COUNTRIES AND US

What's Wrong with the World

How many of us have anything but the vaguest notion about the United Kingdom's conduct of foreign affairs, except for a small number of celebrated cases like Iraq, where Prime Minister Blair declared war without the approval of either Parliament or people and it all went tragically wrong? In effect we have yet another democratic deficit in that governments once elected seem to have carte blanche to act in the international arena in ways that suit them, rather than having to answer to a people's mandate. The fuss over Brexit is not typical, partly because a referendum is such a rarity here. One assumes, therefore, that what we do abroad, in relation to hundreds of separate countries, is an amalgam of factors such as past practice, any treaty obligations, our commercial and military interests, the attitudes and behaviour of other nations, and so forth. But we don't know. And anyhow, whatever it is, we haven't voted for it because international affairs are rarely a prominent election issue.

I am very gloomy about outcomes here, even where I can see we are probably proceeding in the right direction. The reasons are obvious. Very large numbers of people throughout the world are living in economically poor countries, their problems compounded by natural disasters, or human ones like famine, and/or warfare or terrorism, genocide, or displacement. Some are failed States. Some are ruled by tyrants. Nasty ideologies and primitive thinking can be dominant, be they religious or secular. There are few democracies and it is doubtful whether any are thoroughgoing. Some nations seem to be hundreds of years behind in terms of attitudes. But all, as well as the more civilized and affluent countries, are subject to weak international laws and very inadequate enforcement thereof. We do not have the institutions, the machinery, or the collective will to bring these about, and so, as Ian Goldin puts it in his excellent book 'Divided Nations', 'societies retreat into nationalism, protectionism, and xenophobia'.

But:

> 'globalization with increased integration is simultaneously the source of our greatest opportunities and threats'.

As he explains:

> 'our vulnerability is most acute, as in the case of cascading financial crises, climate change, and pandemics, when the threat is spread via our global networks'. And there is no 'all-encompassing cure', because 'each of the challenges…is compounded…by the complicating factors of…interdependency'.

We have ample recent evidence, also, of our vulnerability to terrorist activity. Powers of surveillance, even by a determined State, can never be one hundred per cent successful. One incident that gets through is too much, and it could lead in some cases to an extreme loss of life. Nor can we solve the problems of mass migration, some of which will adversely impinge on security questions, of course.

That we need reliably effective trans-national agencies is obvious. Equally so is the realization that none of the existing institutional structures and organizational arrangements are adequate. The United Nations will not do. Neither will the World Bank. It is naïve to believe as idealists once did in a World Government. Any 'solutions' will be incomplete, but rely on a balance of interests being properly represented in international arenas that respect the nation state (because it is here to stay, like it or not). Having said that, it might be too sweeping a judgement to conclude that these supra-national, peace-keeping bodies have had no influence on events. Maybe they have delayed conflicts, brokered cease–fires, negotiated safe passage for victims and the like.

Ngaire Woods has enunciated sensible principles as a necessary (but presumably not sufficient) condition for success. The first is one of subsidiarity, dealing at the lowest applicable level, for not all issues need collective, worldwide action. Where countries are included, they should to be the ones most affected by the problem as well as those best able to provide a solution. So different players would be leading depending on the issue, with representation of all everywhere an impracticability. In addition we need prior agreement over rules of engagement to underpin their legitimacy. Finally, and hardest of all, there has to be 'enforceability at the global level, visible to all'.

Whatever institutional arrangements supplant the United Nations will, on this reading, require sub-groups of nations working and reporting with recommendations on specific issues. The choice of nations must be subject to regular review; selection criteria will have to be on the basis of most relevance or expertise rather than size or perceived importance; vetoes will need to be outlawed. It is very difficult to see how this will work, given that no nation surrenders its own individual paramount interests at the door these days.

Niall Ferguson has cast a damper on idealistic notions that a well-connected world, through global internet communications and so-called social media, will be a more understanding and peaceable one. On the contrary, he sees pathologies in networks. They polarize their communications, turning away from all the rest in favour of like-minded people 'in confirmation of their certainties.'

Dealing with Foreigners

A key problem regarding international affairs is the preceding history, especially with a nation like Britain, which has a very diverse and complex long history behind it. Some of this inevitably colours future policies and seriously affects the manner in which we are perceived by foreign powers and ways in which we ourselves behave. In Britain's case, of course, there have been fluctuating alliances and fallings out with our near neighbours, the French. We have a so-called special relationship with the United States (probably almost entirely fictitious) because of our intertwined colonial past and deemed cultural sharing of taste and interest. It is made much more complicated still by virtue of our position as head of the Commonwealth of countries which we formerly conquered all over the world, vestiges of the British Empire. Our legacy as the leading nation involved in colonialism historically is laced with truly shocking crimes against humanity, if we did but acknowledge the fact. One such was the partition of India following crude lines drawn by an ignoramus on a map, as a result of which millions died, or were displaced from their homes and family by mass migration And in modern times the referendum decision by the British people to leave the European Union, if radically implemented, is massive in terms of our future development when we have shared laws and trading agreements for over half a century.

Others will have better things to say about international affairs; my life has been rather parochial and my travel, starting relatively late, confined to an array of countries in Europe. So I shall restrict myself mainly to points of broad principle which I would advocate.

The first is that Britain must in future learn to punch at its weight and not above. Saddled with a rich, complex, and not altogether glorious history of Empire, with the world benefits of our colonialism much disputed, we have among the political and establishment class vestiges of grandeur, delusions of remaining glory and a force that has in reality ebbed. We can no longer claim to be a world power, nor should we try. We have neither the resources nor the vigour or vision required. When we were 'top nation' we had the massive relative wealth forged in our industrial revolution, able to afford the most potent armed forces anywhere. But the trick now will be to cut our cloth accordingly, trying to retain influence where it is in our national interest to do so, commensurate with our status as others see us as a rather small and querulous island just off mainland Europe.

However, since the world cannot be trusted, with a good few nations ruled by madmen and megalomaniacs, extremist terrorist groups abroad, and insane individuals seemingly all over the place, the first duty of Government – to defend its people – remains prescient. How this is to be done I cannot spell out. Yet it seems clear that the armed forces need to be kept in a state of readiness, with properly trained personnel and modern equipment provided in a way that should essentially transcend party politics, to be guided by a genuine national policy of consensus along with adequate long-term funding. We must keep up with changing threats, such as the emerging need for rapid response capabilities to guard our borders from smuggling and illegal immigrants.

Whilst the good name of the country is an important consideration that the Foreign Office could learn to foster better than its somewhat woeful, darker past performances, this will have to be done in future much more via advice and expertise to developing nations than through direct help and our foreign financial aid, which we cannot afford. Nor can we ensure it is well spent, as the record will show. The agenda must importantly include progressive abolition of our arms trade profiteering.

There ought to be a cessation of involvement in all foreign wars, whatever our perceived international obligations, except in the extreme circumstance when the physical integrity of the realm is under attack, or the very real threat of it, when a (constitutionally required) free vote of Parliament and ideally prior public consultation, must precede the commitment, if at all practicable in the prevailing circumstances, or as soon afterwards as may be managed.

By the same token we must surrender our crude attempts at building nation states after destroying their infrastructure and accept that we have in the past been too easily led into actions of folly in countries whose history and cultures we just do not adequately understand. Our military actions in Egypt, Iraq, Afghanistan, Libya, and Syria are sad and complex cases in point. All have destabilized the countries concerned and led to untold misery for their peoples.

This may be the time to mention that it is dangerous to be too much in thrall or beholden to countries which seem friendly enough, but whose interests sometimes deviate from our own. The 'special relationship' with the United States is an obvious example, where we could prudently cultivate more distance and reserve, whatever the respective economic realities. We are frequently used.

Crucially, the United Nations, just like its forerunner, the League of Nations, may well be a dying duck. Nevertheless, we should keep our seat at the tables of progressive international forums, mediate and forge carefully worded alliances and legal agreements where we can.

We are historically a mongrel race, with much interbreeding from earlier influences, be they conquerors, invaders, asylum seekers, refugees, or economic migrants. So current preoccupations with immigration can seem both exaggerated and xenophobic. Nevertheless, we do have a big problem, to which I shall return.

In dealing with foreigners we have to be realistic in admitting that problems could easily prove to be very long-run, perhaps intractable. Another likelihood is that so complicated are the tangled issues in many an international situation that it becomes well-nigh impossible to maintain a consistent moral stance right across the world. Matters are not solely for moral consideration, of course, but it says much that it figures so low in our priorities.

So we turn now to a way of proceeding politically that is anything but moral, though it may be close to our normal mode of conduct, namely 'realpolitik'. According to Professor John Bew, realpolitik probably originated with Machiavelli, whose vintage political book 'The Prince' gave advice on how to gain and wield political power, surviving in the process. Certainly Machiavelli is associated these days with a kind of pragmatic approach to politics, wherein problems of the day were addressed, apparently of necessity, by methods difficult to square with religious values and private moralities. It is a classic statement of the idea that dirty means are often required in this dirty world to attain maybe noble ends.

Bew bemoans the lack of a satisfactory definition of the term realpolitik and suggests that it could be best grasped via modern studies of the history, along the lines of Ludwig von Rochau's treatment, the 'Foundations of Realpolitik'. He highlights Foucault's problem that many accounts of historical 'truth' are dependent on subjective and time-bound vistas rather than revealing fundamentals about the nature of international affairs per se.

By way of justification for his actions a politician will say that he had to face the facts and act accordingly, so the idea has taken hold that realpolitik is a manifestation of realism. And yet, from Rochau what we have rather is a procedure for analysis when political problems become complicated. You have to understand the 'context of operation' so as to work out how to adjust to change. It is the art of the possible, with the acceptance of partial results if these are all that may reasonably be achieved at the time.

So, in conclusion, realpolitik may serve us usefully, as part of our armoury, but it is neither a theory nor a movement. Never can it be claimed as antidote to poor analysis, self-delusion, bad judgement in political decision-making, but it does emphasize the value in good ideas. It also takes a multidisciplinary approach to situations, so that what is relevant to politics from other subjects such as economics and sociology is also prayed in aid. Acting as a corrective to the notion that a particular morality (no doubt one of many)should invariably guide all political decisions, its danger lies in the seriously erroneous and seductive conclusion that ethics may be discounted from the political arena altogether.

That said, I will briefly sketch a few comments about different parts of the world, so as to try and initiate an appropriate stance to each.

Concerning the British former colonies and dependencies our legacy for them has often been to build a financial sector based on tax havens. As part of a new ethical stance towards the world we must close these down, or clean them up, or sever all links.

The Middle East we should withdraw from, stop meddling in nation-repairing, and refuse to touch their problems in future with a large barge pole. With the notable exception of Israel these are generally primitive states run by dictators of one stripe or another, royal or otherwise, on medieval lines with brutal religious ideologies and tribal separatism. Our masters may cry 'oil' and I say 'too bad'. Get it elsewhere, including around our own shores.

I would make two further comments about countries in that part of the world. Firstly, the lure of oil should not blind us to the fact that American-driven friendship with Saudi Arabia is morally repugnant. Secondly, whilst Iran is certainly dangerous as an emergent nuclear power, its fundamentally Shia Muslims would oppose the extremist threats of the likes of ISIS. They are also a democracy, more of a natural ally for the West, potentially, than the Sunni Muslim Saudis, and they do not seek to convert or kill.

Concerning siting naval, air and other military bases abroad, apart from pulling our weight in organizations like NATO purely for defence, we should retain none. Once you have such a toehold in an unstable part of the world, the temptation to become embroiled in local action can become too much, it would seem.

We need to exert governmental force to clamp down on dodgy commercial operations undertaken by multinational and British companies abroad. Exploitation of mineral resources by Shell in Nigeria is a case in point, with serious environmental pollution one adverse consequence.

Our best way of dealing with foreign countries as a rule is through cultural and scientific links, and honest trade. Pariah (and now nuclear) States such as North Korea we should have no truck with at all. Nor should we indulge the Americans by backing up their dangerous sabre-rattling.

An emergent superpower, like China, needs especially careful attention, but our relations should not be based on subservience – trade at any price – including allowing them to buy our nuclear power stations, whilst at the same time flooding the international market with cheap steel, sinking our heavy industry on Teesside. The disgraceful genuflection of Chancellor Osborne springs to mind, in exchange visits with the Chinese leaders.

Where we seem to be at our worst in the opinion of many a poor English subject is in our intransigent policy of very generous overseas aid. The Cameron government policy was of stubborn ring-fence protection to the international budget. This was quite inflexible, with exemption given from the draconian cuts repeatedly visited on most other departments of state. The way the money was allocated it had to be used up by the end of each financial year irrespective. The objects of expenditure, how they have failed to be monitored, the uncertain outcomes, the allegations of misappropriation of funds, propping up tyrants have all contributed to a widespread feeling of dissatisfaction. People think charity should begin at home and I also think it should end there until we can decently look after all our own people here in Britain, which we are a long way from doing.

What we could do, however, is contribute our proportionate share to foreign aid dispensed by a new world body financed on the basis of levies from the better-off countries, rather than ostentatiously try to outperform them in gifts. Another pipe dream? Of course it is.

Now a sobering fact about other countries we are reluctant to accept is that some of them are better than us, at least in doing certain specific things, such as mountain railway engineering in Norway or Switzerland. What we should do is study and learn from them, borrowing their best ideas. Conversely we should avoid the pitfalls some have experienced elsewhere. Where to look in particular is anywhere that pioneers a new social reform or technological idea. Britain established riches during the industrial revolution by trail blazing, but subsequently we rather lost our way as other nations capitalized on our ideas with better designs. This was especially true of transport infrastructure and factory manufacturing equipment. Since we are increasingly unlikely to be in the van of much successful innovation as we retreat remorselessly towards third world status, there should be considerable scope for development in its wake. But we must first value and reward our engineers, scientists and original thinkers, instead of sportsmen and celebrities, many of whom in any case have little talent and are all engaged in doing trivial things for personal gain.

Our Divided United Kingdom

People tend to take it for granted that we do and should live in a nation state. It seems natural, and it is a very convenient way of organizing large groups of people, whilst giving them a sense of identity. But nationalism can lead to dangerous delusions, as Pankaj Mishra illustrates well in his book 'Age of Anger':

'Anglo-American achievements cannot be seen in isolation from their ambiguous consequences and victims elsewhere; why many assumptions, derived from a unique and unrepeatable historical experience, are an unreliable guide to today's chaos. Pointing this out might offend the fierce partisans of nation or civilization – the people who bring sectarian passions into the life of the mind, and present their own side as superior and blameless. But a curious and sceptical sensibility would recognize that to stake one's position (thus) or turn to the accident of birth as a source of pride, is intellectually sterile.'

The concept of the nation is problematic, not least because it does not always form a coherent whole and it can foster the emergence of a bellicose nationalism, as the extreme manifestation of petty tribalism. It is not only Sunni and Shia Moslems that cannot live together, or Israelis and Palestinians, but we ourselves in Britain are much more divided among ourselves than many would care to admit. This is fine if it stops at friendly rivalry, a celebration of cultural and regional differences, but when it is enshrined in deliberate economic inequality, as between North and South in England, it becomes a matter for serious concern and opposition. Example are legion, but look at the vast expenditure on Crossrail, the East-West and North-South London tube projects, whereas electrification of important inter-city rail links in the North was suspended. At least they thought better of the London Mayor's vanity plan to build a Garden Bridge across the Thames at a cost of over £200 million, but not before £37 million had been wasted on planning. Before I expand on divisions in the United Kingdom, though, I want to talk about Catalonia, because the happenings there in October 2017 were worrying indeed and carried very significant political messages on a much wider scale. The Catalan region has a history of difference from the rest of Spain in culture, language, way of life. Its economy is strong, output accounting for around one quarter of Spain's total. It held a referendum on the subject of independence, but this was immediately declared illegal by the Spanish Government and unconstitutional by its highest court. Interference with the polls was on such a scale that the feelings of the majority of Catalans remains unknown. The King weighed in for good measure. And the importance of the rule of law was stressed.

Now as the Catalan people sought to vote they were subjected to a vicious physical backlash from the national police force, who closed polling stations and attacked ordinary people, old and young, men and women alike. The Government's 'justification' for this naïve action, which of course had the contrary effect of hardening attitudes among Catalans previously not enthusiastic over the issue, was that it was defending democracy and the integrity of the State. Shamefully, the European Union refused to intervene, regarding it as a domestic matter for Spain alone. This demonstrates another good reason for leaving the EU, given the obvious and immoral reluctance to involve itself in difficult political issues. On the other hand it may just have been realistic: its record in solving international disagreements is poor.

I have little doubt that the Spanish Government were correct on the letter of their law, but what does this tell us about the nature of a country that will seek to justify violence against its own peoples by appeal to abstractions, as though constitutions are inviolate and the state of law inevitably right? Worse still, the Spanish Government then refused talks with the Catalans, and invoked a completely draconian law allowing them to take whatever measures they wish to suppress the Province. At the time of writing this involved removing the Catalan leaders from political office and replacing them with their own politicians. It is entirely possible that some of the prominent Catalan rebels will face legal sanctions, perhaps including prison sentences following the immediate arrests. And there has been talk of a State takeover of the Catalan television and radio stations, so censorship and suppression of opinions they don't like is something the Spanish Government evidently has no qualms about. Whatever view you take on the rights and wrongs of the ends here, there is very little democracy involved. Spain has shown itself to be a Parliamentary dictatorship.

There is a further worry that the same thing could happen in other Western 'democracies', even here in England (as, of course, actually did happen when Thatcher used the police to physically smash the Miners' Strike in the 1970's). It is very concerning that the Spanish authorities are not willing to enter into devolution talks to see what further powers Catalonia might enjoy within the Spanish State, but rather seek to criminalize their leaders and threaten sanctions. Is this insecurity disguised as noble nationalism? Seemingly, the world over there are populist movements pressing for more freedom, or even independence. The bottom line appears to be a perception that the centre does not give them a big enough slice of the national economic cake. In other places there are the kind of problems such as the British created where they divided Middle-Eastern countries crudely on maps, leaving religiously warring factions cheek by jowl.

Granted the powers of nation states are weakening in the face of large, multinational companies, we will still continue to live in a nation state for some time to come at least. Even if Scotland, Northern Ireland, and Wales eventually leave via devolution processes, the rest of us will still have England, albeit that more power may have been devolved to the regions by then. Looking just at the indigenous English population there are many tight regional identities, like Cornwall, and inter-regional disparities, partly based on historical and cultural factors, as well as significant variations in the local job base and traditions. But I think these are less marked than the profound economic divides which threaten to sunder and the very poorly planned transport infrastructures which geographically isolate. Fail to address these matters successfully, you politicians, and the very integrity of the nation could come under fracture.

When I say I am in favour of devolution, I mean to a maximum extent in Scotland, Wales, and Northern Ireland. Let's see Whitehall fork out large budgets instead of mean ones on five and ten-year plans to these countries along with the widest range of delegated powers. Of course, once out of the lamp the genie cannot be put back. But I would go much further. These satellites share in common with English regions outside the Home Counties a relative starvation of central interest, planning, and resources. The problems associated are of such long standing over centuries and have received such false promises and miserly action in addressing them that the moral case for ruling from London has arguably collapsed altogether. Unfortunately for those who wish to see devolution developed further, their legal authority in the present constitution has not. Nor is it at all clear how the process can be brought about against the will of the ruling party, unless public clamour and concerted media campaigns are able to dent central resolve, which seems mighty unlikely.

Assuming a democratic majority in favour, which is a big assumption, the devolution case is at its best when asserting that locals tend to know better what their region wants and needs; at its weakest when looking at their economies. The idea of the so-called 'Northern Powerhouse' was a clever one, giving as it did the lure of fool's gold to ambitious provincial politicians and businesses. Tying it however to partial local government structural reforms involving the creation of empowered American –style mayors to run city regions was a recipe for dividing and conquering. Politicians from the various towns, cities, and counties in the North of England found agreement somewhat difficult. And the people were neither consulted nor particularly interested. The reality will be a distorting effect on local democracy, as these new autocrats take decisions previously under local democratic control, with evident risk to the prospects of rural and outlying communities. Crucial for performance, of course, will be the pot of money available, liable on past record to be derisively small. Whilst places have their own separate sub-regional identities and cultures, there is an unfortunate tendency to fail to see their interests in common. For example, it would make economic sense for Wales and the Midlands to combine, Scotland with the North of England also. But it is somebody's pipe dream.

There is little doubt that the North could go it alone It has over fifteen million people, powerful traditions of engineering and industrialization, de facto separation already in matters geographical, cultural, historical, linguistic, and economic. Devo-max to a new regional assembly of the North could provide a fitting vehicle within which local authorities as traditionally organized could cooperate. They would need to be able to plan their own infrastructure, housing, education, social services, health, and police as a minimum. Even Yorkshire could do it and a strong group of councils there wants to…

If the Government takes this sort of thing seriously from the security of Westminster, it might embark on integrative measures of its own to counteract the sentiments. I was pleased to see two little such seeds in September 2017. The Government announced the creation of a 'Whitehall of the North' by the placement of around 6,000 civil servants from HM Revenue and Customs in Leeds. Such measures have been tried before and failed before, so it will be interesting to watch how things develop. Secondly, the Ministry of Defence has a proposal to involve shipyards around the country in building a new generation of warships, for final assembly in a central hub. It is a crying shame they were ever left to rot in the first place, but the regeneration will no doubt be welcome as far as it goes and subject to the areas still having a trained and dedicated workforce. A proper indicator of spending balance would be if each of our regions was to be systematically provided with key wellbeing resources, such as Olympic-quality athletic facilities, velodromes and swimming pools, symphony orchestras, and theatres. Don't forget that following the enormous claims for the legacy of the London Olympics in 2012 the Sheffield track named after our most famous athlete, Jessica Ennis was closed owing to lack of funding.

I am not talking further of Northern Ireland in this section. I would myself prefer to see a united Ireland, though I do not support Sein Fein, but the Irish question is an utter mess. They are a quarrelsome people who donkeys' years have shown it is fairly pointless to negotiate with. The North was without a government for well over a year because they could not agree to cooperate with each other and the UK Government believed the restoration of Direct Rule from Whitehall would be retrogressive. Whilst in the rest of Britain Catholics and Protestants have learned to rub along peaceably, religious rifts and historical grudges ruined them long ago on the island of Ireland and I do not go there.

The European Union

When I first envisaged writing my political statement at book length there were two rather unexpected and major Western developments yet to occur, and, as I write now, most of these remain to be played out. I refer, of course, to the election of Donald Trump as President of the United States, and the Brexit referendum by which a majority of voting United Kingdom citizens decided we were to leave the European Union. These topics have become fascinations to the point of obsession for the British media, which are increasingly long on speculation and short on solid factual information, as well as, for the most part, having ideological stances of their own against both Trump and Brexit.

For my part, rightly or wrongly, I do not intend to say much about Trump. He is difficult to predict, but he may come to be seen as a discontinuity, a phenomenon with a lot of obnoxious views, yet a refreshingly irreverent approach to the rather mundane business of government. Hopefully, he will not destabilize the world in the process. It is likely he will achieve much less than his purported agenda, as is the way with the American constitution in practice, given its checks and balances, the enormous strength of the opposition, and the difficulties of successful policy implementation. A very fast learning curve would have been needed to come to terms with the new regime. Nevertheless, the uncomfortable truth stands out here that, albeit the American voting system and its primaries is itself bent, the American people saw fit to elect such a man as their President. So the cardinal weakness of democracy is perhaps that the will of idiots can prevail if there are enough of them.

Few topics elicit as much evidence of the obsessive extremism of the UK media and of the insincerity and bumbling incompetence of leading politicians as 'Brexit'. Constitutional aspects of referenda are dealt with in the first chapter, but here I want to address in very broad terms the journey into the future. Experience suggests it will neither be as rosy nor as disastrous as the doctrinaire pundits assert. Most large-scale long-term changes historically were a very mixed bag.

Part of my reasons for approving of Brexit in spite of opposition from younger members of the family were to do with the immigration question. Leaving the European Union seemed a necessary prerequisite if we as a nation are to have any hope of controlling our numbers, because of their insistence on freedom of movement. Another was the constitutional matter of wresting back control of our law-making, though it remains to be seen how many and which foreign laws we shall repeal, because our starting point was to adopt them all. The European Union is so difficult to move and change also, whereas it is in sore need of massive internal reform in a democratic and less bureaucratic direction.

Whether the EU will remain and, if so, what sort of organization it will become are moot questions. So far its record has not been impressive on any yardstick. It is full of political dissent, bureaucratic, legally unresponsive, economically unstable, constitutionally moribund, and unclear as to its future development either in terms of the nations that may join (or leave) and whether its direction of travel is to a federal state. I was concerned about the latter possibility if we remained, as all I wanted were trading agreements and cultural exchanges among friendly countries. I was worried, too, about basket-case economies, countries with large populations, even Islamic states among joining and existing member states. Most certainly, in the longer run Britain should be able to develop good trading links all over the world, not fettered by European policy, but influential media try to indoctrinate us otherwise.

The worry persists, however, that the strong political opposition to Brexit still entrenched within the Establishment will prevail to ensure that the kind of severance we actually get is minimal. Will there be the transparency of decision-making to ensure we know clearly what is being done in our name even? We did not know when we voted the extent to which Parliament would be involved in approving any final settlement there may be either. We did not know because we have no constitution to cover even such fundamentals. Parliament itself did not yet know either.

In practice, whatever the official deadline markers put down, it will all play out over many long years. I shall therefore need to consult my crystal ball before commenting. I predict, not with total confidence, that in the fullness of time the United Kingdom will weather the storms of Brexit. And it remains to be seen whether our leaving will be more nominal than thoroughgoing. To aid the task I have turned to the expert opinion of a moderate, Roger Bootle, author of the book 'The Trouble with Europe' and founder of Capital Economics, Europe's largest macro-economic consultancy.

What Bootle's analysis shows, rather against his pro-European dispositions, is that the European Union has not so far delivered the growth and standards of living hoped for. Its scheme to run its own euro currency has not attracted anything like all EU members to join and has proved an economic disaster, with weaker countries like Greece in serious debt and default, testing beyond destruction the notion that other countries would bail them out.

It is clear that other economic blocs and areas of the world are successfully competing over share of world gross domestic product and this could intensify as Europe's working population ages and falls. There are serious internal disagreements, between those who wish to press on to a federal Europe ideologically opposed to those who aim to preserve strong elements of national sovereignty and just enjoy benefits of trade, tariff—freewith economies of scale. When we joined I was in the latter camp. A major rift since opened up over freedom of movement as a result of uncontrolled mass migration from the ever-ongoing war conflicts of the Middle-East.

There is growing realization that the EU's undemocratic governmental structures, virtually unconnected to national electorates, are too unwieldy and inflexible to brook the prospects for early and substantial reform in the face of a rapidly changing world context. The institutions are badly run, rigidly regulated, and driven by an integration agenda, not economic growth.

More countries seek to join. Some are large. Some are politically unstable. They may be Islamic, like Turkey. None have rich and successful economies. Whilst the EU may gain credit for having brought together countries that were mutually hostile factions through two world wars in the twentieth century it has of itself provided no military buffer against Communism or Islam.

Of the three major economies in the EU apart from Britain, Germany has a powerful manufacturing base, export-oriented, building up a large surplus that its people are understandably unwilling to see lost to subsidizing the weaker brethren. France and Italy run deficits and have relatively unstable and corrupt political systems which rarely satisfy the demands of their electorates.

Other reasons for inherent instability of the EU include the unsettling effect that Britain's leaving may have on some of those who remain. Countries might try to extract worthwhile reforms in their own interests, like Cameron spectacularly failed to do for Britain. They too might then leave. Most would go from a position of weakness, of course, but they would at least be able to plan their own destinies. A North-South split is possible, the economies in the North generally being the stronger.

In the coming decades the former dominance of the United States will probably subside and, although India, and especially China are predicted to rise, perhaps no nation will become pre-eminent. Whether as a unified bloc, or as separate nations, Europe, and that includes Britain in or out of the EU, may become so small in economic terms that it will cease to matter particularly to the larger world economies. So our ability to forge satisfactory trade deals with the big battalions will become progressively harder. Whether we are in or out of Europe will be much less relevant in international terms.

In the meantime, however, it is important to be realistic (not wildly pessimistic or optimistic) about the United Kingdom's chances outside the European Union over the foreseeable future. No existing trade model will fit, but we must strive to negotiate as good trading arrangements with them as possible consistent with our being outside their jurisdiction. We should re-join the European Free Trade Association, EFTA, which includes Iceland, Norway, and Switzerland. We need enhanced economic ties with Commonwealth countries, building on any funds of goodwill, binary free-trade agreements with as many countries as can be attained world-wide, together with agreements with the United States. Whether we could join their North American Free Trade Association, NAFTA, should be explored. At worst we would come under World Trade Organisation rules, perfectly workable, despite being little talked about, and applicable almost everywhere. The main problem is likely to be tariffs, very variable from one industry to another.

Finally, when we look at British firms, we see a mixed picture over support for Brexit. It should be remembered that the private sector always acts as far as it can on self-interest. So this is not the same as the national interest and might only rarely approximate to it. Firms that do little trade in the European Union and those adversely affected by their regulations (such a fish quotas, for example) may be broadly in favour of Brexit, as would ones seeing particular niche opportunities on the continent. At first there will be winners, such as those whose major trade is elsewhere than Europe in the world, and losers, where the reverse is true. It needs to be realized that business leaders are at best good at business: they are not experts in political matters, though some seek to manipulate these in their favour via lobbying systems and other methods. For all their apparent positions they might be no better judges than ordinary citizens when it comes to weighing up the likely medium and long-term consequences for the nation as a whole.

A single industry may not provide a decisive argument one way or another on Brexit. Nevertheless, the case of agriculture is instructive. When we joined the Common Market all those years ago they had a system of farm subsidies aimed at ensuring a stable supply of food by protecting farmers against loss from such risks as bad weather. Over the years, however, the European Union has moved to a system which bases subsidies largely on the size of the land. Whilst landowners nominally have to be 'active farmers' in reality the test is so weak that the model rewards already wealthy landowners, such as members of the aristocracy and, of course, the Royals. We can only hope that one consequence of Brexit, if it ever happens, will be the reform by the British Government of the system of farm subsidies in such a way as to support instead the small and needy farmers within a national policy of sustainable land management. We should aim to become self-sufficient in the staples of life. Don't hold your breath.

A tantalising early move regarding Brexit, however, was the announcement by the Government of repeal of the convention whereby Britain grants access to other nations' fishermen within twelve miles from our coast. Of itself this measure will not be enough to protect what is left of our fishing industry following its decimation by EU policy and national neglect. Quotas need rebalancing to serve the interest of the small armies of local fishermen nationwide, but will they be? And in any event just who and how does the Government propose to police the waters? There will then still be the need to negotiate suitable terms with the EU regarding the seas between twelve miles and two hundred out.

Mervyn King, former Head of the Bank of England, spoke on the BBC Newsnight programme on 20th March 2017 about Brexit. His concerns were quite moderate. He was sure we could survive and prosper beyond the European Union and recommended short negotiations, so as not to become tied down. But he also made a few points about the state of the United Kingdom more widely, saying our leaders seemed to be in danger of devoting themselves almost exclusively to Brexit, whereas he thought we faced far bigger problems. These he correctly exemplified as paying for an ageing society – its pensions, NHS, and social care.

This book will probably be published before negotiations for the terms of exit have been concluded and was mostly written before formal negotiations were even under way. I will therefore confine my speculations to a minimum. There must be an end to free movement to comply with majority wishes in the referendum. This will presumably mean we can no longer access the single market. There will inevitably be a net financial cost of leaving. We do have assets to offset it, but will want to go on paying for some benefits, like cooperation over combatting crime and terrorism, and on science, education, aviation and space. There will probably be reciprocal rights to remain for EU nationals already here, and for Britons currently residing in Europe. We will doubtless keep a large dollop of EU law and my hope is that this will include their higher environmental standards, which we regularly breach. At the time of writing legitimate concerns surrounded the perceived incompetence of our negotiating ministers, and the uncertainty of resolve caused by the government's propped up Commons majority. The absence of voices for the devolved administrations of Scotland, Wales, and Northern Ireland, as well as the other denial of representation to a much strengthened Labour Party, and, where reasonable, arguments from those who wish us to remain in the EU, does not augur well for a satisfactory democratic outcome. Further down the line it remains to be seen how much the parliamentary process will be allowed to shape the evolution of our own laws coming out of the EU shadow and how much the Government will seek to push through without debate or vote.27 other nations are bound to ensure that the EU stance is fairly inflexible and that they will want Britain to be made something of an example so as to discourage the rest. They are plainly worried by the financial black hole arising from our withdrawal too. Having said that, Europe has its own development agenda and internal problems, which we are too self-centred to fully appreciate. Many of them are weary of the nuisance we keep presenting and angered by the foolish, jingoistic rhetoric adopted by our gutter press and politicians who should know better. It adds up to show just how foolish our populace has been all these years to ignore the remorseless way our laws and administrative arrangements have got so entwined.

One deep concern over Brexit is that our more deprived areas in Britain currently receive aid from the European Union for specific development projects, whereas commentators in the provinces are sceptical that the UK Government will in future fill the gap with match funding. They are more likely to shelve the projects indefinitely or altogether.

Immigration

All political commentators these days seem to have to say something about immigration, so, with some trepidation, I will too. Rather than moralize, or talk about legal principles such as human rights, which have dubious philosophical grounding, I find it easier to view matters from the standpoint of practicality. Bluntly, we are a small, very overpopulated island. In the modern world of high-speed transport and communication links, it is very difficult to fulfil that first obligation of governments to provide a secure environment for its citizens. Nevertheless, we do need considerably strengthened border controls, better powers to police our boundaries, and a large force of well-trained and highly mobile officers to protect us.

We ought to have an ongoing national debate, not just sprouting by the press, since we are supposedly a democracy, and need to decide just what levels and types of immigrants we want. There are obviously shortfalls in labour at any one time. As we are in danger of being swamped by the large net influx, we obviously have to make the country harder to reside in legally, and easier to turf out of legally.

This means seceding from any international agreements and laws which would in principle require us to take in various categories of immigrant. Currently, a distinction is made between so-called 'economic migrants', who there is a claimed disposition to exclude, and 'genuine asylum seekers', who allegedly qualify by virtue of atrocities elsewhere in the big bad world. I would have done with both concepts, along with any treaty obligation concerning privileged access for types of applicant from countries where, say, we have colonial connections, or from areas of the European Union. The onus of proof would rest with the migrant in their country of origin; at any rate not here. Our admissions criteria would relate primarily to national and local regional needs for skilled labour of various kinds, notably at professional and technical levels for specific industries and employment streams, and a population of balanced age and ethnicity.

For our self-respect and to avoid undue exploitation (there will always be some from the desperate and the criminal) our regulations need to be altogether tougher than hitherto. For example, bona fide examination qualifications, severe visa restrictions and on sending earnings abroad, adequate proficiency in both written and spoken English, would be prerequisites. And I like the Australian idea of enshrining in law automatic disbarment for would-be immigrants who enter the country illegally, or who try to deceive the authorities about themselves. Marriages of convenience and any arranged marriages would disqualify. We are in trouble because of both the sheer scale of net influx and the dubious or unsuitable qualities of some of the migrants. Many come with criminal pasts, minimal education and skills, dangerous political and/or religious ideologies unlikely to mesh when they arrive here. What we can do about it nobody yet seems to know, though there are theories a-plenty. Meanwhile the composition of the population has been transformed, quite irreversibly.

Our asylum system is far worse than a national disgrace. It is a growing threat and danger to us all. As Harriet Sergeant pointed out in the Spectator in September 2017,'nobody arrives in this country without the help of people traffickers.' Most are economic migrants whose family have paid the traffickers. They are young men, not children, neither are they refugees from some kind of oppression in their countries of origin. Typically, they destroy their papers, take assumed names, and spin a yarn, lying about their identity, age, nationality, and plight. The immigration authorities are by and large not fooled. They even know the traffickers, whom they cannot touch. Basically they are politically gelded, for whatever (sinister) motives. They are forced to work within a corrupt and broken system, which makes us a soft touch for much of the world's riff-raff, some of whom have already made a Devil's pact with ISIS to do us harm when they get in. The ones who miss out as a direct result of this false humanitarianism are our own indigenous youth – the vulnerable teenagers too old for care homes anymore and the many unhappy teenagers who simply leave home and disappear, without benefit of the fostering system supposedly designed for our own.

Whilst we do not wish to appear lacking in humanity or compassion, we must be careful to explain a cogent and defensible position if we can arrive at one. Likely some of the pressures will fade away in time without our understanding or much impact, as international problems sometimes can, but we would be foolish indeed to rely on it. There has to be a firm but fair approach developed, one which nevertheless takes away the right of would-be immigrants to sue the government and in British Courts at that, one which denies them legal aid, one which deports immediately anyone failing new stringent tests of right to remain. They must not be allowed to crawl away into the shadows, their whereabouts and behaviour unknown.

Of course, once illegal immigrants have been caught, the Home Office has a woeful record in not deporting them. Not only that, as often as not they continue to move around freely, whereas they should be detained. Complications over deportation evidently apply to thousands, whether EU nationals or otherwise. Sad to say, official statistics cannot be relied upon, but there is no doubting the scale, nor the long-term nature of the problem.

What the humanitarian do-gooders forget when they look at would-be refugees from some horrendous conflict or natural disaster in a faraway land are the sad cases of United Kingdom nationals already here and living lives of poverty, neglect, exploitation – slavery even. And they fail to realize that some years down the track a lot of these new immigrants will have significantly outbred us. Neither will they have helped us create an integrated multicultural society. Draw your own conclusions.

The people who turn into violent random killers in England are typically young men, Muslim, either Middle-Eastern in origin or in that of their parents. We hear with depressing regularity after an atrocity that the perpetrators were already known to the security services, who either failed to see them as a threat, or who were continuing to 'monitor' their activities (not closely enough). There had usually been some previous history of violent crime, or religious radicalization, sometimes associated with insurgent, often Saudi, Imans at the local mosque, and usually in a network, or family, swanning in and out of terrorist haven countries with impunity.

It is of course easy to be wise in hindsight. Except that we are not. We do not appear to learn the lessons – that those who make the decisions are being too readily fooled, that not enough resources and intelligent manpower are being dedicated to our safety, that our wishy-washy liberal laws are too weak to protect us, the standards of evidence too onerous. For those suspected as potential terrorists we need to decide as a nation whether their liberty is a superior value to champion than our safety and peace of mind.

The potentially helpful powers we have we rarely use, such as temporary exclusions from the country, removal of right of return for those travelling to places that ferment and train jihadists, house arrest and internment. It is clear for undisclosed reasons that the Government is not really serious about controlling immigration and clamping down on criminal suspects from abroad, despite the persistent loud clamour of the citizens. It allows proselytising on our streets, the setting up of religious schools, freedom of operation of mosques, implementation of sharia law. It has enacted anti-racial laws which override the rights of free speech and muzzle the indigenous population. Even as the US-backed forces effectively defeated ISIS in their Syrian strongholds, the head of MI5 calmly pointed out that our struggling Security Service would face greater challenges still as hundreds of British Muslims who had joined ISIS came 'home'!

When the Manchester bomber of May 2017 murdered 22, mainly school kids, and injured 166 more, the country reacted in interesting, but largely irrelevant ways. There was intense and ghoulish media interest, publicizing private grief, a temporary show of solidarity and defiance by citizens, the absurd and cosmetic deployment of thousands of police, some armed and accompanied by soldiers, patrolling dangerous locations such as Scarborough beach to show a visible presence. Whereas our reservoirs and power stations, for example, went undefended. It was said that we would never be beaten by the terrorists. Yet this has already happened. We live in fear of the next atrocity to get through, our freedoms are curtailed, decisions on where to go and what to do become more cautious, the costs of protection get higher, there are more searches and long delays at airports.

Weak laws compound the danger, limiting as they do such useful measures as powers of detention, interrogation, restriction of movement, deportation, house arrest, removal of passports and citizenship and the like. We are just pathetically soft with those among us with alien backgrounds who wish to live by their chosen laws, not ours, and in segregated quasi-religious communities, preferably speaking their own native language.

In 2016 naval commanders and the immigration service both warned the government that much of the British coast is wide open to people smugglers who seek to bring in migrants using small boats. The 7,700 miles of coastline were currently being patrolled by the only three ships possessed by the Border Force, a derisively small number wholly inadequate to the task. This was said at the time the Government's latest token measures were announced, comprising supposed new maritime powers for the Border Force to arrest, search, and detain suspects. They do not seem to have grasped the monstrous fact that a systematic and widespread network of slavery has been established in our larger towns and cities run by foreign gang masters to make huge profits from such activities as drug trading, prostitution, and free labour.

The loophole of immigrants getting through the channel tunnel, and the intimidation of intercontinental lorry drivers to smuggle them into the country via Dover, seemed to recede with the French authorities' action to destroy the Calais camps, but the inmates were merely dispersed and would try again. The fact that it disappears from view as a media preoccupation is sadly little indication that the problems have gone away. Certainly, if they have it is small thanks to the British government, or the European Union.

As a final example of EU ineptitude in the face of mass migration to Europe, there is the influx from the

North African continent to Italy and Spain. I do not pretend to being anything other than at a loss how to solve this problem, but I would say, however, that it is beyond the powers of any one nation, however affluent. Unfortunately, where you are reliant on international cooperation much is honoured in the breach. And humanitarian efforts can be worse than counter-productive in such a case. What do I mean? Well, there is a disconnection between non-governmental charity organizations and governments, so there are clashes of intention regarding the refugee boats. The agencies occupy the moral high ground as they rescue the desperate from unseaworthy craft and deposit them alive on the European coast, but the countries cannot cope. In reality the charities are helping the traffickers by not taking the migrants back where they came from. And Britain with the USA has an undischarged obligation to help solve the problem of traffickers by cooperation with what passes for the rudiments of good government in North Africa now we have destabilized the region.

Defence of the Realm

Defence has to be seen in military terms regarding the perspectives of army, navy and air force, but rather more widely, too, concerning risk management. Dealing with defence first, the government's basic duty is naturally to protect us. Throughout history until the twentieth century this could broadly be done by dint of the invariable sacrifice of the expendable ordinary people: modern conditions and technologies, however, render keeping us completely safe almost an impossibility. So we must strike a note on realism whilst doing what we can.

This requires eternal and collective vigilance, the perennial evaluation of risk, and a deep understanding of foreign countries, their needs, aspirations, and mutual interactions. We must also be alive to threats from terrorist groups as well as extremist individuals. Sadly, they will always be with us in some incarnation or other. We must remain alert and be able to respond rapidly in any crisis.

One thing we must utterly avoid is short-term budgeting and crude percentage cuts. Quinquennial defence reviews are a good thing so long as their purpose is primarily to evaluate changing need for personnel and equipment: finance should not be the driver. Whilst I am incompetent to make technical suggestions in this field, it is clear that we need considerable professional expertise to monitor and make recommendations. Weapons procurement prudently requires a sophisticated arms industry of our own, but this is too strategically important to be allowed in the hands of private firms. Nor must we warmonger, or sell arms abroad anymore.

Although attitudes of the general public towards our forces personnel are very supportive, not so the way our wounded heroes are dealt with by government, which often appears callously indifferent, secretive, and penny-pinching. They have always to our shame been regarded as canon-fodder throughout our history, an unpalatable aspect of the nasty and hypocritical country we have always been.

I have a lot of other worries about the armed forces apart from the above, not least their adequacy for the primary role. The country's culture makes it very unwise for senior officers to stand up to politicians, even when they know them to be misguided. In recent times we have seen a worrying feature whereby military commanders have resigned or retired and then made the kind of criticisms that would repay our close attention. And today politicians tend to be out of touch on military matters. They make sometimes crucial decisions with no real understanding, quite a change from the days after the Second World War, when many of them had direct personal experience of the services. What this leads to can go way beyond embarrassing shortfalls in equipment and training for our forces in conflict zones to being given ridiculous goals or none at all, so that they reflect their democratic masters in being unsure what they are there for. Because the services are command structures with rigid hierarchies, the ordinary soldier, airman, or sailor has no voice. He cannot even complain up the line without risking disciplinary action and career blight. Dawning recognition renders recruitment more difficult. Later on the distance from civilian life makes the youths going in unable to adapt to life on the outside when they come out.

It is expedient for the nation to provide proportionate assistance to any bona fide and credible international peace-keeping roles and to retain active membership of international defence organizations of significance like NATO, yet it is also important not to overcommit or to lead. We cannot afford to be seen as striving for world influence way beyond our capacity and capability. Wherever possible we should maintain neutrality like Switzerland.

With regard to risk management more widely, we have to be prepared for contingencies of major natural and man-made disasters, about which more will be said in the chapter on the Environment. Both relate to keeping us safe and we must not assume in either case certainty of disaster or our ability to avoid it totally. The area is potentially a considerable worry, because our blinkered five-year term governments do not naturally incline to plan ahead to consider future possible problems. Not only do the relevant agencies – national, regional, and local – require sustained resources, but they also need mechanisms of coordination and cooperation which now barely exist. They used to, to some extent, when people worried about the 'bomb'. Unfortunately they require a sustained continuity of policy which transcends the insular and small-minded nature of current party politics.

The lure of money makes us fools to ourselves. The extent of the UK government's complicity in selling arms and other 'strategically controlled goods' is truly staggering. In 2013, for instance, there were over 3,000 government-approved export licenses amounting to nearly thirteen billion pounds' worth of equipment for no fewer than twenty-five countries on the Foreign Office's own list of countries, like Saudi Arabia, whose policies were of concern over human rights. They behead people like ISIS do. Licenses have even been granted to actual or potential enemies including Russia, Syria, Iraq, Pakistan, and Iran, not to mention China.

Weapons of Mass Destruction

In the Cold War days the focus was mainly on the hydrogen bomb and the atomic bomb, but more recently have arisen the spectres of chemical and biological warfare in addition. There is no doubt that their killing capacity is awesome, truly on an unimaginable scale, and so it behoves the world bodies to monitor what nations do and to intervene appropriately before there is a serious risk where WMD programmes appear to be ongoing. Peaceful purposes are always claimed by the miscreants, of course, and it is far from clear how they can be stopped before they join the nuclear club. In the case of North Korea, as an example, it is conceivable that their young, dynastic leader is deranged, or at least is reliant on militancy to sustain his power base at home, so this adds irrational and unpredictable elements for consideration. Stakes could not be higher, since in the worst scenario the future of the entire human population is at risk, given that conflicts could plunge the planet into a nuclear winter which, lasting years, might kill everyone, friend and foe alike. President Trump's crude and irresponsible comments in the face of repeated missile tests by North Korea have rightly alarmed the world. It might be a comfort to suspect that powerful internal forces may conspire to unseat Kim Jong-un; his brutal and repressive regime rules by fear and keeping the populace largely unaware of the outside world with its considerable relative benefits and ways of life. Modern communications will gradually breach their curtain of ignorance. Additionally, South Korea and the USA could plan to assassinate Kim using commandos or strike weapons, on the theory that his demise would defuse the nuclear threat, at least temporarily.

Deterrence is the fundamental policy by which we attempt to safeguard our futures. Broadly it means building up such a large strike capacity as to deter a would-be aggressor, who would know that after his preemptive strike our retaliation would be severe enough before we died to cause grave, even terminal damage to his own country and people. A stalemate and uneasy peace would therefore alternatively ensue, neither side being willing to take the risk. Rationally, there is little point either in winning such a conflict if the enemy does not fire back since the country of the vanquished would be irradiated and uninhabitable for hundreds or thousands of years to come. It is said that the strategy works. At any rate, nobody has started a nuclear war since the Japanese cities of Hiroshima and Nagasaki were completely destroyed by very much less devastating weapons than we nowadays possess.

In my pessimistic and suspicious way, I am not so sure. I am far from sanguine about the situation, mainly because of the human preoccupation with wars for political power, the fact that deterrence theory plays to psychological makeups which we do not all have, and by observing the painfully slow progress of the superpowers in their mutual programmes of planned decommissioning of their WMD.

To use deterrence effectively as a shield you have to play as thoroughly immoral game of poker. You have to say to the other side that you will use your WMD under certain circumstances and you have to persuade him that you will. Consequently, it does not work if your leaders take an ethically humane position and say they would not use WMD under any circumstances. It puts the nation in relative weakness and thus serious vulnerability. It is better to bluff convincingly and not mean it. This is at the core of criticisms of Jeremy Corbyn's perceived pacifist stance over the Trident missile.

My own position is no help at all to gung-ho nationalists. With a mixture of moral preference and pragmatic assessment of likely outcomes, I conclude that it could in no circumstances whatsoever be justified to press the red button. Even if we ourselves had to die, it would still be better for some human beings to survive, albeit that they were on the other side and their leaders wished us dead. In other words the normal psychology of war has to be set aside because the nature of the conflict would be like no other in its extreme severity. There are only two justifications for war: self-defence and the defence of the helpless. If we can do neither there is no justification for war left.

Cyberwar

Philip Hammond, as sometime Tory Defence Minister, announced in 2016 a large new programme to put the nation in a state of readiness for cyberwar, especially to combat attacks sponsored by unfriendly foreign governments and aimed at disabling our strategic infrastructure. I think this strategy is right in principle, but it remains to be seen how effective the government measures, both defensive and offensive, actually become. A major problem with the Conservatives is their ideological aversion to public sector expenditure, so whether the right level of resources will be allocated, sufficient numbers of staff of the requisite calibre recruited and trained, seems to me doubtful short of a spectacular national disaster to concentrate public opinion, media pressure, and recalcitrant politicians.

'Cyberspace' to quote experts Singer and Friedman:

> 'is…an information environment …made up of digitized data that is created, stored and … shared'.

It is a new major threat in the computer age:

> 'It comprises the computers that store data plus the systems and infrastructure that allow it to flow. This includes the internet of networked computers'.

So 'cyberwar' is conflict between enemies via cyberspace. All advanced nations are building cyberwar capacity, both for attack and defence, as well as terrorist groups and individuals with a range of motives. And in case this fact seems somewhat abstract and remote it should be mentioned that such developments have the potential, like conventional warfare, to cause serious loss of life. We are used by now to hearing on a personal level about people whose identity has been stolen, or whose bank account has been emptied. We are perhaps less aware that banks could be made to collapse, hospitals to lose their energy supplies, the national grid to be disabled, transport coordination jammed, key defence secrets stolen, and much else besides. Whether cyberwar will actually replace conventional war remains to be seen, yet it has the potential one day to be able to disable whole nations without reducing their buildings to rubble or rendering them irradiated nuclear wastelands, so it would be an attractive alternative proposition to political megalomaniacs.

There is a classic dilemma. To be useful information has to be shared with somebody. But there is no way possible to do so with perfect security. There is always a degree of risk. The difficulties of preventing a cyberattack are more problematic than with conventional warfare, unfortunately. Notably, it is very hard indeed to ascertain who the enemy is, or quite what his goals are either. There are also far more enemies possible in principle because the cost of necessary equipment is quite low. And the speed of attack is phenomenal – a matter of seconds only. As is common in war, the collateral damage to innocent civilians is likely to exceed that of the official combatants, although governments naturally perpetuate the contrary myth.

Given that the scope and scale are global, the prospects for avoiding massive catastrophes seems low. Many factors militate against adequate defence, among which I will just cite a few prominent ones: governments are ponderous in thought and deed, they are notoriously slow to cooperate with each other, they prefer talk to action, they are frequently scientifically illiterate, and they mostly have a plethora of other priorities that keep them in blissful ignorance or denial.

The philosopher A. C. Grayling, in his thoughtful book 'War – An Enquiry', ranged widely across the world and back through history trying to understand war and how to limit it. Of his conclusions one of the most comforting is that war is not caused by human nature but by political institutions. 'Aggression is a feeling of an individual, but it is a choice in a State.' And again:

'if most people are traumatized by war, and if almost every idea of human good and flourishing is negated by violence and destruction, loss, grief, and premature death, then war is not an expression of human nature.'

He continues:

'although anger, aggression and a desire or willingness to fight an opponent on occasion are human characteristics, the overwhelming evidence (is) of cooperation and mutual interest among members of our essentially social species.' So 'this feature of human psychology (is put) in its place, along with ...allied features such as greed and selfishness.'

He therefore prescribes de-institutionalizing war, which means getting away from government military contracts, and the arms industry playing an important role in the national economy, and overturning the general social approval they command. He also advocates not romanticizing war by the simple expedient of ceasing to censor news. As he so graphically states:

> 'how about the aversion therapy of truth-mangled bodies, blown apart children, blood running into gutters, people screaming in pain or terror?'

There are other crucial philosophical concerns here too, namely about the need for fresh modern analyses of the definitions of war, not revisited since early times, despite the vastly changed circumstances that advanced technology dictates. Cyber-activity blurs the understanding of what should constitute war, when we can say it is occurring. Adversaries no longer have to declare themselves or their intentions, where they are operating from. Again, in what way are consequences relevant to such a judgement? Do people have to die, for instance? What is the status of hacking, of espionage, of disrupting infrastructure? How do we accommodate to the fact that vast numbers of ordinary citizens will potentially be affected, no longer as unfortunate 'collateral damage' from misplaced attacks on the military?

CHAPTER 5

CONTROLLING CAPITALISM

The Dismal 'Science' of Economics
Capitalism
Anti-Capitalism
Post-Capitalism
The Entrepreneurial State
The Tax Man Cometh
The Global Village
Trading Partners
Multinational Companies
Business Behaviour
Bonkers Banking
Worthy of Our Hire
Pensioning Off
Deeper in Debt
Who Needs Charities?
What of the Future?

The Dismal 'Science' of Economics

Economics is broadly the study of how to make good choices for deployment of scarce resources, of which money is but one such. This applies at all scales from the individual to national concerns. It uses such concepts as the 'supply' of goods and services. When this meets the 'demand' for them it supposedly determines an agreed 'price' or cost to be paid for the transaction to occur. 'Competition' between suppliers tends to drive down prices, whereas scarcity of goods and services drives them up. Firms produce, households work for an income, then spend or 'consume'. Employment levels vary depending on the money available to pay workers. As they fall, incomes reduce households' capacity to buy, and so demand drops, causing a reduction in prices to try and stimulate the demand. Extreme cases result in a 'slump' or 'depression'. Higher prices (called inflation) are another way of reducing demand. A 'boom' is the opposite, when investment rises and higher income levels generate greater demand.

That will have to suffice as a basic description of the bare bones of economics. The subject has been much elaborated and refined, with the development of further concepts. In some cases mathematical, both geometric and algebraic, quantification has been added, but it is not within our scope to discuss such specialist topics. I suspect they have led both economists and politicians into serious errors at times, as too much reliance has been placed on formulae and dubious theories.

One grave problem that occurs is that the subject is neutral as to morality. So what happens to people in the grip of economic forces they deplore? Where politicians can see nothing wrong with the way matters are conducted? Another problem is that the assumed psychology of how people act is flawed. To give an example: people do not necessarily seek out the cheapest or most available goods. They may be snobbish. They may be lazy. They may believe that paying more gets better quality. They may be swayed by advertising and so on. A very serious objection to economic theory is that markets are assumed to be 'perfect', whereas they are far from it usually. A perfect market would bring supply and demand together smoothly and totally, as well as automatically, but this is the real world of imperfect and false information, not an ideal one where things never go wrong.

Now a major problem for societies is that economics is regarded as subservient to politics. Politicians frequently advocate and implement economic measures on political grounds first. Few have proper training or grounding in economics either, so they can and do utilize wrong measures, or measures wrong at the time, or with insufficient degree of application.

A further important problem concerns economics itself, an academic discipline which has pretensions to being a science, but is in reality very much in its infancy as a means of explanation and prediction. Novel situations have a way of coming about, sorely testing the economic theories available. This, of course, allows for much difference of opinion among even the most distinguished economists.

We the public are in double danger as a result. Politicians can use the disagreement among economists as an excuse to do what they like. Secondly, they are not all above using the mystique of the subject to blind us with science.

Nevertheless, we should all be obliged to be responsible, to try and use the best of our modern economic understanding to solve our real life difficulties. There is the hope that as time goes on the subject will be better understood scientifically and that more politicians will try to apply its advice objectively instead of through the distorting lens of ideology or expediency.

The very fact that values have to be reckoned along with the facts naturally is the main reason why progress has been slower in the social sciences than in the physical and biological ones. In my philosophical worldview values as such do not exist, except they are invented and constructed. There is no grounding in the way that facts and truth are anchored. Values occupy a different realm –

that of meaning imputed by humanity and underpinned by emotional attachments of varying strengths, for which reasons and arguments are then elicited. In this worldview obviously values can occur and be used across the whole range of human experience. What I am saying is that a great many values are not financial. Whereas those that are form the subject of interest here in the present chapter and politicians frequently act as if nothing else matters.

It follows that values, if not exactly arbitrary, will vary a lot between individuals and among groups, as well as between nations. Which is fundamentally why there can be no ultimate agreement in politics, or within its economic sub-sets. A further difficulty is that values can clash, so need to be prioritised in a hierarchy to solve the more complex problems.

My financial values are fairly straightforward. Broadly speaking, I want to live a free existence, equal under the law in theory and practice with all other citizens, whether high-born or more lowly, with the right to pursue my legitimate interests, including career, within a culture that rewards fairly without huge disparities, and which has excellent and humane welfare systems in place should I falter or flounder along the way. My more detailed value preferences, those concerned with particular economic facets, will no doubt become clear as the chapter develops.

The Archbishop of Canterbury, Justin Welby, himself a former executive in the oil industry, claimed in September 2017 that Britain's economic model is broken. He wanted the implementation of proposals recommended by the Commission on Economic Justice, radical measures massive in scope to raise living standards for most of the population, a huge redistribution of wealth to narrow the gulf between rich and poor, a reduced and socially redefined role for the banking sector, and action to curb the financial and moral excesses of internet giants like Google, Amazon, and Facebook. I am not a Christian, but so do I.

Unfortunately, perhaps, politics to be successful must be informed by the best of economics. Whilst this subject contains much that is pre-scientific, or ideologically warped, it cannot unfortunately be dispensed with either, where we are hoping to set down remedies for our failing society. It is important in this context to pay particular attention to the theories of what I may term 'alternative' economists; that is, those outside the prevailing paradigm of received 'wisdom' who nevertheless have imposing academic credentials and requisite international experience. Justification comes from the fact that politicians struggle to make a success of managing the economy with the aid of conventional economics. One rebel is perhaps the economist Michael Hudson, an American non-establishment figure who, addressing the mighty problem of international debt, argues in 'The Bubble and Beyond' that there is no legitimate debt repayment option, only variations on 'debt forgiveness', to avoid economic catastrophe. The austerity agenda is shot: elected governments should on the contrary determine policies in the best wide interests of their citizens, not the narrow ones of firms.

There are some key economic ideas that underlie debate and which should be teased out for clarity. Firstly, there is the bedrock assumption that we must have free markets. But only the purists will surely be so naïve today as to believe that unfettered free markets will always turn out the best possible consequences. Try telling those who lost their jobs when their firm went bust, for example. So my vote is for free markets, but subject to the appropriate nature and extent of regulation and intervention by the State's organs to give Capitalism a human face and protect people from its worst excesses. The key question is of course what is the right intervention?

I am by nature a planner, so am appalled at the fact that the country is run largely on the basis of short-term tactical vision, with but hazy notions of desired end-point; without strategy in other words.

I deeply resent the unfairness built into the country by State controls on public sector worker incomes with a hands-off laissez-faire attitude to anything the private sector does.

I am not doctrinaire about privatization, but sick of its polarization between right-wingers in favour and left wingers against. There is to me no right and wrong here. Both have some place in the armoury of governments to tackle economic problems, but there is nothing wrong in principle with mixed approaches in some industries. The strategic national self-survival industries such as agriculture, fishing, steel, ship-building and vehicles manufacture, building of infrastructure, energy, natural resources, should, it seems obvious to me, be under national control, not at the mercy of foreign owners, a major risk with private firms. Other areas in which public ownership is potentially advantageous are all those where pseudo-markets have been created. Current notorious examples include the malfunctioning rail franchises, water boards, and, par excellence, the 'big six' energy companies, which have fleeced millions of customers. Where these ideological stances are dangerous is in their unthinking application to sector and circumstance. State control can lead to inefficiency and waste. Private sector involvement can put profit above service, as well as distributing employee rewards far too unevenly, skewed towards the top, and pricing less well-off customers out.

Another area of doctrinaire economic ideology doing harm is the right-wing espousal of monetarism against the left-wing turn to Keynes, respectively favouring manipulation of the money supply against that of taxation and public expenditure. Both are certainly needed: the economy never ceases to throw up novel combinations of problem beyond whatever the current thinking in this 'dismal science'.

There is a depressing consensus among national politicians that the general public would not stand for a wholesale redistribution of wealth. The result is that substantial checking measures are not deployed, so the inequality gap in Britain just grows and grows. All the tinkering, ideally exemplified by the Chancellor of the Exchequer's periodic 'budgets', ducks this important question, fuelling discontent and division, consolidating the unjust society.

There are key economic areas which are malfunctioning because they lack the proper regulation. One such is monopoly. There are laws against monopolies. Either they are not strong enough or are inadequately enforced, for we still see the merger and takeover of enormous firms. It is an economic article of faith that all monopolies are bad, because they are less accountable: if they are private they become exploitative without competition; if they are public hopelessly inefficient. Monopolies need not be that large as to be the only player in a given sector, they just require the capacity to distort the market in their favour, singly or together with a small number of others within a mutually cooperative cosy cartel, such as the so-called 'Big Six' energy companies. These set ups are not in the public interest, but weak governments allow them, usually afraid of possible adverse effects on jobs should they intervene.

According to David Orrell, as set out in his book 'Economyths', economics is a bit of a con, essentially an ideology not a science, although it has scientific pretensions and these days makes copious use of mathematical formulae and statistical data. The first myth he exposes, therefore, is the one that claims our economic behaviour is regulated by laws, ones which are even quantifiable, whereas the truth is that human behaviour has an unpredictable, irrational quality causing features to emerge as a result of complex dynamical interactions. Secondly, the economy is falsely taken to be the outcome of individual, independent self-interested actions, so underestimating the importance of herd behaviour. A third conventional (mythical) claim is that the economy is fundamentally stable, being subject only to minor fluctuations. The truth, that it is inherently unstable, that 'bust and boom' are normal, is presumably too terrifying for us to accept, though history clearly points to it.

Orrell demonstrates, too, that we are bad at risk assessment, tending to downplay it and to use suspect methods. We also sometimes act irrationally and place too much store by emotional reactions like trust and confidence. Those who claim that markets are fair are wrong; income distribution skews badly, so that the rich get richer at our expense.

The notion of merit, though frequently preyed in aid as justification, comes little into it.

Growth is worshipped by most economists, yet it is a false God. It has no regard to more important concerns such as the environmental health of the planet. It is neutral on depletion of resources, climate change, pollution, and so is contributing to our eventual downfall.

Economics aims to provide plenty, through goods and services, in order to bring happiness via higher standards of living. Whereas, the relationship between money and happiness is 'fuzzy and often contradictory'. We may be more interested in fair pay for a day's work, security in the face of economic shocks, a job that is socially worthwhile and emotionally rewarding. Money and happiness are in any case in very different categories of concept, so comparisons are strained.

Finally, Orrell draws our attention to the Establishment claim that the way the economy works is for our own good, that market forces, if left alone, will deliver 'the best of all possible worlds'. People all over the planet are, however, beginning to see through this. They increasingly think they are being lied to, with bogus statistics, and manipulated in the interests of those who have the power and dominate the resources. And they are correct, terrifyingly. Since we live in such a capitalist economy, we had better give it a closer look.

Capitalism

The understanding of capitalism that I shall be discussing here is simply characterized as follows. According to James Fulcher, in his book 'Capitalism', its 'fundamental feature' is 'the investment of money in order to make a profit'. That money is called 'capital', and it might be available in the form of other non-monetary assets, such as property. Capitalism comes in various forms – notably 'merchant', whereby goods are traded, 'industrial', where goods are produced, and 'financial', which exploits the changing worth of instruments like shares. Because production and consumption are separate they need to be brought together, so this is done via a 'market', where exchanges occur between parties by mutual agreement of the price and quantity of goods. Although the systems operating in the United Kingdom are obviously considerably more complicated than the above description would indicate, that is nevertheless their basic nature.

We shall proceed next to a critique of Capitalism, for not all is well with it, by any manner of means. There is a sense in which we are all critics of Capitalism, whether we realize it or not, because we either suffer from its rougher edges, or feel a preference for features that it does not presently manifest. A few illustrations will be given below, citing various prominent people.

In 2012 the then Archbishop of Canterbury, Ronan Williams, talked about the need to constrain markets by an ethical overlay. He warned against the pervasive adoption of 'the principle of universal exchangeability', whereby attempts are being made to assign almost everything a commercial value. He cites Michael Sandel, political philosopher, who gives the example of commercial blood banks which, in America at least, result in 'a large-scale redistribution of blood from the poor to the rich'. He also warns using a wonderful quotation from Robert and Edward Skidelsby: 'capitalism has no spontaneous tendency to evolve into something nobler'. Governments must not be neutral here, but implement such measures as advertising curbs, greater emphasis in developing economies in local production and progressive taxation of consumption. With these sentiments I profoundly agree. Most certainly, I see the damage in the Education system that stems from its commoditization, and I grow impatient of the feeble interventions of governments to rectify palpable injustices across the piece.

Lord Mandelson, a Labour Peer, made some observations following the 2007 credit crunch about how they should do so, pointing out the dangers of an ideology of regulation sweeping government. His views of the government's role was that of support for the market, support in the form of 'infrastructure', education, technology and export promotion'. This would of course include 'good regulation', whatever

that might mean, and could almost be seen as a
Conservative standpoint.

By contrast Tariq Ali in 'The Extreme Centre – A
Warning' describes as offensive the current nature of
Capitalism in Western countries:

> 'The astonishing development of technology
> undoubtedly created the material basis, but not the
> distribution, to satisfy the needs of all its citizens' 'but
> the economic structure based on maximising profits…
> divides the top layers from the rest. The cost of production
> is now so low that the practical value of the commodity
> has to be ignored in order to keep prices artificially
> high…The parasitic marketing and advertising industries
> are among the largest in the world, second only to arms
> production… Consumerism has conquered all. Our
> needs are manipulated. The market itself is controlled
> by the ruling elites, via a set of mechanisms such as the
> acceleration of in-built obsolescence'.

Tariq Ali points to resistance movements within the
economically weaker countries of the European Union,
like Greece and Portugal, and democratic parties trying
to make changes in South America:

> 'The attempts to roll back neoliberalism are gathering
> momentum, but what to put in its place, and by what
> means, remain subjects for debate. The most successful

movements are targeting the political structures of the state. Taking on its socio-economic base and transforming it on the South American model – state ownership of utilities and heavy regulation of capital – is an essential next step. This will not be easy in Europe. The power of the world financial system has been on display…The few control the wealth and have a military to back up that control'.

As Lenin realized, it is not sufficient, though necessary, that the lower classes want to live differently. It is also an essential prerequisite that the upper classes should be unable to rule as they do. Yet they still can.

If we go back to our original definition of Capitalism it is basically about financial exchange, deals to make someone a profit. And how could such a fundamental phenomenon ever stop so long as humans walked the earth, it might be asked? And we know there were markets before money, and before money became 'sophisticated'. And so it will endure, whatever the political system it operates within and however far from serving the people as a whole, as opposed to the minority who are the beneficiaries.

The troubles with Capitalism include the fact that it provides manna from heaven for the dishonest, there being legion ways to cheat consumers with impunity. One we rarely think about occurs when a firm goes bust. There must come a point where they know they are going under. Yet they will often still trade, taking full prepayment on orders they know they will be unable to honour. I'm sure that contract law has got this covered, to ensure they can't be touched for such villainy, but isn't it nevertheless to laypeople a nasty kind of fraud, extraction of money by false pretences?

If people have any doubts about claims that our capitalist financial institutions are not fit for purpose, they have only to look at the statistics on complaints. Record numbers of these were received in 2013 running into many thousands, ranging widely from bank accounts and store cards to insurance policies and private pensions. This holds true even when you factor out the mass fraud that was payment protection insurance, which at least they are paying compensation on. The Financial Ombudsman Service received 264,375 new cases in the year ending March 2012. Mortgages were one area, with administrative errors and failures to find individually tailored solutions being bugbears. Credit cards are notoriously another, with firms trying to wheedle out of their joint legal responsibility when customers are let down by goods and services.

Anti-Capitalism

So capitalism has so many seriously adverse effects for individuals and society as a whole that an anti-capitalist movement has sprung up in opposition to it. The sentiments are expressed and the ideas considered in works like 'Anti-Capitalism' by Simon Tormey. They are agreed that the present system, usually called 'Neoliberalism', has failed. Opinions differ, however, over whether it can be replaced. I myself am gloomy over the feasibility of the prospect, believing that some minor ameliorations of its worst effects are about all we can expect, but within an ongoing unstable context where Capitalism itself is likely to generate serious crises from time to time. Where it does, such as with the banking crisis of 2007, we are unlikely to learn the lessons and take the necessary preventative measures for the future, sad to say, with too many vested and opposing interests within a power-diffused society. In other words, if we tear down the status quo, we do not really know how the future will pan out; it is the familiar devil we know of today, but the future is uncertain, and probably compatible with many alternative structures.

Tormey's analysis cites two key obstacles to reform at the global level which he calls 'externalities'. These are the 'dominant position of the USA in global politics' (we might add the rising influence of China now), and the fact that money can be moved round the world instantly by computer. He cites other difficulties he calls 'fault lines', the principal ones being dualisms like North/ South, reformism/radicalism, ideological/non-doctrinal.

So, inevitably, any agreed programme of action would have to be a compromise. It might well look like Tormey's list:

- improved representation of groups and regions in global institutions,
- introduction of fairness measures such as debt relief, trade tariffs, more equitable trade agreements, bars on dumping of subsidized goods (like Chinese steel),
- global treaties to end labour exploitation,
- arms trade controls,
- environmentally sustainable development policies.

I think a lot of people, me included, might well sign up to a programme such as this without any conscious belief that they wanted to act against Capitalism, or were in fact doing so. But if it was branded as Anti-Capitalism they would not. It has a somewhat derogatory ring.

Naomi Klein, though a celebrated market critic, sounds notes of caution that to her the Anti-Capitalist movement so far is just a kind of 'serial protesting' which effects very little improvement and does not seem to have any clear idea of where it is going. So another fault line, for Tormey, is one between those who want the movement to become 'a conventional political organization' and those who want to build on its present 'disaggregated, dispersed and decentred character'. They would wish to have resistance developing organically out of the grass-root concerns of ordinary people, with corresponding flat, flexible, non-hierarchical organizing structures. I don't see why it cannot be both, though turning people's collectively enlightened attitudes into movements that direct whole governments and crack the excessive behaviour of multinationals seems fantasy-land to me, much as I might like to see it happen.

Post-Capitalism

It is my deep conviction that Capitalism has to be controlled somehow for the good of society as a whole. The interests and legally-defined purposes of firms are so simple and self-serving that to allow them to be unfettered ultimately does great harm to the rest of us.

The term 'Anti-Capitalism', as we have seen, is not a happy one, suggesting, as it does, a movement with an entirely negative agenda, one bent on destroying rather than creating. So Paul Mason's term 'Post-Capitalism', explained in his eponymous book, may fare somewhat better. It suggests the total or at least partial replacement of Capitalism with something else. Unfortunately, the history of use of similar terms from other fields in the past is against him. 'Post-Modernism' and 'Post-Structuralism', for instance, may have quite loosely come to mean just what came after Modernism and Structuralism in time, whereas we are looking rather for a coherent concept which makes a difference.

Does Mason provide it? Well, there are many clues, but arguably they do not stack up to a comprehensive picture. Firstly, Mason usefully characterizes Capitalism:

'– the whole system – social, economic, demographic, cultural, ideological – needed to make a developed society function through markets and private ownership. That includes companies, markets and States'.

Although he concedes that 'Capitalism is a complex, adaptive system', he claims, but not conclusively, that it 'has reached the limits of its capacity to adapt'. And that Post-Capitalism offers 'a clear alternative', which will abolish Capitalism:

'by creating something more dynamic that exists, at first, almost unseen within the old system, but which breaks through, reshaping the economy around new values, behaviours and norms'.

Mason relies a lot on new technology to make this happen, citing three impacts of information technology in reducing the need for work, corroding pricing, and producing goods, services and organizations not responsive to markets. He correctly chides the left for its hopeless reliance on a working class proletariat that has lost its collective values, despite its economic woes and failure to find the good life.

New factors combine to change the economic landscape, says Mason. We are 'global, fragmentary, geared to small-scale choices, temporary work and multiple skill-sets'. For millions 'consumption has become a form of self-expression', so that they now have a new stake in the finance system. (You might have thought that would strengthen the hand of the bankers, one of the key citadels of Capitalism). He camps on the term 'network', which he sees leading to more and more free goods and services, collapsing their market.(This has certainly happened a lot to the book trade already, also dumbed down through people's poor education).

Mason recognized that 'progress' so far has been piecemeal and uncoordinated. But he does set out an outline of 'what a large-scale Post-Capitalist project might involve'. He believes that to be successful it must be in tune with people's psychology, be ecologically sustainable, lead to accepted new ideas and behaviours, running in accordance with scientific principles to attack each problem from all angles. This sounds encouraging, though vague.

His 'top aims' would be the rapid reduction of carbon emissions, stabilizing the world financial system to account for addressing debt (mostly by writing-down), delivering:

> 'high levels of material prosperity and wellbeing to the majority of people, primarily by prioritizing information-rich technologies towards solving major social challenges, such as ill-health, welfare dependency, sexual exploitation and poor education'.

Movement would be aimed at reducing necessary work with:

> 'transition towards an automated economy. Eventually, work becomes voluntary, basic commodities and public services are free, and economic management is then primarily an issue of energy and resources, not capital and labour'.

Obviously Mason puts more flesh put on the bone than I have space to describe here, but the main features are clear enough. It comes across to me like a collection of disparate, often small factors, which certainly complicate parts of an already prodigiously complex world. And isn't that rather the point. It is hard to see how mere networks can coordinate them to a common purpose, supposing all parties were willing, always a big 'if'.

A second point of departure for me is that Mason seems bewitched by the new technology. He is by no means alone in making sweeping and exaggerated claims for it: witness those who predicted the demise of books in the face of the e-book, or the enthusiasts who said that millions of people using anti-social media like Facebook and Twitter would force Parliament to change its policies.

But perhaps the largest flaw is in the idealistic claims he makes for major reform within the world's banking sector. Admittedly he produces far more technical detail than we need in the present text, but he has to accept that the reform programme must inevitably start with individual countries, where the government is knowledgeable and assertive enough, in the hope that practice will spread in time to all the rest. It is not clear where the drivers will come from, given the enormous vested interests, the economic, political, and social differences, inertia in the face of seemingly insurmountable odds.

Optimistic is the implied assumption that all can be under our control, where 'our' means just a handful of experts with the standing to influence the major political agents. What I am saying is that change is undoubtedly rapid, yet it is largely outside control, even if it is capable of rational description. And our powers with the crystal ball are weaker still. Mason has produced an intriguing mental map, which simplifies so we can get our heads around it. But is it real? Nevertheless, there are utopian elements in the mix, ones which the left-leaning can happily subscribe to in principle at least. So Mason's book is a noble effort, yet it falls short like all the others.

The Entrepreneurial State

One very depressing dichotomy for me in the United Kingdom is the enormous chasm between private and public sectors. Whilst the one is relatively affluent and unfettered, the other is very much the poor relation, overregulated, under-resourced, and endlessly disparaged by government and media alike. The private sector of industry and commerce is lauded for its wealth-generating capacities, whilst government fails to pass adequate laws to protect citizens from its worst excesses, like being thrown out of work, robbed of their pensions, cheated over goods and contracts, exploited by profiteering and criminal fraud…the list of atrocities is endless. The public sector on the other hand is mistrusted, cut to the bone, considered an unnecessary drain on the economy, regarded as inefficient and incompetent, and payments for it and its staff are resented and restricted.

But in her book 'The Entrepreneurial State', Mariana Mazzucato dispels the myths and prejudices which centre round the public/private sector divide. Her starting point is that entrepreneurs are always reliant on public investments to provide their framework of operation. Out of taxation the State contributes such basics as the transport infrastructure, the education of the populace, financing of research in science and technology. Much of the essential risk-taking is by government, through its various agencies. State initiatives, for example, have been behind important developments in computing, notably the internet and Apple, biotechnology, and green energy. This turns conventional understanding on its head, of course, if timidity and short-sightedness are hallmarks of business, whilst boldness resides in the public sector. When it is not cowed by the cries of the free marketeers, who fear incompetence and waste, and brow-beat them into cut-backs, which endanger new breakthroughs and inhibit public recruitment of talent.

Mazzucato has strongly critical things to say about the way rewards are distributed. Whilst much of the risk-taking is by the government, the private sector keeps most of the accruing profit, very inequitably distributing them with a high skew towards top management. Tax evasion then starves the government of the public funds needed for further investment on the public's behalf.

The function of government, Mazzucato contends, goes way beyond bailing out the inevitable 'market failures' of industrial firms, be they bureaucratic, lacking in dynamism, badly or corruptly run, the victims of competition fair or foul.

But if the current vogue is a ruthless cut-back of the State, we shall no doubt observe the wanton destruction of the organs and institutions of government that can plan ahead. Where will be the counter to media-dominated prejudices, the shirt-sleeve Tory nonsense that seeks to belittle State employees as lazy and inept 'jobsworths'?

What Mazzucato is proposing is nothing short of a (hopefully peaceful) industrial revolution. First, she wants to spread the economic truth that value is produced by our collective efforts, not just by 'entrepreneurs'. Secondly, she tries to repair the frightful misunderstanding over the causes of the financial banking crisis. Contrary to government claims, it was private debt not public that was responsible. And the way to cure it is not to load it all onto the public sector and make the poor try to pay it off with harsh years of austerity, but to invest in:

> 'long-run growth areas that raise real incomes, and reduce reliance on speculative credit'.

This requires putting a stop to the industrial hoarding of cash, the excessive profit-taking by executives, and ploughing the money into investments in productive capacity instead, new technology, together with research and development. Government would pump-prime, encourage, and collaborate as necessary with companies to tackle the big social and environmental problems of the age.

This is still 'alternative' economic thinking, but it rings true to me. In order for the State to be able to fulfil such a new role, however, it needs to ensure that it collects all the tax due, which is far from the case currently.

There may seem to be an inconsistency between what I said here about promoting the Entrepreneurial State and negative remarks in my book 'Radical Bureaucracy', arguing for local government to remain outside the role of promoting local business. I do not believe there is any inconsistency at existing levels of funding so long as local government continues to be cut to the financial bone, such that its statutory duties are at risk. That would remain my position. Ideally, of course, the Entrepreneurial State should function, in a coordinated way, at all three levels – national, regional and local.

Ed Balls became a famous dancer on 'Strictly' after he was an infamous Chancellor. He was poor at the former, which the public loved him for, but good at the latter and rejected by them for his pains. Such is life and the judgement of our voters, yet only one role was a bit of fun. The other was deadly serious. We could have turned our back on austerity through an exciting national programme of infrastructure investment if we only had the Balls.

We have talked of Tory ideology encouraging the doctrinaire privatisation of public services. Unfortunately, whilst British jobs remain in the short-term, the government are quite happy for the profits being made by these companies to go abroad. The list of foreign owners is impressively long, ranging from rail, water, electricity and gas, to nuclear power. Tellingly, a good few of the foreign companies are financially backed by their own governments, something we not only do not do, but even ban by law our own companies from competing for contracts. You might be forgiven for believing that the Conservatives were working for foreign powers, but the wilful selling of our national silver has been ongoing since Mrs. Thatcher in the nineteen seventies. When will it become a major election interest? I conjecture when it is too late, if not already.

The Tax Man Cometh

Call me old-fashioned, but my starting point is still the 'canons of taxation', which lay down principles which should be followed by all good taxes. Note I do not take the irresponsible view that we should keep all we earn and avoid paying tax whenever possible. Some taxes are good for society if not for me. I firmly believe in a welfare state, which means we should each and every one of us pay according to our means into a central fund, which is then used as a comfortable safety net to help the old, the young, the weak, the disabled, the mentally ill and the disadvantaged, as well as providing funds to generate the Entrepreneurial State.

Here then are the canons, which are about all I seem to agree over with their liberal-conservative originator, Adam Smith, written many years ago in his classic text, 'The Wealth of Nations':

equity:	the subjects of every state ought to contribute towards the support of the government, as nearly as possible in proportion to their respective abilities,
certainty:	the tax which each individual is bound to pay ought to be certain, and not arbitrary. The time of payment, the manner of payment, the quantity to be paid, ought all to be clear to the contributor, and to every other person,
convenience:	every tax ought to be levied at the time, or in the manner in which it is most likely to be convenient for the contributor to pay it,

economy: every tax ought to be so
             contrived as both to take out
             and keep out of the pockets of
             the people as little as possible,
             over and above what it brings
             into the public treasure of the
             State.

I do have some unease about the convenience canon, in that we have seen the lengths some, usually rich, people will go to in the avoidance of their financial obligations. The current law disgracefully makes a (dubious) distinction between tax avoidance and tax evasion, only the latter being illegal.

The canons have received acres of discussion. It is said that as modern economies have become more complicated there has been a need to add to the canons, which seems plausible, so some of the main candidates will now be set out:

productivity: the tax system should be
                  able to yield enough revenue
                  so government can avoid
                  borrowing,

elasticity: the tax should be capable of increasing or decreasing according to the requirements of the country's circumstances,

flexibility: this is needed so that the tax system may be easily adjusted for changing times,

simplicity: the tax system needs to be easily understood, so it can be administered without problems of interpretation and dispute,

diversity: the sources from which tax is collected should be diverse, so government does not rely on one single source, and no sector of society pays disproportionately.

Now when we look at this list I think we can probably readily agree pragmatically to elasticity and flexibility. But it is obvious that the productivity one is just a pipe dream. The country, so-called austerity policies notwithstanding, has not lived within its means for years, and seems very unlikely ever to do so, unless forced by international action. Moreover, governments control the public sector, but at best exhort the private sector, so the debt in this latter sector is massive, though partly hidden. Every now and again, of course, a company overreaches itself and people suffer as the redundancies mount and the receivers are called in.

The simplicity canon prompts a wry smile or two. Though eminently sensible it has no chance of coming about, because the present system of United Kingdom taxation is almost too complex for human understanding. Certainly, it is in practice beyond the kind of drastic reforming that would be required to meet the canon's tests. And this because successive governments since time immemorial have taken the easy way out and piled new regulations on top of old. They would be most unlikely to agree to such a systematic review, which would certainly give them many a headache and take donkeys' years to do.

Diversity, we will seemingly never agree on. Every section of society always regards its taxation as unjust. Yet if we could agree we should have taken a big step towards being a civilized and others-regarding society.

When we look at our actual tax system it is obvious that lip service only is paid to the canons, old or new. This is primarily because the British public tend to want their cake and eat it too: they wish to pay very little tax, yet receive generous benefits. But only growth or borrowing can fill the gap. The Conservative Government was elected in 2015, for example, on an election pledge not to increase income tax, national insurance, or VAT during the five year lifetime of the parliament. But both the first two taxes are progressive in ensuring that the better off pay more and all pay proportionately to their income, though many argue for lower percentage takes at higher incomes than I would. VAT is not progressive in that sense, but very many kinds of goods are available over a range of prices hopefully to suit pockets of different sizes.

One tax which is very unfair, however, is the Council tax levied on domestic properties in (wide) payment bands related to their worth on the market. As is often said, people of low incomes can, and often do, reside in expensive houses. Which makes their ability to pay sometimes problematic. The business rate equivalent for the premises of firms similarly fails abysmally to meet the basic fairness test of ability to pay. Reform is needed, but governments lack the wit and the energy. They remember Mrs Thatcher's famous demise over the former Council poll tax.

Another (brutal) tax is stamp duty, now paid on the purchase of a home. Whilst there are some exemptions for lowly first-time buyers, revaluations, owing to uncaring government, have not kept pace with rising house prices. A simple reform which would be more socially just would be to levy stamp duty not on the buyers, but on the sellers, who already own a house.

There is also the very widely understood fact that whilst the little man is forced to pay his taxes, however reluctant or compliant, and will have received nasty threatening letters from Her Majesty's Tax Inspector, the big international firms get away with paying vastly less than their due. They enter into accommodations with the Tax Man to let them off because the Government fears they will take their business elsewhere. So I look forward to the day when I can negotiate my tax bill too!

Nobody knows for sure but it is plausibly estimated that the money stashed away by the rich in off-shore tax havens is about ten percent of what the entire global economy makes on goods and services in a year. Now this is enormous and although some of it may be there for legitimate reasons it is fair to question most of it. Because the only clear reason for putting money there is to hide it from the tax authorities in the countries of origin, so that the wealthy can pay less tax than they ought. The sheer size of the problem suggests government tax policies would be well advised to recover as much of this money as they reasonably can. It would be fairer than putting up tax rates for the rest of us, though doubtless much more difficult to do.

Some insight into the problem emerged in 2016 with the leaked publication of the so-called 'Panama Papers'. These were confidential documents from a firm based in Panama, Mossach Fonsea, which revealed how the firm used shell companies to launder money on behalf of powerful international clients, including some near the top of the political elites in Egypt, Syria, Libya, and Russia. Tax avoidance would be bad enough, but there are other aspects just as serious: another reason that money is hidden is that its 'owners' acquired it in dubious ways, such as via drugs and bribery. It is said that the wealth of the City of London has been substantially built up by offering United States banks an escape route from tax regulations there.

There are many other connections between this sordid world and Britain. When news of Panama broke, Prime Minister Cameron was forced to admit his own father had actually run a tax-free offshore fund. It also emerged that many of the companies assisting the Panama firm were incorporated in tax haven countries within United Kingdom administrative jurisdiction, Crown dependencies such as the British Virgin Islands and Gibraltar.

Another dirty feature of British involvement in tax haven transactions is the ease with which foreigners can hide their money here. In London, notably, foreigners have bought the most expensive houses and few questions are asked, or at least answered, about where their capital came from. The scale is such that it has completely distorted the market. As available properties have become scarcer this has pushed up prices driving the cost of houses beyond the realistic lifetime aspirations of thousands of ordinary British citizens.

British company directors commonly avail themselves of the tax privileges of living in the haven countries, enough of the year to qualify, that is. Switzerland and Luxembourg were especially popular on figures released for 2014, as were the Channel Islands, Monaco, the Bahamas, and notably the British Virgin Islands.

For the laundering to occur, the rich of course need to enlist the professional expertise of armies of lawyers, accountants, and estate agents. They should be proceeded against vigorously and the firms' licenses to trade revoked, but don't hold your breath about reforms. Plenty of other countries will seek to benefit if one of Britain's biggest industries is put under scrutiny and restriction.

We do have bodies whose job it is to oversee the industries through which the incoming money flows, but in 2015 they were declared by Transparency International to be in need of a complete overhaul for failing in their tasks. As testament to the lack of serious intent by the Cameron Government to take effective action, the level of fines remains woefully small and there is nothing to stop members of these regulatory bodies taking jobs working to advise the companies they have been monitoring!

Threatening to dwarf the scale and gravity of implications of the above in November 2017 came the revelations by a German newspaper known as 'The Paradise Papers' and relating to transactions in the offshore jurisdictions of the Cayman Island and Bermuda. These concerned clients among the world's rich and powerful. Two Brits were immediately called out, the Queen herself via her financial agents, the Duchy of Lancaster, and Lord Ashcroft, the businessman and Tory Party donor. Sir Vincent Cable immediately complained that David Cameron had prevented him taking requisite action following the earlier Panama Papers affair when he was in the Con-Dem Government. It was naturally claimed by interested parties that what was being done was quite legitimate, being tax reduction by legal avenues. But it was even if so being quite deliberately hidden from scrutiny for whatever reasons. That the offshore outfits were selling secrecy to those with something to hide was the popular conclusion.

It might be unfair not to mention that progress has been made on international agreements to make tax information exchange between countries more systematic and complete. Then there is the transparency movement that is supposed to expose who owns what. Nevertheless and notwithstanding these, hopefully more than token first steps, the right-wing Prospect magazine was forced to remark in June 2016:

> 'Given that the UK's network is the single biggest player in global financial secrecy, and the biggest driver of

corruption around the world; it is uniquely well placed to act and it has a unique responsibility to do so.' Unless it does it will be seen by other nations that offshore trading with all its unsavoury practices are truly part of the much-vaunted British values, as they have been since the old colonial days.'

In conclusion it seems to me that policy on taxation is all over the place, although the Conservative Government remained very resistant to the modest increases in income tax that would help ease our national burden of debt. From the standpoint of the ordinary citizen there must be an uneasy feeling that he is fair game for the loss of his money. In addition to the ad hoc policy decisions of the moment there are the underlying threats of being unable to fund his retirement, when his income will continue to be taxed, of perhaps losing his house and the children's inheritance to long-term care taxation, of his estate being stolen via inheritance tax.

The traditional way to build up his coffers by prudent and regular savings is now denied him owing to deliberate Government policy to make him stimulate the economy by immediately spending what he earns. Inflation is inadequately controlled, so that it usually outstrips the derisory returns that savers get when the interest rates are kept artificially low. It is a catch 22 situation in that millions are so close to insolvency that rises in prices, especially of mortgage costs, would break them. It is perhaps fitting that the recommended antidote is gambling, although it is actually called investing in stocks and shares. For this is what the toffs do for fun and the Government does with much of our taxation too.

The Global Village

Financial economic articles frequently mention globalization. So what is it? Well, according to Manfred Steger, author of the book 'Globalization', it is far from a clear and simple concept. He sees it as:

> 'a multifaceted process encompassing global, regional and local aspects of social life'.

Or rather, he considers it as a set of processes which are features of different disciplines – 'economic, political, cultural, ideological, and environmental'. Later he adds 'technological' for good measure. And doubtless there are others too. This is probably too wide and heterogeneous to track, so I am not going to try. Additionally, as you will have noticed, globalization is not merely factual; it has a value-laden component also. For a purist, therefore, it is one of the elusive terms in modern thought. Unsurprisingly it 'remains a contested concept' with no 'scholarly consensus on what kinds of social processes constitute its essence'. I myself would tend to disavow it. When a concept becomes so wide it usually misleads.

Why is it considered so important? Partly, its multidisciplinary nature lends itself to research in teams over conventional subject boundaries, thus hopefully improving communication and collaboration. Secondly, it is concerned across world, regional, and local dimensions. Thirdly, it deals with (accelerating) change, implying more networks of interdependence and internationalism, transcending boundaries, both physical and ideational. Fourthly, people as they become aware of it, can sometimes be influenced to alter their perceptions of 'individual and collective identities' within the global village. There is a kind of shrinking effect, possibly an integrating one as well. People have a developing worldview and they see evidence of other cultures, some of which they might even visit as tourists. A fifth reason is that:

> 'globalization – characterized by roving capital, accelerated communication and quick mobilization – has everywhere weakened older forms of authority…'

according to Mishra.

Within our United Kingdom press globalization has to a very considerable extent been considered as a predominantly economic phenomenon (which, as we see above, it is not only). Despite this, and whilst recognizing there are dangers of grappling with concepts we do not yet properly understand, and which may have uneven effects in place and time for all we yet know, I am notwithstanding going to confine my own remarks to the economic field, which you could argue in any case leads the others here. We shall therefore look for globalization's potential and perhaps actual insights into some of the issues of:

> 'international trade policy, global financial markets, worldwide flows of goods, service, and labour, transnational corporations, offshore financial centres, foreign investment, and the new international economic institutions',

as we go along.

Trading Partners

One of the inhumane aspects of the laissez-faire capitalism beloved of Western 'democratic' governments, and discussed in globalization circles, is free trade. In this model any weaker local firms may go to the wall as a result of competition without government rescue or even help. Those who have argued for State interventions to ameliorate the damage to families of their breadwinners being pitched out of work have been howled down by conservatives and liberals with the claim that their discomfiture will be short-term as they retrain and then acquire alternative jobs.

However, in early 2016 a paper was published by American economists Autor, Dorn and Hanson from the National Bureau of Economic Research called 'The China Shock'. Whilst this was primarily concerned with effects in United States communities of Chinese competition, it found that:

> 'adjustment in local labour markets is remarkably slow, with wages and labour-force participation rates remaining depressed and unemployment rates remaining elevated for at least a full decade'.

They went on to say that this had led to poorer physical and mental health, as well as reduced social standing of individuals and indeed whole communities. In turn the process of political estrangement, with concomitant rising anger and a tendency towards militant extremism, had set in.

It is what the inhabitants of Redcar faced after the closure of their steel factories, and what a generation earlier came to afflict the Durham miners when their collieries were shut. All sorts of excuses for inaction were conjured by the Conservative Government, but the bottom line is that their economic ideology overcame a sense of humanity.

What all communities need, especially those with large populations, are broad and diverse industrial bases, where not all employment opportunities are funnelled into one narrow sector. Towns where most have to find work within one dominant industry are very vulnerable to its changing fortunes. Whole families come to depend down the generations on the same firm for all their wages.

Now it is hard to demonstrate during my lifetime that UK governments have ever payed more than tokenism to the idea of genuinely helping these communities when the axe falls, let alone taken the kind of State-primed steps to ensure local structural resilience to buffer against hard times. And the reasons are not merely money and incompetence. There is a cultural indifference from the unaffected Establishment, who are bolstered in their confidence by a public without the imagination to care enough if it is not on their own doorstep. Some are too dumb to recognize the signs that they might be next.

It is, however, a matter of balance, adjustment and fine tuning. If a country puts up barriers to free trade then reprisals can follow, maybe making the overall situation worse. As usual in Capitalism, deals need to be struck, but in future involving representatives of the interested parties and with transparency. Without the latter, accountability becomes harder to ensure.

Multinational Companies

As briefly alluded to in the section on taxation, one very serious consequence of globalization is the failure of HMRC to recover the statutory amounts of tax from multinational corporations who trade in this country. Partly it is owing to the ineffectuality of government and the laxity of regulation. But, in the absence of concerted action by the main nations affected to clamp down, firms like Starbucks and Vodafone will continue to launder their accounts to show merely nominal profits in the countries where their tax bills would otherwise be highest. Another fiddle is shown by Amazon's agreement with HMRC, wherein they give shares to employees and classify the cost as an expense, thereby reducing taxable revenue. Governments fail to punch their weight for a variety of reasons. Conservatives in office, for example, are disposed to let even the dishonest trade. They believe in unfettered Capitalism as a matter of ideology and value more highly the job creation which they dubiously assume would otherwise disappear. An indication of national subservience elsewhere was the decision in 2016 by Ireland to waive a substantial element of the tax due to it by Apple under a European Commission decision. What is also hard to condone is where rich individuals are let off the hook, though in some cases they too are responsible for large numbers of employees.

This is perhaps the most serious manifestation by the multinational companies, namely, that they intimidate even national governments into merely light regulation of their activities. So keen are we to show gratitude to these giant firms for the jobs they bring that we accept the dumbing down of labour skills, their low wages and job insecurity, as prices worth paying. We are then powerless to stop them when they close our local factories and take the work abroad, as indeed happened with our beloved Cadburys shortly after its American takeover.

Morozov has declared a method whereby the problem of regulating multinational technology giants like Google can be addressed realistically and successfully. He says their power lies in the 'big data' they accumulate and the potential profits from usage. A national data bank is envisaged, co-owned by all citizens, and only available to private companies in exchange for fees plugged into profit-sharing. This, he says, would be far more effective than fining them for breaches of competition law following lengthy and wasteful investigations.

Business Behaviour

Not too many industrialists come out and admit that there needs to be a fundamental redesign of the purposes of private companies, one which pays particular regard to improving relations between business and the general public. An exception is John Browne, former CEO of the oil giant BP, in his timely book 'Connect', who wishes to reconcile the 'rift' between big business and society. He realizes that in so doing firms can gain tangible benefits beyond the 'feel good' factor. This is contrary to conventional 'wisdom', but needs to be done anyway as an issue of justice. It is an old problem, of course, but depressing to think how little has been done about it over the years. And this in spite of the fact that good will is slow to nurture, yet can be lost in a flash.

Browne refers to the concept of 'corporate social responsibility', CSR, which he describes as

> 'the standard system for major companies to handle the connection between business and society in the twentieth century',

so as to act like 'a responsible citizen'. He claims it did a little good, but is now dead. Too often their successful work with stakeholders was confined to improving employee morale, but it could not prevent adverse effects on company reputation 'in the face of corporate scandals'. CSR was seen as cut off from core business, too remote from the local situation, too involved with limiting the negative.

Browne's alternative prescription is, as he freely admits, an extremely difficult one in practice, namely to 'integrate societal concerns deeply into commercial strategy and operations at every level of the company'.

To achieve all this requires 'connected leadership', which has four main tenets: 'map your world, define your contribution, apply world-class management, and engage radically'. Less grandiosely the tenets boil down to identifying the firm's core commercial activities and for every item deciding their engagement strategy – whether to contest, collaborate, or concede. 'Radical engagement' is where we would notice the most difference, for 'complete openness' is being advocated. To win public trust and gain credibility they must scupper climates of secrecy, abolish the insincere chicanery of the public relations department in their quest to create image by propaganda; instead becoming 'open, proactive and constructive'.

The people expect business to take its profit granted, but to serve society, and in a world where people are better educated and informed, they are more demanding. When firms can meet these expectations and rise to the challenges, Browne believes they have enormous scope to help forge a better world. Among the scourges he would importantly like to address are 'global burdens' such as war and terrorism, obesity, smoking, alcoholism and other drug abuse, illiteracy, climate change, air pollution, road accidents, poor sanitation and malnutrition.

This will not happen overnight, naturally. Nor will it happen at all, except in rare cases where strong individuals resist the norms, while firms look over each other's shoulders, judging the new ways as not in their own interests, so long as the rest of the competition continues as before.

To make things happen first there has to be a growing recognition across the country, especially within government, that companies have a variety of purposes, which must be compatible and balanced. They include, as now, profit for the owners, shareholders and employees, added value – be it in goods or services – to the consumer, tax for the social infrastructure, activities which benefit society, not reduce its quality. So that in extreme cases we could see a firm not being allowed to trade should its products be anti-social. The deeming of them thus would be hugely controversial, of course, but ethical teeth are needed, or we get guttersnipe behaviour mixed in with the more savoury operations.

We also need to know who we are dealing with, so ownership and formal interconnections with other firms through key players should be a transparent legal requirement. Currently it is far too easy to hide.

As Browne's agenda above may mostly sound somewhat abstract and visionary, let me say that it should be accompanied by concrete structural changes in the managerial organization of companies. Obviously we need workers on the Board as of right elected by their fellows, a proposition too much for many Conservatives. We need to cut out bogus paid positions like non-executive directorships, where a name is offered for advertising and prestige purposes, but little work. These are an insult to employees and doubtless have a demotivating effect.

Relationships between shareholders and senior management ought to be radically rethought to stop the former being taken for a ride, starved of dividends whilst milked for capital and enormous salary hikes. I therefore like the idea of limiting top salaries to a reasonable multiple of what the humblest worker in the company receives.

Structurally, to help with such plans we need to look to legally imposed new ways of constituting the management of companies for greater balance between the interests of the legitimate parties. These could take various forms, but would definitely include the compulsory placement on Boards by peer election, of the workers, blue and white collar, a proposal kicked into touch by Teresa May, as new prime minister in 2016. Out should go symbolic gravy train positions, such as non-executive directorships designed to use the names of well-known public figures for promotional purposes. And away too should go the ability of incumbent management to 'out vote' the majority of shareholders at the annual general meeting regarding remuneration packages and appointments, as now regularly makes a farce of bank and building society decision-making, for example.

Social Democrat theorists in the Corbyn era argued the case for Britain to move towards 'coordinated market economies'. These are described by Kevin Hickson in 'Rebuilding Social Democracy' as having larger trade union membership, with workers encouraged to join cooperative not conflictual relations, and an integrated system of collaboration over economic planning between firms, employers, and employees. Some capital would be provided in longer-term time frames, so allowing for investment in new technology. Vocational training would be less transferrable than now, more geared to the needs of particular industries, where employees would tend to stay longer. Two-way loyalty and greater job security would be obvious spin-off benefits, and companies would be more willing to invest in training if it did not feel employees would soon walk out of the door. The stakeholder belief – that parties on all sides have a mutual interest in success of the venture – should be altogether easier to foster. Unfortunately, much practice is culturally and historically determined, so that previous bitter experience will inflame prejudices and colour judgements. So even if there were a national will, development would likely be slow and uneven. We have seen for years the downright wilful obstruction that firms put in the way of policies on equal pay between the genders and their open use of ageism too.

Finally, a distinction needs to be made between small and large businesses, as the former need more help generally and provide the backbone of the local economies. The unremarkable kinds of support they need are lower corporation tax levels and rent relief. I like the idea of a national investment bank being set up to lend to small businesses, filling gaps left by the private sector. This would enmesh with regional subsidies from central government agencies in deprived areas and for other firms in economic slow-down or recovery. Annual plant and machinery allowances would also aid the necessary investment, as would strong legal enforcement of prompt payment by their larger debtors.

In contrast I mentioned the revolving door between politics and industry. Here is a very good illustration. In August 2013 Chris Huhne, the former Liberal Democrat MP and ex-minister for climate and energy, was appointed as European manager of Zilkha Biomass Energy merely months after completing his prison sentence for perverting the course of justice over his driving offence. Writ large this kind of thing helps ensure that government keeps business sweet against the time they themselves may be looking for gainful employment beyond their political days.

We must never again allow ourselves to be duped by big business with regard to building public sector provision like schools and hospitals, something first started in the years of the Blair/Brown governments – under the Public Finance Initiative, PFI. For communities were ripped off. The attraction, the fools' gold if you like, was that much of the capital was delivered up front by the private sector so that taxes could be kept down. And it looked as though a nominally left-wing government could cooperate with the business world, contrary to public fears.

But Mary Dejevsky, writing in a newspaper in April 2016 referred to the 'prodigious amount of borrowing'. She went on:

> 'central government, local councils and health authorities all signed away not just the ownership of fixed assets but the right to arrange or subcontract the servicing. They now find themselves liable for escalating bills for decades – bills in which they have little or no say'.

Consumers can be treated abysmally by companies in this country, all too easily, especially when things go wrong. A classic example occurred in May 2017 when British Airways had a massive worldwide failure of their computer systems over the bank holiday period. This resulted in the disruption to, and ruination of, thousands of holidays affecting 75,000 passengers.

You can talk about passengers' legal rights to refunds and cancellations all you like. The fact remains that on the days in question, the BA hierarchy took no responsibility for customer care. They kept them starved of information or explanation, in effect placing them in temporary detention of indefinite duration at the airports. They were denied transport away, or hotel accommodation, and did not automatically receive food and drink. In short they treated their clients in ways it would be illegal to deal with animals. It subsequently transpired that the company had recently outsourced its IT system management to a firm in India, and power failures were claimed to have occurred. Whatever the actual causes, obviously, this was the worst sort of attempted abdication of responsibility, motivated by saving money, and, in the absence of contingency planned backup, the loss of control proved their undoing. Needless to say, the Government, despite the obvious potential damage to our national reputation, was no help at all. And the public go on using British Airways, which turned a nice profit over the ensuing quarter!

It seems to me that we could hope to grow closer in mutual understanding with industry and commerce through a variety of measures which now exist in small degree, but are needed much more. I refer to work experience schemes, where teenagers from school spend quality time learning about the world of work in situ with proper mentors. We need systematically organized visits for adult parties to experience at first hand.

And we need an end to the intelligence-insulting and psychologically sinister, underhand way they try to brainwash us about the merits of their advertised goods. Overwhelmingly, advertising should be unacceptable in its present manifestations. Most is imbecilic, annoying, exaggerated, deeply uninformative about the product, and appeals to our emotions without, they hope, engaging our reason. Legal protections are woefully inadequate. We are being manipulated so effectively that we do not even realize it. We are passive recipients rather than the actively questioning, and at times aggressively hostile, resisters our education should have prepared us to become. But this is another nasty aspect of Capitalism; it encourages sales in the immediate interests of the seller, not the buyer.

Perhaps the cardinal illustration of disgraceful business behaviour and public ineptitude in the face of it is to be found in the energy companies – especially, but not exclusively – the so-called 'Big Six'. We have had years of rapidly rising prices, feeble government action, and an industry regulator which has failed to act in the interests of consumers. The Government has in vain encouraged the public to shop around, and its sole achievement in the field has been to force companies to simplify their tariffs and provide the public with clearer information, despite regular 'pledges' around election time. They are also administratively incompetent: research revealed that during 2016/17 more than a million customers had been overcharged substantial sums because of 'billing errors'.

According to economic theory this is what happens with a cartel. There is not enough competition, demand is fairly inelastic. Hence they charge what they like. Although the wholesale energy prices they pay go up and down, these fluctuations are not passed on to their customers, as they would be with vehicle fuel at the forecourt pumps. And when they bring in smart meters on a large scale the public are likely to be given no choice in the matter and charged high installation fees and an ongoing rental.

I myself have an account with an eco-friendly smaller supplier. I joined because of all this and its reputation for good customer service. But it has not saved me from expensive bills or the unsatisfactory behaviour of the industry, for when it comes to computer billing they are all alike. I used to pay by direct debit, but that meant subsidizing the company with interest-free loans in the summer months when our usage was low. They would project forward unrealistically high estimates of usage for the forthcoming year, based on simplistic calculations they were reluctant to change when challenged. When I cancelled my direct debit, deciding to pay monthly in arrears, they sent me bogus bills based on estimated meter readings. I asked them to come and read my meters and send me accurate bills, but of course, despite their huge profits, they no longer employ someone to do the job. Behind the scenes are the far-from-transparent dealings these companies have with the Government, whom they all blame for levying high 'green investment' taxes. Are we seeing the benefit of any of this, I wonder?

A major problem in the accountancy world is that the cartel of big four players, such as PwC and KPMG, are not properly regulated. An illustration came in October 2017 when the City's Financial Reporting Council, FRC, the main watchdog, dropped its third investigation in a matter of weeks, arguing that no tribunal would 'make an adverse finding' against PwC, having spent three years looking into why PwC failed to notice that Barclays were in serious breach of the financial rules. Similarly, it exonerated KPMG over its audit of HBOS, saying how could it have known the bank was in difficulties? The issue may seem somewhat obscure, but isn't. A pattern is being followed here of regulators deliberately not being given enough powers by Government to do their job (they cannot bring fraud charges, for example), of them having no accountability to the public, and operating largely unseen. To be effective, a regulating institution also needs to be wholly independent of the industry concerned, which the FRC is not. My advice is to examine carefully the remits of all watchdogs that affect your life and ask awkward questions about the obvious weaknesses. For this, I would wager, is no isolated, accidental case.

One final example of bad business behaviour may seem like an odd choice. I refer to the holiday industry generally, although their poor behaviour is partly down to pathetically meek and accepting consumerism, as well as the way the law is framed on their behalf. It starts with the brochures, which are quite inadequate as sources of information on which to decide. Most of the travel agents are not independent and tend to back up the holiday companies. A lot are London-centric and do not bother themselves with the transport difficulties of those living in the North. They all expect wacky deposits, and full payment ahead of the trip, with extremely mean refunds in the event of default, whereas they can sell your holiday again. We see them in their true colours with untrained guides who do not know the place, dodgy hotels, and their uncaring self-protectionism when things go wrong. My advice would be to do your own thing, by thorough research, design the holiday to suit you and not the masses, and go freelance wherever possible, provided you can get bonding cover. But it is disappointing that we do not have an effective watchdog for the industry and that there appears insufficient concern to call for worthwhile reforms. Public complacency here, as in so many areas of life, lets us all down.

Bonkers Banking

Professor Lapavitsos wrote a paper in 2014 for the Centre for Labour and Social Studies about the phenomenon of 'financialization', ongoing in the United Kingdom since the Thatcherite years of the 1970's. The item refers to 'the exceptional rise of finance in terms of size and penetration across society, the economy and policy'. The phenomenon has been aided and abetted by the Government in a variety of related ways. It has given the central Bank of England the power to set interest rates and provide liquidity, reduced the regulatory framework, and bolstered bank deposits from taxation. Lapavitsos unceremoniously blames financialization for increasing inequality and reducing the size of the public sector, thus jeopardizing social housing, health, education, pensions, employment and welfare benefits. There is a vulnerability for a country like ours so out of balance that other economic sectors like manufacturing industry are in serious decline.

It seems too much of a commonplace nowadays to heap criticisms on bankers, their high-pay and bonuses, their distaste for regulation of their activities, the way they expect the Establishment to bail them out using ordinary people's money when they are in trouble, yet have the incompatible belief that they should keep almost all the profits the banks make. They claim success is all personally down to them, while failure is the fault of other people.

Elizabeth Anderson, writing in the 'i' newspaper on fourth August 2016, told of a rogue trader, formerly imprisoned in America for illegal activities at UBS that nearly brought down a Swiss bank. On release he made a press statement warning that the culture has not changed and the same sort of crime is liable to happen again. Staff were still under pressure to make money no matter what the risks. His claims were met by the usual complacent remarks from the British Bankers Association.

Ben Chu, (the 'i' newspaper in July 2014), was pessimistic about bankers changing their spots:

> 'Ultimately, the attempts to regulate banks into good behaviour are doomed to failure. And the threat of legal sanction is always going to be blunt except in clear cases of fraud such as the fixing of interest rates'.

The culture inside investment banks can allegedly be nasty. Former Goldman Sachs executive director, Greg Smith, in the Daily Mail in March 2013, for instance, explained why he left the firm, having become disillusioned with the changed leadership vision. He said it had moved from ideas generation and ethical conduct to manipulating their clients, regarded as 'muppets', for maximum commercial gain.

The culture is also reflected in feeble law making light of what we the people consider to be white collar crime.

This is in stark contrast to America, where huge fines and long prison sentences are regularly meted out.

It is important to make a key distinction between the two main types of bank; namely, the ordinary high street bank that serves the personal banking needs of the public at large, and the investment or merchant banks, which deal in financial instruments like shares and derivatives, and is a major lender of capital for industrial investment.

For years after the clear evidence provided by the 2007 crash the regulatory argument to segregate ordinary from investment banks has failed to convince those in power. Opponents have pointed to various measures designed to separate their respective dealings within the company instead and claimed they would be quite adequate. Welcome has been the prudent introduction, though, of a requirement for high street banks to hold a certain proportion of their worth in ready capital against a run, and the national body established to protect ordinary savers against concomitant loss.

Ben Chu continued to advocate structural reform of the banks to change their behaviour somehow. You give them different incentives and reduce their opportunities to misbehave. The types of bank would be institutionally separated, retail from investment, and the maximum allowed size of a firm's balance sheet would be kept in proportion. It would be made crystal clear that incompetent banks would be allowed to fail, not bailed out in future by the taxpayers as before. Earnings ceilings would be at maximum no more than x times the pay of the most junior employee and this would be the law of the land, not confined alone to the banking sector. Labour's idea of a national investment bank to work with major infrastructure regeneration and development projects is also a good one. There is, however, a need for more competition in the banking sector, because it is not sufficiently accountable or encouraging of economic stability to have so few and so large.

Finally, on the domestic level, I worry that increasing use of computers and telephones to carry out personal banking will continue to cause both temporary, minor inconvenience and sometimes major problems for consumers, when systems crash or are hacked. Time and again we have had warnings that data is not secure, that firms can be irresponsible over encryption, and that villains are perennially ahead of the game. Unfortunately, government understanding and sanctions are weak. Young people especially have known no better, so life goes on largely without effective reform. It does not particularly affect me directly, because I won't entrust data to the internet, or undertake financial transactions on it. Yet the options for living in the old financial ways are unhealthily diminishing, with such silly suggestions as the removal of cheque books and even cash being rife. Try contacting many an organization nowadays by letter or telephone and see how many route you onto one-way contact web sites. So much for progress here!

One adverse consequence of all of this is going to be the retreat of the banks from the high street in small towns, thus rendering access almost impossible for 'switched off' older people. There seems to be a blasé, uncaring attitude of well, they will be dead soon anyway.

Worthy of Our Hire

If you look at salaries and wages, the way they are distributed across the various walks of life, enormous disparities will be seen. Whereas there is understandable and justified concern about the great gulf between the pay of those at top and bottom within organizations, we hear much less about differences between types of employment. None of this, the result no doubt of myriad forces over generations, stacks up under any possible yardstick of fairness you could devise. Call me a dreamer, but I want it to. It seems deeply offensive the way things are, because it provides real barriers to what people can achieve in their chosen field. It ultimately reflects a rotten value system, one which we haven't the power to stand up to, or which we willingly acquiesce in. I am not going to give a catalogue of comparisons here: it would take too long and, in any case, we all have our ready examples. But look at the way we fawn at celebrity, be it royal, aristocratic, or from the worlds of entertainment and sport. Then reflect on the meagre rewards given to nurses, teachers, probation officers, prison staff, local government workers.

Just as everybody thinks apple pie is a good thing we all want decent incomes too. My judgements on this matter are coloured by a lifetime of working in the public sector in local government where successive governments invariably held down our pay. We looked in vain at the private sector where rewards were much higher, and even to more favoured areas of the public sector like hospital consultants. There was no independent national body to advise on parity. Since I was a good graduate from a top university and had excellent professional qualifications too, it more than rankled. My union, Unison claimed that a pay freeze followed by a 1% cap had resulted in public sector pay rising by 4.4% in the years 2010 to 2016 against a cost of living rise of 22%.

Anyhow, in my universe incomes in the United Kingdom would have to undergo a massive overhaul. Not only would I be looking at fairness between public and private sector at the different levels, but also to reduce the pay gaps on hierarchical ladders to reasonable widths in place of the present yawning chasms between top and the rest. I will repeat:it seems to me that the often striking disparities between different professions are seldom justified either. They say quite indefensible things about our relative valuations as a society. Invariably any job that involves caring for others or improving society is underpaid, it would seem.

The summer 2017 scandal over the mandated disclosure of top BBC salaries for their so-called 'stars' also showed how precious some people can be over keeping this kind of information private. It remains to be seen whether in time it will have any effect on reducing the huge, unjustified inequalities – between men and women, and between the 'talent' and the rest of us poor bastards. I beg leave to doubt it. The BBC apart, and once again something of a law unto itself, it has long been the practice for humble public sector employees to have their salaries a matter of public record. So let's have the private sector follow suit. Will we then, as many of us suspect, lay bare widespread private greed and outrageous opulence alongside the massive inequalities?

Government behaviour is inconsistent. For example, it did take steps to require the BBC to publish its top salaries, but is leaving any consequential action regarding anomalies to the corporation. On the other hand, with regard to universities, it is threatening financial sanctions unless the pay of vice-chancellors is moderated, many having been seen to be receiving upwards of £200,000 per year (whilst undergraduates pay course fees through the nose).

What John Mc Donnell aptly called 'serfdom' are the brutal conditions often found at the bottom end of working life in Britain today. Unpaid interns are employed at their own expense in order to gain experience. There are also zero-hours contracts making for weekly uncertainty as to how many hours people will be called to work and how much income they will accordingly receive. Then there is bogus employment, where firms claim the workers are self-employed, so they can be free of any obligations to them under employment law. Many a firm illegally pays lower than the national minimum wage, which itself may or may not constitute a living wage. In my world all this would cease, civilized laws would be passed with draconian punishments routinely handed out to the exploiters.

We must wake up to the realization that the staffing behaviour of large firms is crude and unfeeling. Top management can be so poor at assessing market trends and competition that in good times they take on far too many workers that they then discard when times get tougher. It just won't do. People have families and take on commitments. They cannot adjust at the drop of a hat to rip-off redundancy. The State needs to protect them, at least for a while, and it could do so from an industry levy on profits, together with rules on sensible expansion.

Many matters would have to change for a move in this general direction. We would need legislation to limit levels of pay as well as pay gaps, proper employment legislation more generally to look after workers, including democratic representation in the workplace and renewed respect for the unions. We would need somehow to stop the race to the bottom, whereby multinational firms strive to de-skill jobs and pay low wages. In this they are aided and abetted by the United Kingdom government, which pays in-work benefits to workers, in effect subsidizing firms irrespective of merit. The excuse is globalization. There will be cheap labour available in countries to which the companies could alternatively decamp.

Ensuring a sufficient supply of good quality apprenticeship opportunities in the key industries is a central duty of government in my book. There will be times, left to their own devices, when companies will be reluctant, or exploit the trainees, by lower wages or indifferent working experiences. It is not therefore simply a matter of providing state grants at appropriate levels to ensure skills learning on-the-job.

Pensioning Off

Pensions need to be given urgent and serious consideration. I do not shy away from the so-called 'nanny state' here: people in some cases need to be protected from themselves, especially where they have financial dependants. All who work should be in a long-term pension scheme, flexibly transferable from the day they first start. Legal compulsion will be necessary to ensure this. We need the umbrella of an independent Savings and Pension Commission, one which would uphold individual and group rights. It is also sadly the case that close scrutiny and regulation of pension funds investment is long overdue, to ensure it is safe and responsible.

In a civilized society pensions would be part of our welfare umbrella. Nobody in old age would be without the wherewithal to live decently. There is no excuse. The United Kingdom is one of the richest countries in the world. The trouble is that pension provision has failed for a lot of our citizens. Here, as in so many aspects of life, the State has lost the plot. What we used to do well we no longer seem to know how.

When I worked in the public sector, in local government, our pensions were based on simple principles. We compulsorily paid in about six percent of our salary monthly, the employer contributed similar, and we accrued entitlement annually over a maximum of forty years to give a final salary pension at a maximum of half pay. However, the government frittered away the money raised. Instead of investing it properly and soundly for growth it met the yearly bill from general taxation proceeds.

In the private sector there were at that time more generous schemes. Some were final salary ones based on attaining pensions of two-thirds pay. Some did not require employees to contribute. Following government deregulation, though, and especially after the 2007 banking debacle, firms gave up on final salary pensions and demanded larger contributions from employees. Government tightened the screws in the public sector also. So it is fair to say that the best schemes are those no longer available to new retirees in either sector. What they had found, and had no satisfactory solution for, was that pension fund investments in an era of low interest rates were no longer adequate to meet the legitimate claims of retiring workers.

Joining pension schemes increasingly became optional, so that the cash-strapped young, unable to secure mortgages in the stock-shortage housing market, tended to defer commitment in the (forlorn) hope of making up the lost ground in later working life. This was always difficult, but when it is policy to have very low interest rates it becomes well-nigh impossible for most.

As the Tories encouraged personal freedom, so they also enabled a climate of exploitation. Hence pensioners were now lured by attractive-sounding offers to cash in pension pots and home ownership in favour of once-in-a-lifetime high seas cruises. And the more unscrupulous firms raided their own employees' pension funds in order to finance other aspects of the business, or simply take their wacky 'profits'.

A notorious example came in the shape of Sir Phillip Green, former boss of British Home Stores, knighted for services to the retail sector. Just after he sold the company for a nominal sum to a new owner, a former bankrupt, it collapsed, revealing that hundreds of millions of pounds in the company's pension fund had been purloined by Green for his personal expenditure. To the nation's shame months went by after eleven thousand staff had been made redundant before Green made any sort of offer in financial reparation, too small for acceptance by the HMRC as it transpired. Media fumed, a government sub-committee castigated him publically, there was talk of removing his knighthood, whilst he retreated to one of his yachts in the Mediterranean. The House of Commons deliberated, but by our pathetically lax and immoral laws they could find nothing illegal in his conduct. Green finally caved in, partly to retain what he could of his good name, but that he did not have to do so is the point.

You can tell by my tone that I do not think much of any of this. I want laws toughening up, I want pariahs jailed and financially ruined, I demand their honours be stripped, I require full financial compensation for victims, as much paid from the private sector as possible, I insist on tripartite financial arrangements with compulsion to ensure all can afford a ripe old age. But will it happen? I doubt it very much.

If I were young again one thing I would be watchful of would be government movements in relation to state pension. It is obvious that huge numbers of the next generation when elderly will have no occupational pension in place as we did. There will be a variety of reasons for this. If regular pension savings in a properly regulated scheme is an optional choice many will not make it at all, or until it is too late to safeguard their (statistically longer years of) old age. Secondly, more will have been in short-term employment, or working for small firms not legally required to run pension schemes, or their pension fund will have collapsed when the boss ran away with his loot.

And so the state pension will be their last resort for millions. Just watch my predictions. I think that as the proportion of old people in society increases government will take ever more drastic measures to control expenditure. State pensions will probably be reduced or withdrawn altogether for those who actually have an occupational pension. People will be forced to pay much higher proportions of their working life incomes in national insurance, and the official retirement age will creep ever upwards. Keep complaining, or they will do it. We shall then return to a former, unenlightened, time when pensions did not have to be paid for long because the recipients mostly died before or shortly after retirement, worn out by lives of hard graft.

Since there is never enough money, one useful policy proposal to consider is to remove all state pension entitlement from the higher earners, as the international Organization for Economic Cooperation and Development (OECD) has suggested. There are legal and moral difficulties, however, because employees were led to believe they were building up pension entitlements via up to thirty or forty years of national insurance contributions. We would need new understandings for the future and a phased in scheme.

But do pensioners need the winter fuel allowance? Well, I don't and I think it should be means-tested, along with local transport passes. I know that the trend is for people to live longer on average, but raising the age at which a state or occupational retirement pension is paid requires very cautious handling. It is not simply a matter of money, but quality of life, with people ageing at greatly different rates and with jobs making very variable demands.

The much-argued-over triple lock raises the state pension annually in line with the greater of inflation, average earnings increases, or 2.5 percent. I do not see where the third element justification comes from and for me the moral case only covers the other two.

A lot of Capitalism is needlessly corrupt, partly because the Establishment likes it that way and does not frame laws designed for our protection as hapless consumers. Pensions by the private sector are one large source of fiddles. It is true that when you take out a pension agreement they are obliged to tell you the annual management charge. The trouble is they are not obliged, and so may not tell you about all the other deductions they make. Some are large ones, such as costs for taking advice from the investment banks and sometimes lavish corporate hospitality. No wonder our investments seem to underperform professional expectations. Why does the Financial Conduct Authority not stop it?

As the population proportionately ages the extra burden on pension providers becomes more onerous, obviously, so government looks to the policy potential of raising the state retirement age in order to maintain affordability. This seems rational and responsible from a utilitarian perspective, but it conceals a crime of incompetence, whereby government year on year failed to take any heed of the demographic trend and plan ahead for it. So the action they nowadays contemplate seems draconian and characteristically fails to provide sufficient lead-in time for couples and individuals to adjust to harsh new realities. Part of the lack of enlightenment too includes such assumptions as one-size-fits-all and rigid age cut-off dates. Needless to say this can have differential effects on people. Jobs take different tolls and people age very differently too, so although some sixty-eight year olds may welcome continuing with their work, others could well be burnt-out at forty in demanding roles like teaching, nursing and social work. So take all this cant about creating a fairer society with a large dollop of salt. We need, for example, far more flexibility over retirement and partial retirement regulations, so that people can obtain their occupational and state benefits when they need them, whilst still being able to continue with part-time employment and without having earning ceilings imposed on them as local government currently does.

Adding to the sense of chronic miss-management, the Government cannot stop tinkering with the system. It planned to introduce changes to national insurance in April 2018 which would make the contributions of the lowest paid subject to a four-fold increase. The target group earned under £6025 per year and comprised a fifth of the self-employed workforce-tens of thousands of people.

Deeper in Debt

Government and the people have not learned their lessons from the credit crunch, which precipitated the banking crash of 2007. Put simply, mortgage lenders loaned money to people who could not, or who had no intention to keep up the payments. The traditional safeguards involving financial checks on borrowers had gradually been eroded in the new, computer-led spiv economy, so that people overreached themselves. The banks would have collapsed without massive public sector handouts by government from tax reserves.

Since then there have been some attempts made to restrict mortgages to those who are financially secure, but the general climate of borrowing up to the hilt for all sorts of expenditure has not disappeared. Credit is still far too easily made available, with a lot of spastic plastic on the high street. It has been calculated that in 2016 in Britain the average household, apart from mortgage borrowing, owed over £7,000. There are lots of financially ignorant, greedy and downright irresponsible people out there. The old-fashioned virtue of saving up until you can afford it is now seen as silly by the impatient must-have-it –now brigade.

In mitigation, government encouraged retail spending to help economic growth. By the same token it did nothing to increase interest rates, so that safe saving could not keep pace with even the low levels of prevailing inflation. As usual, what we need is balance through effective micro-management of the economy – something the Government cannot or will not do. What is also distressing is the feeble reaction of government to the loan sharks who prey on the hard-up and those who have lost their jobs.

With a society like ours, where the population is up to its eyes in debt, it is hardly surprising that payday lenders thrive. And as usual the government puts their rights to trade and to turn a fat profit ahead of protection of the public against exploitation, not to say downright racketeering. It is always the same. Cries for an industry to clean up its act are followed, after pressure, by government statements exhorting the companies to put their house in order by self-regulation. This can go on for years before action is taken, typically to give the job of oversight to a non-government body – in this case the Office of Fair Trading – carefully set up to have very limited teeth to enforce anything. Typically it took them two years to revoke a licence. We are now promised tougher action by the replacement body, the Financial Conduct Authority, but a raft of measures would be needed to prevent such common practices as misleading advertisements, to impose lending ceilings and interest charges, require proper affordability checks and bring in tough legal penalties.

In 2013 one continuing nasty practice was for payday lenders to take money out of clients' accounts without warning or permission, the bank being far from blameless in such situations either. In fact banks could do a lot more to provide affordable short-term loans as an alternative to the unscrupulous charges of firms like Wonga, where interest rates could reach over 5,000 percent!

I would want from personal debt legislation a regime that ensures that bankrupts can get back on their feet, whilst protecting from financial loss as much as possible the legitimate creditors, especially individuals and small traders. But although some people go bankrupt through no fault of their own, others are culpable to varying degrees. Their treatment should reflect the facts of the circumstances. In appropriate cases rehabilitation should include attendance on a prescribed course to learn preventative skills and good financial management for the future. Nor am I a believer that discharged bankrupts should just be allowed automatically to re-enter their previous working lives, with the possibility of history repeating itself and innocent people being hurt in the process. What we need here to protect society is a sensible measure of proscription. Having failed before, you rule yourself out of entitlement to be a player in certain risky financial enterprises. So I would like to see discharged bankrupts, for example, disbarred from setting up their own businesses or becoming company directors.

Two aspects of the present law that I particularly find nasty are the fact that bankrupts have to pay court fees through the nose. The State could exercise a little humanity here. On the other hand court orders for the bankrupt to pay debts out of earned income can only last a maximum of three years, which seems to me too much of a let-off.

And we need to look quite closely at reforming the law governing companies in debt. If they go into 'administration' under insolvency legislation the aims are to try and ensure the companies' survival in whole or part as a going concern and achieve a better price for creditors. It might seem to the layman that these objectives are liable to conflict and that creditors tend to lose heavily. Those to whom money is owed are divided into groups, with a batting order of entitlement to reimbursement, at whatever proportion in the pound can be managed. The Government takes first bite, which always strikes me as the opposite of what should happen. Instead of raiding the depleted coffers of failed companies at the further expense of legitimate creditors why doesn't it make successful ones pay their just taxation dues?

There is clearly something very wrong with the way debt in professional football clubs is legally handled. Clubs, often mismanaged, frequently rack up millions of pounds in debts and apply to be taken into administration. First call on any resources is required to be the players, the most expensive commodities and usually the main reason, along with their agents, why the club is in debt in the first place. At the end of the day many creditors, some of whom will be local fans supplying provisions through small businesses, miss out, while the club is triumphantly re-floated, albeit sometimes relegated to a lower league for its sins off the pitch. I would not have this happen. Let them all go to the wall, as a firm in the real world would probably have to. Money has corrupted the game, at the best of times a trivial pursuit, mostly for men who should have better things to do.

The biggest debt of all is, of course, the national debt, defined as 'the total amount of money the British government owes to the private sector and other purchasers of UK gilts' and seemingly governed by entirely different laws to debt in the personal sphere. By way of illustration this stood in September 2016 as £1,627.2 billion, comprising some 83.3% of gross domestic product, GDP, a measure of our current national worth. It does fluctuate considerably, but has been steadily rising from 30% in 2002. Why?

Well, between 2002 and 2007 the national debt rose in spite of a long run of sustained economic expansion, owing mainly to increased government expenditure on health and education, as well as social security. But from 2008 to 2015 national debt soared to its present very high levels owing to the banking crisis, followed by their financial bail-out by the public sector and a long period of recession thereafter.

A sense of proportion may be provided by the facts that after the war in the late 1940's our national debt was over 200% of GDP, and that quite a few other countries have much higher national debt than ourselves – Japan at 225%

in 2016, for instance. Care needs to be taken, though, with such comparisons, because the capacity to borrow and its cost will vary greatly depending on the economic conditions affecting potential lenders at the time and the reputation of the country for financial competence.

It is a comfort, however, to note that in principle, and to some extent in historical fact, a high national debt has not been incompatible with high economic growth, rising standards of living, and the setting up of major public institutions, such as the NHS and the welfare state. This is emphatically not what Chancellor Osborne told you when setting his Tory austerity budgets year after year. Nor did he remind us that after the First World War the United Kingdom's adoption of austerity policies failed to reduce the national debt in relation to GDP. In fact, the best way to do so is the way it was done post second-world-war, by maintaining economic growth at reasonable levels for a prolonged period of time. Osborne's method was to cut government spending, whilst maintaining tax levels, but this failed as economic growth did not pick up. The method of substantial, but justly progressive tax rises has yet to be tried, being ideologically against what Conservatives stand for as unacceptable to industry.

One worry perhaps is that future debt payments the government will be committed to when the time comes, like public sector pensions and private finance initiatives for public building projects, are falsely not presently calculated as part of the existing national debt. In this way future national expenditure is already to some extent fettered.

Now when the government borrows it issues bonds and other gilt-edged securities (so called because payment when due is never defaulted on). These are bought by the UK private sector, especially insurance and pension funds, and foreign investors. Increasingly, though, the Bank of England also buys gilts, now holding some quarter of their total worth. One problem is that when, as in recent years, companies have wanted to save more, they have fuelled government borrowing at the expense of their own investment and private sector spending more generally.

Debt should possibly be seen in total for the country, in which case it is made up of government, household, business and financial sector debts, amounting to a huge 500% of GDP altogether.

The Government does not on the whole like to talk about the national debt, but it is quite capable of using the concepts for its own purposes to deceive. Notably, the national debt may be rising, but the Government will not mention this, instead pointing to the fact that the budget deficit is getting less. All they mean is that the annual borrowing has fallen from the previous year, or more likely, that the forecast of annual borrowing for the forthcoming year is lower. The unbounding anger when it begins to dawn on the public at large that all their austerity privations occurred for nought, whilst the Government continued its habits of profligate borrowing, may be something dangerous for our society.

In order for governments to resist the temptation to deceive the public with regard to the national debt it will have to become much harder to do. Which requires a financially more informed public. And we need a national debate over a long-term policy, which of necessity would have to transcend party politics, and which would move us in broad unison towards a goal deemed desirable on the best of economic advice, at a viable, much lower level of national debt. As a layman I get sick and tired of the short-term expediency, the endless political scheming which glosses over the underlying economic situation. It gives me the feeling that we do not know where we are going. There is a sense in which the concept of national debt is so remote and abstract, so seemingly lacking in adverse consequences for the population at large whatever its actual level, that to pursue its reduction at all has to square with people's ideas of public-spiritedness and self-denial. I think a lot of us only really understand debt at the level of personal finances within the family, and sometimes not even there.

Manuel Arriaga talks of a real danger very rarely mentioned by the political commentators, namely that the cumulative effect of years of excessive borrowing has put the United Kingdom at the mercy of the international money markets. Private creditors could ensure that we are paying off vast public debts on a permanent basis. Debts can be reduced to some degree by renegotiation or reneging. Either course naturally increases our risk to lenders and so makes borrowing more costly or in some quarters impossible. Much of our reputation depends on past behaviour to fulfil our promises. Ultimately, the only way is to live, like domestic households, within our means. Which for comfort requires generating handsome budget surpluses through increased economic output and sales to pay off debt.

Yet concerning the balance of payments deficit and the national debt it is clear that the brutal austerity experiment of the Con-Dem and Cameron governments was a damaging failure. One characterization of it was the way deceptive comments were used. Little attempt was seemingly made by politicians or media to explain the salient facts to a long-suffering, nay, persecuted general public. The view was driven home that private debt was their business, public debt a disgrace. It was an area subjected to a quite arbitrary setting of (an optimistic) deadline date target for repayment. They could recalibrate this at will, but while it lasted people were rigidly kept to it. The financial squeeze was visited on public sector institutions, notably local government, the NHS, and the Police, with crude percentage cuts imposed and the invidious choices of adverse impacts left to the institutions to decide – a library closed here, a youth club there, and so forth. Ultimately, we have somehow to restore the public sector cuts made to our essential services, disallow government borrowing for everyday spending, and considerably reduce debt as a percentage of gross domestic product.

What happened over the 2007 banking crisis is well-documented and reasonably well understood, but unfortunately it has led to endless political disagreement over what should be done to reduce the ongoing and likely risks of it happening again. So far, the Conservative right, in both the United States and the United Kingdom, has prevailed, with the result that not much regulation has been put in place to fetter the operations of all concerned, including the general public. Whilst they rail (rightly) against the obscene levels of bankers' bonuses that continue to be paid, citizens mostly fail to realize or accept that their own credit needs to be seriously curbed as well. We are continuing to live way beyond our means as a nation, so there will be a reckoning sometime in the future, although nobody can predict when.

Adair Turner, who as former chairman of the British Financial Services Authority, which set and monitored standards, was very well placed to advise on the way forward. And he has done just that in his book 'Between Debt and the Devil'. Turner, for all his experience and expertise, was nevertheless at the time of writing firmly in the minority camp of economists on such questions. Which is a good reason to become more concerned and to take what he has to say seriously.

Fundamentally, Turner argues that credit needs to be firmly managed. If it is not, we will over-borrow, which leads inexorably to the housing booms and busts of financial crisis and a depressed, recessive economy. In order to shore up the stability of banks they need to be made to hold more capital – enough to underwrite their loans – and it would help in this regard if the relatively higher risk-taking 'investment' banks would be structurally split from the high-street banks dealing with the little people, as I have said elsewhere.

Much of the failings stem from prejudice about the shortcomings of the public sector, including government, and a greedy desire to remain unfettered to make money for private gain irrespective of the consequences for wider society, which can be seriously adverse. Left to their own devices, the private sector financial institutions will create too much credit and distribute it with little sense of responsibility or social purpose. Such inefficient lending produces excessive debt, and eventual personal default on repayments. So this needs to be carefully controlled by state intervention. Conversely, however, if the state prints money through its central bank to stimulate the adequate demand needed for growth, it can likewise be ill-advised and inefficient in the extent and timing of its lending, and generate too much demand, or not enough, and for the wrong ends. So a careful balance is needed, which requires skill, knowledge, close ongoing monitoring and timely interventions – a role for the State that sadly remains in most people's eyes yet to be legitimated.

Turner does not see an evil per se in central bank creation of money, the so-called 'quantitative easement', regarding it instead as an essential tool in the armoury of government. One crucial use for it can be to reduce or eliminate debts racked up nationally by post-policy errors. Debt is a bad thing and the message has yet to get across. Turner regards debt as a form of 'economic pollution' and does not hesitate to prescribe taxation to rein it in.

There are a lot of little people and they all need somewhere to live. A majority still crave to own their own homes, driven on by tradition and government aspirational propaganda. But since population is rising unchecked by restrictions on immigration, and house building is at a relatively low ebb, house prices inexorably rise in the high demand areas of the country where jobs are plentiful. Hence the clamour for still more credit, because the low-wage economy reduces affordability. So the big-ticket loans, for houses for the actual borrowers to live in, sadly have to be rationed to those statistically most likely to repay. A growing number of young people will therefore be denied the prospect of life outside the rented sector, an ambition their parents succeeded in.

Unfortunately, as lots of manufactured goods, especially the IT related, become cheaper, house purchase borrowing becomes the largest factor. Such capital investment is obviously very uneven across the classes, so leading to the increasing wealth inequalities within society which the right-thinking deplore and the I'm – All- Right- Jacks could not care less about.

Who Needs Charities

Charity, as the old adage has it, 'begins at home'. And maybe it should end there also in rather more cases than it does. It strikes me that there is a large surfeit of so-called 'charities' in this country. There must be a sensible limit on the number of 'good causes', and dubious justification for several covering broadly the same area of interest. Too small is too ineffective also.

I don't know much about charity law, but we have the familiar complaint from other fields that some charities lack both transparency and public accountability. And, of course, there is the popular yet seldom examined view of an excessive proportion of income being spend on (that dirty word!) 'administration'.

The reality is, of course, that government will put the charities through a nominal procedural hoop for petty constitutional compliance and financial probity, whilst seemingly indifferent to the gross misapplications of funds that can actually occur.

It seems to me that in a rich society like ours the need for charities to cover the basic essentials of the population should be low to non-existent. It is something of an indictment that it is not so. But most of the money is in the hands of the few, and the government wastes a great deal of its tax take on such scandals as foreign wars, uncontrolled overseas aid, and military projects instead. Then there is the outrage that public schools qualify for charitable status, thus giving a tax benefit to the already privileged.

It does not seem to me to help that, whenever the frequent cry goes up in our community for donations to prominent causes or emergency appeals, usually abroad, the cash-strapped, long-suffering British public dip their hands into shallow pockets without complaint. This, of course, encourages the Chancellor of the Exchequer in his conviction that there is plenty more slack where that came from…

I still have a hunch that charity law and practice is in need of serious reform. The fact that in 2013, according to the Charity Commission itself, there were around

160,000 registered charities in the United Kingdom, should provide a clue. The reason is that there are lots of little organizations, some no doubt scrambling for the privileges of tax relief, whilst preying on the generosity of our consciences. There is nothing quite like the word 'charity' for pulling at our heartstrings. Many a worthy organization exists, possessed of impressively 'noble aims' (not difficult to think up), variously to do with the amelioration of multifold human miseries.

What typically happens is that somebody dies, often in tragic circumstances – a victim of a rare disease perhaps, or of a terrorist incident, let's say. So the nearest and dearest relatives decide to set up a charity in their honour. Their plans do not have to be realistic. You can undertake to raise millions in the cause without a cat in hell's chance of ever doing so, travelling in hope, but never arriving.

The Charity Commission is a typically inept quango, set up with duties and powers, as well as resources, far short of what would be necessary to stop the rogues and charlatans. The legal requirements for keeping and publication of records are minimal and easy to comply with. So it is all too simple to register a new charity, and there are provisions for a salary to be paid. Like my mother, who did a lot of charity work, I have never been quite at ease with the principles and practicalities of professionals and volunteers working together.

There is a sham regarding Cameron's 'Big Society' as it relates to small charities. These used to work alongside local authorities in providing public services. But as the functions of local government are increasingly required by the State to be farmed out to private firms, small charities can end up in effect acting as sub-contractors doing their bidding. If they speak out they are liable to lose their role, perhaps needless to say. Some national umbrella organization should be looking at the whole piece with a view to effecting mergers and rationalisations for improved effectiveness, efficiency, and to avoid overlaps.

Another sound reason to be suspicious of charities is their general lack of transparency. To keep them honest we should want to know such information as what they spend their money on, analysed into areas including administration, advertising, and salaries. We would feel entitled to be able to evaluate the outcomes of their expenditure in relation to the objects of the charity. Unfortunately, there is no legal requirement for charities to operate this way, so a lot of them don't and could not provide the information even if they wanted to…

What of the Future?

In summary there is a growing recognition that the capitalist system as operated in the United Kingdom is not fit for purpose, both unjust and ineffective.

Certainly, this is a considerable part of the reasons for public disquiet, although they may not see things in these terms and mostly protest against rather than positively adopting unorthodox political ideas.

Perhaps unfortunately, no new radical system waits in the wings to be tried, nor would the majority of the voting population wish to witness a full-blown socialist alternative. It is perceived that communist economies have all failed, and have usually been accompanied by rigid rules and oppression as well.

So there is a tentative view emerging among a minority that the balance between public and private sectors needs to be altered in such a way that the worst elements of the private sector can be reformed and the best elements of the public sector can be harnessed in symbiosis. There must be a patching up. Criticisms of the private sector have included the huge rewards given to top managers, the vast pay gaps between those at top and bottom, and the skew of influence in favour of shareholders and against employees. Stealing from the pension pot and lack of worker representation on the Board are part of it.

So where does a more interactive State come in? Key roles are envisaged to include breaking up cosy cartels, stimulating stagnant demand, areas and industries where there is poor performance, raising private sector productivity, kick-starting expensive infrastructure projects, creating cash. The State is uniquely well placed as the only operator across the board. When the economy or a sector of it is doing well, private firms can usually cope, but when there are problems the public sector could be there with a State Bank to increase investment and business confidence.

CHAPTER 6

SAVING THE PLANET

Introduction

I regret I am pessimistic enough to expect the world to end for human life long before it astronomically should through one or a combination of various sorts of ills of 'biblical' proportions-famine, pestilence, climate change, war, other human mismanagement. Nevertheless, it would be responsible for the nation to act sustainably regarding care of the environment and use of its limited resources. And this would be sensible notwithstanding that many other countries probably will not do likewise, including some who sign binding international commitments. It follows that policies, incentives, prohibitions, and sanctions are all likely to be required in various measure. I have no wish to rehearse again the dire warnings, some unfortunately justified, from the green lobby, however, but to make a few, possibly idiosyncratic and inevitably incomplete, observations of my own. I start with land, since it is one of the obvious fundamentals and in human timescales they are not making any more of it. But for a comprehensive and systematic treatment of the relevant findings of ecological and related environmental sciences, I would simply refer you to the academic texts. There are big issues out there that I care passionately about – from fish-stocks' husbandry to the plastics' industry's poisoning of the oceans, to name but two.

Briefly regarding the latter, Greenpeace have exposed the serious problem of the contribution made by plastic to ocean pollution and squarely placed the blame on the world's biggest producers of plastic bottles, soft drinks companies like Pepsi, Coca Cola, and Nestle. In the main the companies had no recycling or reclamation plans. Needless to say, governments are not doing enough either, such as passing tough legislation to limit production and encourage recycling. The plastic degrades over hundreds of years, making it essential to try and stop its entry into watercourses in the first instance. Parts of the plastic inevitably find their way into fish and large sea mammals like whales. This is in addition to the plastic fragments used commercially, and the microfibers and microbeads from synthetic clothing materials and other household items such as toothpaste. So they will and do enter the food chain and end up being ingested by ourselves. A growing school of thought sadly recognizes that the only way ultimately to tackle the problem of plastic waste is to stop using plastic altogether. Yes, we could possibly design new plastic materials that would bio-degrade very quickly, we might generate micro-organisms that can successfully feed on the stuff, we could definitely recycle a lot more by clever technology, improved public awareness and industrial cooperation, but these measures are not likely to be enough.

I would dip into the agenda of the Green Party to support more research and implementation of renewable sources of energy – solar, wind, tide, hydroelectric – in place of coal, oil, and gas, and especially that obtained by fracking, likely to have the added fossil fuel disadvantage of being unsafe and psychologically disturbing to nearby residents. I like their idea of community-owned energy schemes which can be zero-carbon and take pressure off national sources. A new Clean Air Act would help reduce the enormous loss of life from atmospheric pollution if pursued with zest, an education programme, and draconian powers to fine and imprison serious offenders.

Greenhouse gas emissions like carbon dioxide are also far too high and, unless constrained, will lead to irreversible climate changes beyond our influence and to our very serious detriment, if not actual extinction. So far the international conference agreements have been pathetically inadequate, frequently only honoured in the breach. Nations are so keen to look after their own narrow interests as they see them and too concerned about fair comparisons with how others are affected. One notable stumbling block here is that developed countries have had many years of unrestricted pollution behaviour whilst wishing to deny underdeveloped nations the same free run. Equal per capita annual emissions might be reasonably just, but what price survival?

Finally, I think concerted international effort should be put into research to provide us with defences against objects from space such as large asteroids that may potentially collide with us and wipe out mankind.

Blighted Plots

One of the causes of why Britain is ugly in far too many places is that land sometimes lies idle and neglected for years on end. Now there may be understandable reasons for this. For example, someone who owned the land may have died. Or the owners could simply be holding it in the hope of a rise in market value. Perhaps they wish to block a development they don't want to see. These are understandable reasons, yes, but are they justifiable ones?

I have some sympathy with a Labour Party suggestion that you should have to use it or lose it. From some perspectives land is too precious (especially in a grossly overpopulated country like England) to confer selfish and controlling rights on owners to the exclusion of wider public interests. Money somehow ought to be ploughed back at least into tidying up the site.

Naturally, we do have to be careful. Compulsory purchase orders enforced by State organs when, say, pulling down an awkwardly placed private house for a motorway extension without adequate compensation, can and should be vehemently resisted. Nevertheless, we do have to recognize private, anti-social tyrannies and oppose them on both utilitarian and aesthetic grounds.

Apart from neglected land there is also developed land, of course. A very great deal of this, in private or public ownership, is blighted by untidiness, badly designed and maintained buildings, plant and equipment not appropriately stored. I would like to see a national monitoring agency with very powerful powers of fine and enforcement. You only have to take a train ride through urban environments to see the disgraces we have become inured to, a nation uncaring as to its appearance to self and outsiders. The same goes for the areas bespoiled by industrial waste, such as poisonous metallic residues.

It is really down to government to safeguard us in the last analysis. Part of this role involves a watching brief over emerging trends to see if they are deleterious, so requiring appropriated intervention. One such is that a new generation of householders, doubtless too busy to bother and overprovided with cars, is turning green front gardens into paved over surfaces. This is not just a problem of aesthetics. The trend is taking away oxygen-replenishing plants, the sense of well-being, and the permeability that helps to remove rainwater and prevent flooding.

Give us a Sign

Signs along our roads and streets are a proliferating scourge. Usually starting from such intentions as a desire to inform or advertise, they have proliferated to an extent where many of them can only incidentally do either. Even if you accept the dubious legitimacy of commercial signs, as opposed to public ones, there are still way too many of the damn things, and their positioning, juxtaposition, size, colour, wording, layout, and other characteristics can leave a lot to be desired on humble, aesthetic grounds alone. Unlike other indicators of the way Britain is becoming uglier, such as litter, they are possibly too familiar now for the most part to stand out from their blighted backgrounds and are so not the justified target of mass concern they should be.

Every now and again a local authority, or possible a junior government minister, announces an intention to clamp down by simplifying. Such initiatives are usually short-lived and attract little public interest among the general clamour. Characteristically, these campaigns are one-sided too; they concentrate on public responsibilities alone, whilst leaving the private sector unfettered. For the government's aim is invariably to leave the 'wealth creators' as free as can be. And so they bombard us with tasteless and unsolicited adverts from all angles. In America, and coming here too, because of our special relationship of subjugation and imitation, we have billboards along the major highways so big as to obscure the scenery. Another creeping aberration and danger is the use of distracting commercial advertisements on traffic roundabouts where drivers are supposed to be exercising particular care.

Loutish Litter

One thing I should like to 'see' would be no litter. It defiles and debases our society: the ugly side of Britain needs no help from it.

Litter seems to speak of antisocial elements, people who don't care about the effects of their behaviour on others. It may be too charitable to suggest that a majority of them are merely thoughtless, or perhaps too dim to appreciate what litter can do en masse. And our understanding of the causes of this phenomenon may be a help when it comes to finding a cure.

Evidently the current laws and their enforcement are tokenism. They do not work, and efforts to address the problem seem confined to local initiatives, from hapless Councils or voluntary groups, or are down to conscientious individuals, who make spasmodic efforts, such as 'Clean for the Queen' to mark her ninetieth birthday.

There has to be a political will for serious change to happen across the country as a whole. And that is going to be lacking as long as terrible problems continue to beset us, so that people's priorities are inevitably concerned with fundamentals like economic survival.

Perhaps we might benefit from exploring what other societies do. And the right messages promulgated by education during childhood and adolescence would be no bad thing. Meanwhile we could achieve a lot through the systematic deployment of criminal elements such as serving prisoners and, especially, those doing community service.

It has to be faced that we do not collectively bother enough about this and that there are huge numbers of fly-tippers getting away with it. We are a dirty, scum-ridden society, where litter is our badge of dishonour.

No lesser light than Jeremy Paxman has called for a national litter strategy to help local authorities who are becoming overwhelmed by fly-tipping and fast–food remains. The burden is shoved onto councils by a politically vindictive government and they have neither the powers nor the staffing resources to cope after all the cut-backs. Another problem is that it is not strongly seen as socially unacceptable by the majority. We have little national pride about it to help our tourist trade and it is typical of our culture that we shift the burden of responsibility away from the guilty, who hide behind almost impossible to attain standards of evidence. In reality the mess is generated by dirty, antisocial people, commercial outlets, and the irresponsible packaging industry. We could if we were serious about it legally require shops and restaurants, for instance, to keep tidy the areas around their premises, levy the packagers, drastically increase fines, and empower local officials to impose them on the spot without appeal. But the government actually exacerbates the problems by allowing councils to charge the public and other legitimate operators seeking to dispose rubbish legally in approved waste management sites. There is usually an admission fee, together with extra charges for various different kinds of disposable item.

Tree Tribulations

Let's hear it for trees. We need more of them, lots more. They should maintain the indigenous varieties as well as conifers and other trees that will grow well here. Everyone with a big enough garden should be given incentives to plant some. Encouragingly we seem to have made a little progress, since there has been a wider understanding that trees are our complementary lungs, breathing in our waste gases, breathing out the oxygen of animal life. The Forestry Commission is a wonderful idea and institution. Our stock of trees should be for pleasure, for health, for the raw materials of industries, for shielding fields from soil erosion, for soaking up flood water.

But, and there is a 'but', we have too many of the wrong type of tree in the wrong place. It is not much good uncritically extolling their virtues where they are a nuisance, a menace even. Typical examples, unfortunately widespread, are in the suburban acacia avenues, where municipal planting years ago established the trees. Some are now giants that spread leaves, seeds, block light, and generally threaten to fall down and hurt somebody or damage something. The trouble is that financially weakened local authorities no longer have the money or staff to maintain the existing stock let alone selectively fell and replace with more appropriate species.

One consequence of a lack of national policy, combined with local delegation, is that our trees are put at risk needlessly and wantonly. As councils find it harder to cope with their lot, many are simply cutting down trees rather than trying to keep up with their maintenance. Replanting schemes inevitably lag behind in time and in the short-term replace the trees with relatively immature ones that lack their green lung capacity. Away from the leafy suburbs into managed parks and woodlands the distribution of types of trees also changes. We do not know precisely what is going on because, disgracefully, there is no government requirement to keep and use the relevant statistics.

Farm Fudging

Examples are manifold, but include organic farming methods. These laudably produce healthier food without using pesticides and fertilizers, albeit at a cost. Responsible government would notice the decline in UK organic farming arising from the availability of cheaper imports and plug the gap by encouraging British farmers. But it is too doctrinaire. It would rather our producers went to the wall, or grew something less wholesome at a profit.

Likewise, what does it do to prevent soil erosion? The quality of our soil is vital to a healthy farming industry, yet it has steadily deteriorated as unscientific methods have casually been allowed to prevail in the interests of quick returns. The sort of practices are short periods of crop rotation that do not allow proper soil replenishment and large fields without hedges to prevent wind dispersal. It has been estimated that since 1850 over eighty percent of Britain's fertile top soil has been lost as a result of such woefully ignorant practice. And in effect, owing to the very long time it takes to be produced, soil is not a renewable resource.

The prejudice and regulation against genetically modified crops will have to be relaxed and for a variety of reasons. Principally, the potential contribution GM crops can make to reducing pesticide use, as well as improving plants to tolerate inclement weather and adverse soil conditions, are illustrations of opportunities too good to pass up. And because the fears about 'Frankenstein flowers' have proved completely without foundation. Oh, and remember that without population control we are slowly running short of food…

Waste of Energy

Britain has suffered from a disastrous lack of forward planning and no integrated or coherent policy for energy in decades, so that has to change.

Speaking as a chemist, coal seems far too valuable a commodity to burn away: its constituents were and could again be the basis for a whole chemical industry of useful products. Its abandonment as a domestic fuel is not down to scarcity, the country has enormous reserves, but owing to pollution, essentially by carbon dioxide, a key greenhouse gas. The emphasis here has been too blinkered. Mostly governments and lay people associate burning coal solely with generating the unwanted carbon dioxide. In this regard Britain has largely acted responsibly, attempting to cut emissions to levels set by international agreements, in partial implementation of scientific advice.

But it is also vital to ensure, by government funding if necessary, and ideally with full international cooperation, regular and sustained research into safe and sustainable energy provision. If the holy grail of controlled nuclear fusion could be achieved, it could quite literally solve the wide world's energy problems forever, but short of that we must ensure the more feasible prospects are thoroughly investigated and developed before time runs out. These would presumably include, as well as wind and solar power, wave and tidal energy, an untapped resource of enormous potential in these climatically turbulent British Isles. Electrical options would include progressing battery research into fuel cells so we can effectively store energy, as well as generating biofuels which are low carbon and not a threat to agricultural food production. Fortunately, there are encouraging signs that the renewables industry is making great strides, increasing its percentage contribution to energy generation and becoming a significant player as production costs fall. Fossil fuels such as coal, gas, and oil need not be phased out altogether, providing we can discover ways to severely limit their greenhouse gas emissions. But governments must stop fooling us and themselves and start to act decisively, on the best scientific advice, as a priority and without further prevarication. Carbon quotas should not be bought and sold. They are, when all is said and done, licences to pollute.

Whatever the temptation we must resist going nuclear at all costs. It is not, and never could be, safe. There is no way in the final analysis to prevent severely adverse consequences for human life arising from the inevitable escape of radiation. No matter which technology we choose to design and build an atomic power station, we shall one day be found out. There will be an explosion, or leaking pipes, or corroded valves. However careful we are, circumstances will contrive to cause radioactivity to run out of control. Even if we are lucky for a while and manage to prevent catastrophic accidents in the factories, there is no safe way we can store and neutralize the radioactive waste. In whatsoever vessel, wherever placed, it will remain harmful to all life forms for thousands, even millions of years to come, so slowly do its toxic isotopes decay.

Recycling Tricks

I must say a few words about recycling. We have arrived at a crazy mess. Spurred by the European Union we have legislated in Britain to set environmental recycling targets, then delegated the task to about one hundred local authorities with discretion to do it their way. The result has been a bewildering array of collection schemes. One authority invests in the latest separation and processing equipment (foreign-designed and made) and opens well-designed, easy-to-access public dumps, Its neighbour is more conservative and produces an ugly and awkward–to-deal–with plethora of small bins, plastic boxes and buckets, placing much onus on residents to separate their waste at source in irrational and time-consuming ways. Some even charge extra for garden refuse to be collected. Many have strayed away from the traditional weekly collection to complex timetables with longer intervals. Various threats and penalties exist for non-compliance. Sometimes litter is actually spread by the collectors themselves, exacerbated on windy days especially by the poor design of materials and the thoughtlessness of residents. Overall the record is very mixed and hardly impressive. Admittedly we started from a low base, but perhaps still only collect about half of what we could for recycling.

I have implied what I want to see. My ideal is a very high percentage of recycling achieved at minimal cost and effort to the taxpayer. We should be able to have all our rubbish stored easily and neatly in sensible containers collected regularly without fuss. Not only should it be possible for council and commercial equipment to do all the requisite separating, but with enterprise there should also be money in it to offset the public costs. Recycling household waste in the country lags woefully behind the advanced European nations owing to our old-fashioned and disjointed approaches. The commercial market has not got going properly and opportunities are being missed without such facilities as anaerobic digesters to generate energy from green waste materials and inedible food.

Elixir of Life

Britain is notoriously wet, but somehow the water often seems to be in the wrong place. We repeatedly suffer from droughts and floods, so that the call for a national water grid comes up repeatedly. Experts and private firms are generally opposed, mostly on grounds of cost. Water is heavy to move around and when you do its variable regional composition makes mixing problematic for treatment plants. It is also difficult to predict where the next flood will be, obviously. Nevertheless, it would seem that some places could benefit from linking by grid pipes.

It seems that the rules governing water authorities will not last for long. Currently, a handful of private firms covering geographical areas control our water supplies. Some are foreign–owned, putting at potential risk one of our key basic resources. I would therefore like to see this banned and all of them taken back into public ownership. What is probably going to happen, however, is that they will be made pseudo-competitive, rather like the present system of energy supply. Instead of being tied to one provider we will be able to shop around, the companies by then being released from their limited geographical coverage. But this will not drive down prices as will be claimed. An unofficial cartel will be created, able to fix prices behind the scenes. Just like the energy companies 'Big Six' they will doubtless be overseen by a toothless tiger in the shape of a government regulator.

It would be reassuring if we could believe the water companies to be acting in the interests of our health. Unfortunately this is not always so. In 2017 Thames Water were fined £20 million for deliberately pumping raw sewage into the river. The fine was a record, but it does reflect that the legal penalties are inadequate to deter companies like Thames, which has a history of non-compliance and probably regards the fine as a worthwhile business expense. Environmental pollution cannot be combatted effectively if we let firms continue to trade in such circumstances, yet everywhere the conduct of Conservative ministers will place profit as their higher value.

Ignorance of Risk

Regarding the avoidance of disaster I would not start from here. Once again we have our short-sighted ancestors to thank for the potential tragedies we live amongst. What do I mean? Well when a flood happens we should not have to contend with the added problems of electricity sub-stations being under water. We should have anticipated such events and ensured sub-stations were always built on higher ground. And when there is an explosion, or fire, or severe leakage of gas clouds at a factory, we should not need to evacuate local residents, or in our amateurish, time-honoured way simply urge people to stay indoors and shut their windows. Such actions should not be necessary because the factory should not have been close to houses in the first place. There are worse hazards yet to be realized; for example, when a dam bursts its banks and drowns communities living below it. All stem from rank thoughtlessness, money saving, greed, slack regulations, failures of imagination and other factors that have escaped a scientific risk management that still has little formal and systematic place in so-called modern Britain.

Serious money just has to be spent on proper flood defences. We must start by preventing building on known flood plains. We must develop a national plan, with each region adequately treated, then a costed programme of annual amelioration. Rivers need to be tracked from source to sea to devise successful water volume management strategies for each. Evil and deceitful notions such as the Cameron Government's Environment Agency schemes of work should be dumped forthwith. Contrary no doubt to popular belief to secure funding a flood protection scheme had to show a favourable cost/benefit analysis, so the cost of building and maintaining the defences has to be outweighed by the economic benefits that come from the avoidance of payments to repair or replace damaged property and possessions. Such ideas are not only unfeeling for the disruption to people's lives, the destruction of their ambitions, but they also skew expenditure to the South, where property values are considerably higher.

That isn't good enough. It leaves far too many innocent people at the mercy of changing weather patterns, among which frequent torrential rainfall is an unwelcome feature. Government has not taken the attendant problems seriously. It allows planning permission for new house building on flood plains, it makes derisory one-off payments in a few areas of hardship, but characteristically jettisons the North of England. It could jump on laggardly insurance companies, but does not, and still householders are forced out of their homes for months, sometimes years on end. Neither will the Government intervene to change the building regulations to incorporate water-resistant design specifications. Who needs enemies when we are so looked after? Even the sandbags, those pathetically inadequate reminders of World War Two make-do-and–muddle-through, run short…

Transport Torpor

In this country we have mediocre transport systems, given our claimed status as an advanced nation and considering our impressive history of producing engineers and inventors who have had worldwide and lasting impact. There are several main reasons for this. First is the sheer short-sightedness of our political rulers, the transport infrastructure requiring long-term planning and sustained investment, whereas leaders are here today, gone tomorrow. Second is that the private sector only wants to bet on sure things, so without enormous public subsidy and the generation of false markets to ensure their profit margins, schemes don't happen. We are further baulked by the endless bickering between the political parties which leads to delays and deferment, as well as silly ideologies such as a belief in nationalization as panacea, or alternatively its iniquity. Pioneers are overtaken by those who build on their ideas to produce better ones, never more true than with our railways.

Let's look at a few of the current major problems and defects to see where we might draw together a programme of improvement. Perhaps the first observation to make is that there is little integration between the systems of the different modes of transport. The second is that there is no overall national development plan as such, nor timescale for attainment of those elements that do exist, which are regularly deferred at whim. We do have a number of quite spectacularly expensive follies proposed, however, like the high–speed rail connections from London to 'the North', the idea of building a third runway at Heathrow Airport. With these general remarks as background, I will proceed to comment on some of the main modes of transport separately, starting with air travel.

There is a London-centric political obsession with air flight to and from the capital, whereas what we really need as a nation is a viable airport in each region, subsidized to the extent, if any, necessary. Some of the existing airports are very much more developed than others, so the imbalance needs addressing. Both passenger travel and air freight are important strands in each case. They require adequate road and rail connections to the main surrounding towns and cities, which cannot unfortunately be relied on.

A thoroughly modern problem, hitherto not so much in evidence, is airport security. Here I do not pretend to know the answers, except to say that safe solutions must be found which allow for far speedier 'processing' from arrival to take-off. I fear, however, that air travel is just going to get more unpleasant as time goes on. Some of the main drivers here are increasing pressure owing to popular mass demand, especially at peak holiday times, terrorist activity and the ongoing threat of it, and the development of cost-cutting at the expense of quality and comfort. Extras are charged for, delays become more frequent, and computers increasingly and confusingly handle the administration.

Problems with the railways are legion, ranging from exorbitant fares, service delays and cancellations, overcrowding, poor quality of provision for food and comfort, maintenance problems. The rail industry is sadly a clear example of political ideology overruling sensible action. The Tory Government created an artificial market, whereby running the trains was separated from the company responsible for track and signal maintenance. Franchises to run services on particular regional lines were filled by contracts let by government to bidders for a period of years and then subject to review. Doctrinaire statements against re-nationalization of lines run by bogus commercial enterprises that have failed in consumer terms are ridiculous in this setting, the more so since some of the companies cream off massive profits whilst receiving large state subsidies. Nevertheless, solving the structures and financing involved will not in themselves address the key weaknesses of concern to Joe Public, though state control could solve the ticket pricing problems. Prices are not only too high, increasing beyond inflation, but also very variable between routes and operators in ways that are bewilderingly complicated and lack transparency.

Concerning rolling stock it is another sad story. Britain used to be a world leader in their design and manufacture. Now, with only one indigenous coachbuilder left, and even that in foreign ownership, we have to go and queue for replacement carriages from Europe. We stand and watch rail technology developments elsewhere in the world, like Japan, marvel at their high-speed trains, whereas we have lost the expertise and our lines are too old and damaged to be suitable. Likewise, in our typically blinkered way we resist the investment needed to upgrade our 'lamps on sticks' signals to a modern, intelligently responsive digital control system that would prevent accidents. Then there is the laughable fact that, although we are a country with notoriously inclement weather, we are never prepared for it on our transport networks, the infamous 'leaves on the line' syndrome.

Regarding the road network there have also been some very unfortunate changes in recent times. Main routes have become vastly over-used, so that the congestion leads to unacceptable levels and frequencies of blockage and delay. The standards of driving are woeful, speeds being excessive and tailgating the norm, with due consideration for other motorists declining markedly, as shown by practices like cutting in without warning. EU and other heavy vehicles have been allowed, so leading to early deterioration of the road surfaces. Unsurprisingly, the death toll is very high. Frighteningly, it seems of little concern to the public at large, unless they are in some obvious way personally affected. It has become routine. Media pay little attention for the most part, even though the roads are unsafe. Shock them, I say, by showing the gore on television.

The distribution of population is both historically pre-set and eccentric to modern ways of life, so that even in principle the development of a national network is an overwhelmingly daunting prospect. If we had a choice we would not start from here. To build wide, straight motorways which do not actually go to places, only near them, was a brilliantly simple idea, however, as theoretically it offered fast long journeys and relatively easy connections to the existing historical pattern of roads. But it is clear that road users are not taxed enough for the privilege and that the revenue raised is not being properly ploughed back. The news that one in six roads in England will soon be unfit to drive on because of their maintenance neglect arising from government cut-backs to local authorities is beyond sad. But if they were in some cases to be put out of commission rather than repaired, it would not in my view necessarily be an unmitigated disaster, with certain provisos. I would require a national review, with adequate local expertise, to decide on a pruning policy and programme. This would emphatically not be a Beeching-style operation like the one which decimated the railways during the 1960's. Part of the policy would involve looking at imaginative ways of alternative use. I have often marvelled at our incredibly complex maze of roads that presumably grew historically in largely uncoordinated fashion in accordance with local needs of their times and which we take for granted now. Where demand has atrophied, and where small places are connected by several different routes to the outside world, these are obvious places to review. Perhaps some roads could become alternative cycle tracks, walking routes, or bridle paths, possibly run by regional bodies which would also finance them.

There are things to say about current practice which needlessly renders the lot of drivers more difficult than it should be. To start with so-called 'smart' motorways are being developed (over years and years) to increase volume capacity and ease flow. They involve taking the hard shoulder in and out of use. I await the obvious fatalities for a hoped for review of policy. Secondly, large stretches of road are thoughtlessly put out of commission against the much later rainy day when there will actually be work on them. This is unacceptable and must cease. Exhortations to statutory undertakers to hurry the job when working, together with the threat of fines, is worrying, though. If repairs to gas mains and the like are skimped as a consequence we could have a higher incidence of dangerous accidents. Finally, though I could go on, traffic lights are mostly pre-set and therefore stupid. Modern technology is available and should be installed to make them intelligently respond to traffic patterns, so saving us countless hours in the course of our lives.

For once our government was badly advised by scientists on whose encouragement they promoted the use of diesel fuel, notably for cars and lorries, in place of petrol-driven vehicles which produced carbon dioxide, a greenhouse gas. When diesel engines had attained a large slice of the market, it became clear that diesel produced worse pollution than petrol, notably through nitrogen oxides. Their effect on health is such that they are literally mass killers, especially in crowded cities. The situation was made worse by the discovery that several leading car manufactures, notoriously Volkswagen, had made exaggerated claims for the extent to which their engines reduced harmful emissions. They were abetted by the British Government, then taken to the European Court. Despite proof that legal pollution limits had been significantly overreached, the car firms made a poor fist of their recall and fix programmes, with denial of compensation to car owners whose vehicles were, in consequence of the adverse publicity, then worth less in the market. This is the sort of set-up I have been railing against: firms getting away with it, through a combination of weak regulation, weaker sanctions, and governments without the guts to take the strong measures our health requires. They know their voters are selfishly ignorant and mostly choose their cars on the basis of glossy adverts which sell style and status, not safety.

As a former chemist I must confess to being shamefully ignorant of battery technology and its potential for improvement, which I fear is subject to severe physical and chemical limits. What I do know leads me to be sceptical about the political dream for us all to run electric cars in place of the liquid and gas-driven internal combustion engines. Their range is too small, their recharge time too long, and they would need more and flexible capacity from the national grid, presumably also required to be carbon-neutral in its electricity generation. The rechargeable batteries would cost thousands of pounds and need regular replacement as they deteriorated. Massive investment would be required to provide local recharging points.

It is, of course, laudable that the Government wants to do away with the lethally toxic gases currently emitted from our diesel and petrol vehicles. But the passing of a law to ban their sale from some arbitrary future date places a touching and unjustified faith in science to invent the solution. Meanwhile, vehicle restrictions in large towns and big cities, and a phasing out of the more polluting diesels, with financial incentives to owners, dealers, and manufacturers, would make a deal more sense. It is no use just introducing large daily tax charges with little lead-in time, as the Mayor of London did, thereby putting jobs and small businesses at risk.

In 2013 the Campaign for Better Transport published a report detailing the state of deterioration in local authorities' support for bus services. Since bus transport is de-regulated outside London, bus companies make provision of routes and frequency of services on a commercial basis. Local Authorities then try to fill the gap to provide the residual social needs that do not make a profit. This especially applies in rural and sparsely populated areas. Under government austerity cuts to local authority resources this has become increasingly difficult. And yet a lot of the provision is necessary in that otherwise people are left without viable alternative means of transport. Being thus cut-off can have a serious effect on their mental health too.

I have mixed feelings about British cycling success in the Olympic Games, World Championships and road races like the Tour de France, given the repeated allegations and suspicions about drug cheating by competitors, sexism and bullying by the management. Media have created the impression, whatever the truth of the matter, that an unhealthy and unsporting win-at-all-costs mentality has prevailed, driven on by money, personal ambition, and national jingoism.

Beyond all that, though, there are fundamental questions worth pursuing about the way cycling could be used to improve the fitness and pleasure of the nation. I am all in favour, but worry about the safety aspects, given the poor condition and overcrowding of roads and the hostility of large numbers of vehicle drivers. I suspect that people are leading such busy, miserable lives that it breaks out behind the wheel in snarling anger. With the usual cloth-eared lack of foresight the people who planned our roads gave no thought whatsoever to many important matters such as the vast increase in volumes of usage and the plight of the poor cyclist left without provision of cycle lanes. I don't know what we can do about all that now. It seems altogether too late, except perhaps where new roads are being built. But we could be more imaginative about allocation of facilities in such as parks, as well as providing regional and sub-regional velodromes. One final observation may be apt. In an advanced nation like Denmark cycling is already entrenched as a favoured mode of commuting to work. Copenhagen has more daily bike users than car users and the realistic aim is to make half the commutes by bike. Of course, they do not win so many medals…

To recap then: in summary investment in road and rail has been heavily skewed in favour of London and the South-east. The Institute for Public Policy Research says that the Northern Region has been short-changed compared with London over the last decade by some 59 billion pounds on its transport infrastructure. Redressing the balance is therefore long overdue. We need to concentrate on the North, the Midlands and East-West transport. Run-down railway lines and stations are in need of renovation, with many lines wanting electrification. A proper integration of road and rail transport is called for. National road building programmes would be jettisoned in favour of improving main roads. Somehow driving standards have to be vastly better. Incentives would be given for purchase of electric and hybrid cars and the early phasing out of diesel. Safe cycling and walking networks would be promoted. Uneconomic but necessary urban and rural bus and mini-bus services would once again be owned and run by local government.

If ever there was a clear-cut example of the known London bias of government over infrastructure projects (as well as expenditure generally), it was the announcement in the summer of 2017 by the Transport Secretary, Chris Grayling, of a 31 billion pound Crossrail Link across the capital to complement the one recently finished. This came days after he had postponed indefinitely plans to electrify various railway lines in the North, the Midlands, and Wales. It rightly led to furious protests and a petition backed by regional mayors and MPs calling for urgent 'summit' talks.

A think-tank, the Institute of Government, has warned that the way governments make decisions on infrastructure 'is a serious problem, running the risk of expensive white elephants being created'. Notable here might well be the proposed high-speed rail links from London to the North. The Institute identified several reasons for this woeful state of affairs. Firstly, we are in need of a national strategy for investment, whereas traditionally we see ministers' pet projects and those considered popular with the voting public. Secondly, we need to identify in advance precisely what we want to achieve by the measure on the ground. Then a proposal ought to be tested against alternatives before being adopted. If the Government kept its eye on the ball, and was close enough to localities in its knowledge and understanding, it could anticipate most needs before they got out of hand and too costly to embark on.

CHAPTER 7

OUR WELLBEING

Values
Food
Housing
Health
Education
Culture
Crime
Family
Welfare
Care
Cohesion

Values

When I talk of 'wellbeing' I mean that total situation where people are in good physical and mental health, together with fulfilling social relationships, not in economic hardship, and with time to pursue their interests at leisure. This concluding chapter will therefore explore important aspects of wellbeing, apart from the crucial factors in working life, which were discussed earlier.

But we are too many and growing in number at an alarming rate. Yet still effective measures of contraception are outlawed for millions of Catholics by the Pope on the basis of primitive religious superstition. When will his case come up in court, I wonder…? Nor does he have to cope with or pay for the legions of unwanted babies, even though he also opposes abortion. It is only other people's lives that are ruined, whereas we must approach him with reverence and respect seemingly.

A litmus test of this country's wellbeing would be to ask what is in it for the young people. It is a 'green and pleasant land', unfettered despoliation by legal development notwithstanding. And it is where their relatives and friends are too. Beyond that I have difficulty in being positive. The place is becoming politically unstable, probably less democratic, the welfare state is being stripped back, the NHS underfunded and privatised, employment increasingly low-paid and insecure, house owning a receding dream, the economy stuttering and the cost of a university education is rising into the stratosphere. In particular, the prospects for most young people of ordinary origin appear bleak.

Matthew Norman, writing in the **i** newspaper in June 2014, expressed sentiments I would agree with concerning politicians' regular trumpeting about so-called 'British values'. He pointed out their steady fusion with American values for one thing. For another he mentioned the (Tory) belief in untouched market capitalism, support for bankers, cutting welfare for the disabled, the invasion of middle-eastern states, and the erosion of workers' rights.

Interestingly, politicians deflect the obvious flaws that no country can claim a monopoly on decency, whilst ignoring those many aspects of our culture and behaviour that palpably do not represent the noble and uplifting. The concepts they do pick out are usually very general ones like tolerance, racial equality and fair play. Some will be taken from selected constitutional areas like 'the rule of law', which certainly sound good, even if it does not mean a lot in practice for the vast majority who cannot afford justice.

But one of the major problems for those like me who long for a logically consistent society across all its fields of endeavour is the muddle of disparate values and behaviours that do prevail somewhere or other. Sport provides good examples. Football is a too prominent case in point. The ruling bodies, in addition to being frequently represented by incompetents, operate at considerable arm's length from government. They may, for instance, turn a blind eye to drug abuse and child abuse. Every week the Football Association presides inactively while players commit physical assaults on the field of play that could lead to arrest, charge and custodial sentences in normal walks of life. The Football Association in fact is a very good example of how freedom to make up your own rules within a very loose framework of law has over the years led to ossified structures, and an incompetent Board full of appointees utterly unrepresentative of the modern game. It is incapable of reforming itself from within, while the Government, though critical, remains very reluctant to intervene.

In this context I want to say something more specifically about football – not because it is intrinsically important or worthwhile in the overall scheme of things. On the contrary, it is a rather trivial pursuit, but it has a hold on the majority of men, and says a lot to us about the real prevailing values of our society. I like to watch some football myself and loosely 'support' a professional football team, which experiences somewhat variable success, as most inevitably must. Unlike the large majority of 'fans' I can see that the game is rotten to the core. Clubs have the economics of the madhouse, often carrying massive debts at creditors' expense. It is easy to discern the main reasons why, which are fundamentally due to money or its lack, the uneven way it is distributed within the game, how these factors can be morally corrupting. At one extreme we have a few immensely rich and powerful clubs, owned by foreign elements with dubious financial backgrounds, players being paid obscenely large amounts of money, their agents making a fortune for being nothing more than middlemen. A proportion of the players fail to perform satisfactorily or even at all. At the other end there is a withering grass roots game, for the young and amateur adult players, starved of resources. 'Managers', who are taken seriously by the media, but are often thick, unsporting louts, competent to do little except a bit of coaching, team selection and tactics. With irrational frenzy they are quickly sacked for any shortcomings of the teams. Their silly little jobs are built up by the media into really important positions. With the urgently impatient (and statistically unlikely) quest to succeed, all are encouraged to cheat, tempted on the field and off it, so that deliberate foul play and play-acting to win free kicks and bookings are within the de facto national value system 'justified' as a means to their selfish ends. During and after matches trial by media occurs with television playbacks, while studio pundits, almost invariably ex-players, castigate refereeing decisions after baying crowds have questioned their parenthood. The media sit and reflect these and related values, such as a strong bias of interest in favour of the leading clubs in the highest male league, and a moronic obsession with famous celebrity players. I would wish to stop all this excess. I don't give a fig about how upset the supporters will be, but I should like professional football to end. Let those young and fit enough play the game, while others interested watch their school and amateur clubs.

While we are talking about sport, another plea I make is for Great Britain (which should drop the pretence of 'Great' in its title) to stop hosting expensive tournaments. They have been shown to be largely unaffordable and very poor at providing an enduring legacy for the ordinary folk who also play. I also want to see broadcasters mandated to cover a much wider range of sports as a matter of course and ensure that women's games are promoted into the greater prominence they deserve.

Going back to values more generally as the theme for our overview of the chapter's later details, it seems to me that the worthwhile ones would ultimately be underpinned by a rounded notion of well-being. This is both physical and mental, of course. Far too many indicators demonstrate that ours is not a society where such values predominate, sad to say. We are divided – geographically, politically, culturally, by religion, economically – we mostly live lives of excessive insecurity and toil. Community feeling and activity are diluted, families frequently dysfunctional, struggling with the human condition mostly in isolation. There are enormous disparities of wealth and opportunity, quality of life in sum. Therefore my final chapter is devoted to a few modest ideas aimed at amelioration of our plight.

This will be difficult, not least because a rather disturbing picture emerged in 2015 from a government policy advisory body (the 'Nudge Unit') to the effect that levels of trust between people had fallen markedly from the 1950s to the present day. Their claim that this trend caused stunting in economic growth was dubious, but it is clearly relevant to any attempts at social engineering and community bonding if only thirty percent of the population believe that most people can be trusted. It would appear that dishonesty, theft, fraud, scams, selfishness, insularity, and media exposures, doubtless among others factors too, have taken their depressing toll.

We now turn to a look at our primary human needs to take the analysis further. We shall start with what we eat.

Food

It is difficult to know what to eat because nutritionists are forever changing their minds about which foods are good for us, as scientific knowledge advances. The way matters currently stand, I take it that our diet should broadly include a varied range of fresh fruit and vegetables as the mainstay, with proteins in the form of fish or lean meat, cereals, nuts and seeds to provide fibre. Dairy products are to be in moderation. The intake should be modest in amount, completely alcohol free, with carbohydrates restricted, sugar and salt severely so. There are other recommendations and strictures, such as to avoid frying, but that is the gist.

When you go into a supermarket today you are met by serried rows of junk food, from the unhealthy to the downright poisonous. There are rows and rows of beers, wines and spirits with high alcohol content, lip service being paid to the small number of usually not-very-nice-tasting alternatives. Minorities tend to be persecuted in democracies, or at least not well provided for. Despite the pitifully feeble requirements for labelling it is still difficult, even for the more knowledgeable consumer, to find healthy items with low sugar, low fat, or low salt content, while all sorts of nasty commercial tricks are played on us to convince what is unhealthy is quite the opposite.

Now I am not happy with the monopoly position of the big supermarkets, despite myself being a regular convenience shopper there. Reasons are the usual ones – they are screwing farmers, in some cases out of business, and they are driving the small high street shop to the wall too. It is obvious that the unfettered market will make the situation worse, so, however reluctantly, government will have to intervene with legal teeth.

In my view also it is simply not good enough merely to exhort the public, and try to 'educate' them, so that they change their obesity-welcoming habits in favour of healthier eating. It won't happen. Neither will firms, with the profit motive acting as their conscience, voluntarily give up selling what is bad for us, nor manufacturers making the bloody junk. They do and will try to fool us though, with healthy-sounding advertisements. There needs to be strong regulation with high-sanctioned enforcement, and as a matter of urgency, to ensure private concerns do the right thing by the community. Why must we have to wait donkeys' years so firms can adjust to such government requests as reducing sugar in Kellogg's (killer) cereals?

Another thing that should happen is a strong government-backed movement towards British self-sufficiency in home-grown staple foods. This is important for our indigenous agriculture industry, but also in terms of strategic security and national independence in more than name. We should only be importing the kind of foods we cannot grow here ourselves.

I am unhappy about our animal husbandry: it does not outlaw inhumane practices which cause nasty and painful lives and deaths to many of the animals we exploit for food. Whether it is keeping hens in battery cages, chickens in sheds, cattle unable to graze, pigs standing on concrete, fish caught with hook or nets, it needs a rethink in the interests of animal welfare. Profit will have to be reduced, of course, in order to get rid of factory farms. It is a question of our values once again. While we are at it, we must stop altogether killing animals for materials we do not need – whales and mink come into this category.

I am no agronomist, but it seems we cannot afford to eat meat, principally because its production, distribution, and consumption are too energy-intensive and generate high levels of greenhouse gases. This will be a very hard discipline, given also what our taste buds are used to, but chemists are very good at simulating flavours.

In 2013 a joint report by Oxfam and Church Action on Poverty revealed that more than half a million Britons have had to turn to using food banks, the numbers trebling in one year. And yet Britain is officially about the sixth or seventh richest country in the world. The report squarely placed the blame on government for its reduction in benefits, and processing delays which leave claimants without income altogether at certain times. Firms have also failed to keep up with rising prices for their low-paid employees, so the problems are not solely confined to the unemployed.

Symptomatically, Frank Field, a distinguished Birkenhead Labour MP, wrote to Prime Minister David Cameron in 2014 several times about the issue, but never received even the courtesy of a reply. Characteristically, he then set up a cross-party inquiry which produced the report 'Abolish Hunger' calling for a variety of enlightened measures, including tapping supermarkets' food surpluses and providing free school meals for poorer families during school holidays. I say good luck to him, as our domestic do-gooders seemingly prefer donating to overseas aid and government remains as heartless as ever.

Housing

This is so basic that to admit Britain cannot house all its people is a very serious blow to its claim to be a civilised country to live in. We have lost the plot and it is difficult to see how we may put things right because the housing problems have become such a party political football and because the selfish interests of some fly in the face of what is best for others. The problems have been allowed to accumulate over at least a generation and have overwhelmed both Government resolve and resources.

To begin with, our housing stock is too small, and the rate of new building in no way keeps pace with demand, which at one time it used to. This undoubtedly helps to keep house prices high and to ensure prices keep rising, which is in the interests of the rich, though a body blow to people at the bottom end of the housing ladder, of course. Naturally, with years under the Tories, there have been but token policies, with no serious and sustained attempts being made to solve the problems.

Now, if the Government can be persuaded to address the issues, it will be necessary for it to act, and in a systematic and thoroughgoing way, for quite some years ahead. Left to its own devices the construction industry will not respond adequately to mere exhortation, or probably even the passing of some helpful laws. It is too easy for the building firms to make money at the higher end of the market. If we are to expand building the industry will need subsidy inducements, together with training schemes tailored to delivering a considerably expanded workforce with the right mix of skills. That requires foresight and planning ahead, two qualities British governments are notoriously poor at, unfortunately.

The Government likes to deflect the problem in various shoddy ways, one of which is to blame local authorities over their alleged inflexibility and slowness in implementing the planning regulations. But their powers have been weakened, as can be attested by the local monstrosities we see on housing estates, where people unable to move are adding on. And there never was much of an aesthetic consideration anyway, as witness the generally ugly and depressing state of our towns and cities.

A mixed economy will doubtless be needed, one in which private, public, and voluntary sectors play a (government-coordinated) part. We must address use of brown sites, be more imaginative over design, green belt encroachment, ensure targeted activity to deal with local problems in all regions of the country, abolish and reverse the wicked trend to build new houses on known flood plains, or where there are serious environmental risks generally, like toxic former industrial and landfill sites. It will involve removing the blight of restrictions which has prevented local authorities from building their own houses for a generation after Thatcher.

It is not just about hurling houses up, of course. Great care, backed with serious regulatory powers and penalties, should be put in place to ensure safe and decent building standards are complied with. We all need space for good quality living, which means lowering current high densities of housing and providing the kind of room areas which people enjoyed in the pre-war days in suburbia. Rats living too close fight…

We have seen that builders are told to include so-called 'affordable' houses in the mix, but obviously this policy is not working, no doubt too easily circumvented and inadequately enforced. One help would be to allow mortgages to be inheritable commodities, if buying a house now takes longer than a working lifetime.

In August 2014 Janet Street-Porter wrote disparagingly about modern housing in the 'i' newspaper. She made comparisons only possible from experience for us older ones about how starter homes are too small for furniture or people. She condemns the repetitive, unimaginative designs, but points to glaring faults like the lack of storage or garage space, box rooms in place of bedrooms, combined kitchen and diner. The houses are crammed together, with postage stamp land holdings, reducing privacy and adding stress. According to the Royal Institution of Chartered Surveyors semi-detached houses built in 1924 had nearly double the living space. Even council flats built just after the Second World War to replace slum clearance were relatively spacious, being designed to required Parker-Morris standards.

Of course, just to get on the house-owning ladder today is well beyond the resources of record numbers in their twenties and thirties, who have little option but to live with their aging parents. My prediction is that this will precipitate a good deal of unhappiness, family breakdowns, and mental ill-health. It is yet another symptom of how governments can no longer, or will not get the basics right.

I won't entertain discussion of the so-called 'bedroom tax' beyond saying that it was a vicious and vindictive mistake that says much about the uncaring and uncomprehending nature of some Conservative rulers who brought it in.

When you look at the building industry today, and watch what renovation is occurring in the neighbourhood, it is easy to be struck by the extent to which in the main traditional (labour-intensive and very time-consuming) methods are being used, rather than the much quicker system building. So government needs to steer research into new methods and materials, borrow best practice from abroad, and keep the industry up to date, looking initially to encourage experiment around the margins, with such as factory-built modular units for on-site assembly.

A practice I would stamp out would be the legal right to buy a second home, whether or not this is rented out for profit. In particular I want to prevent villages being taken over by part-time holidaymakers who live most of the year elsewhere and who thereby collectively destroy its community spirit. Also outlaw buy-to-leave-empty operations, beloved of overseas investors here.

Nor should land or buildings remain derelict or unused for more than a very brief period. So clean-up orders, high taxations, and heavy fines would come in to make sure industry and other private property does not look squalid. Owners, such as notably construction firms, would not be allowed any longer to sit on undeveloped land in order to raise its price, but would have to use it or lose it. Wider powers of compulsory purchase would enable (properly funded) local authorities to take on the mantle.

So far I have said nothing about rent, so now is the time. Questions are vexed, the more so since a reducing ability for young people to buy in their former numbers homes of their own has rendered this a growing sector. Thatcher's dream of a home-owning democracy has receded beyond the powers of governments to attain. So, understandably, the spirit of Rackman, a historically exploitative landlord, is alive and well in Britain today, courtesy of governmental support. Local authorities have the legal power to licence private landlords, but in 2016 the housing minister, Brandon Lewis, required them to apply centrally if the licencing scheme was to cover more than twenty percent of such houses in their area. Needless to say, when Redbridge applied on the basis of massive support from the tenants, their scheme was turned down.

The potential exploitative power of landlords to raise rents, reduce building maintenance, and increase rates of eviction, as well as being very choosy over who to admit, will thrive under laissez-faire. Clearly there has to be a balance between rights of the parties. But to be effective and fair this needs to be monitored by a powerful and independent national body in all areas, with a renters' union adding clout. We should trial rent-to-own schemes. Letting agency fees would be seriously restricted and deposits capped. And housing benefit would become available to the eligible from the age of eighteen, to prevent young people starting to live rough.

It has been described as a residual element of feudalism residing within the property laws. I refer to the thoroughly dishonest practice whereby owners can arrange leaseholds within which there are escalating ground rent charges to tenants year on year. These are often hidden in the fine print and can become monstrously large as the years go by. Running into many thousands of pounds they become beyond the capacity of the tenants to service, so their agreement defaults and eviction awaits. The charges are for no services at all, money for nothing because they can. The scandal broke in the press just after the May Government tottered into office and, to their credit, they promised to repeal the offending legislation. Time will tell, but it won't help the existing victims, caught in their spiders' webs.

When people are made homeless the State in common decency has to provide a safety net, though sadly it does not. Housing policies of local authorities can reveal hopelessly long waiting lists, biased pragmatically against the childless couple and singles. We need good quality temporary accommodation, not just the expensive use of private- for- profit hotels. Shelter is required to remove the rough sleepers from city streets. State refuges are needed for the abused, both women and men, in every region.

If we are to aim at having a happy and contented population we have to provide rather more financial security than citizens currently experience. It is estimated from research by the housing charity Shelter in 2013 that eight million people could not pay for their mortgage or rent for any longer than a month should they lose their jobs. Putting it another way, on average four families an hour lose their homes in our supposedly advanced society.

There is a national Decent Homes Standard, which the Government used to fund a programme to keep up. Now they just say they expect 'councils should have the resources to keep all their social housing at a decent level'. But in July 2017 the Government's own commissioned survey showed that half a million of them failed to meet the basic health and safety standards. Half of these were deemed to have the most severe category of risk – the life-threats from overloaded electrical sockets, dangerous heating, vermin, and leaking roofs. Millions more are believed to be living in similarly substandard accommodation rented from landlords in the private sector.

One of the key props in the welfare state is housing benefit. 2017 talk of its being stripped by the Tory government from 18 to 21 year-olds would risk thousands of young adults in this age group being rendered homeless according to charities and so becoming vulnerable to the likely fates described above. Heriot-Watt University's 2016 analysis for the charity Crisis showed high increases in rough sleeping over the previous five years, with 9,100 people sleeping rough in that year, a trend they said was set to continue under existing policies. Ten years ago we nearly had the problem cracked, but since then Government cut-backs have forced local authorities to close a lot of the hostels. Now it is common for them to pay instead for the homeless to have a one-way ticket to anywhere else outside their jurisdiction!

As my book was being finalized something happened so shocking and potentially far reaching in significance as to need extended treatment. I refer to the Grenfell Tower fire which started in a domestic refrigerator and enveloped the high-rise residence in the Royal Borough of Kensington very close to Parliament itself. It slaughtered an unknown number of people probably up to a hundred. As a peacetime human tragedy it is hard to quote a parallel in severity. The Government promptly set up a public enquiry which at the time of writing had yet to make significant headway, but it was already possible to draw a number of important and frightful conclusions from what emerged in the immediate aftermath of the debacle.

Media and government comment seemed to be confined more or less exclusively to high-rise dwellings, to alleged faults of local authorities in flouting building regulations on health and safety, and to rapidly inflammable cladding fitted to the tower blocks. It was, however, clear to me from the outset that very much wider issues were involved, ones which strongly support my sad claim that the country is falling back towards third-world status in crucial respects. In a nutshell, the issues affect a great many buildings, in both public and private sectors, high and low, over a very wide range of functions, from housing, hospitals and schools, to hotels, factories and offices. They also concern the unsatisfactory and ambiguous nature of the building regulations themselves, the unsafe designs of buildings, the methods of approval certification, ongoing inspection and fault remediation. Questions have to be pressed home about the behaviour and attitudes of politicians, mainly but not exclusively at national level within government. We should be beating a path to the doors of material designers, the manufacturing firms, the unscrupulous salesmen who encourage their purchase and use. Cladding is not the only material failing we will find. At the very least we shall see the installation of sprinkler systems to be necessary much more widely, the present use of fire walls, doors and insulation to be woefully inadequate, the availability of escape routes lacking. Notice how little our culture will cater for the prosecution, fining, and imprisonment of miscreants, and how paid officers rather than elected politicians (at least national ones) will be forced to take the rap with their jobs. Watch to see how quickly the feckless media move on, how little is achieved by the (gelded) public enquiry, the modest and minor extent of ensuing reforms. For it is all too much for the ruling classes to cope with, even supposing there is a genuine will, which I doubt.

In fact it was less than two months later before Manchester City Council proudly announced a massive new housing scheme, to be built on the banks of the River Irwell, and involving skyscrapers to a height of sixty-seven storeys, to cater for some four thousand people!

The Grenfell Tower fire was symptomatic of many bad and wholly unacceptable facets of our culture. Not to attempt an exhaustive list, here are a few more. It showed outdated and ambiguous fire safety regulations, the fact that government and local authorities had ignored warnings of experts for years, dubious design of tower blocks, scant regard for the lives of the financially poor inhabitants, an emotionally inadequate Prime Minister indecisive in leadership, a Conservative-run local authority with reserves of many millions and its values skewed towards less important matters such as stimulating opera, a scale of tragedy overwhelming of local resources, a lack of systems for coping with national catastrophe beyond the initial responses of police, fire, and health services. The early decision by Government to hold a public inquiry rather than an inquest reflected the usual establishment instinct to delay, obfuscate and avoid blame. Public enquiries are a misnomer, as the victims and their relatives scarcely get a look in. The Government carefully controls the terms of reference, the chairman, conduct of proceedings, and hence the allowed outcomes. We have a flawed culture of organizations trying to protect themselves against legal comebacks. We shall become aware of yet more cover-ups, refusals to take responsibility, and there will be scapegoating.

When the Grenfell Inquiry eventually opened, in September 2017, it was against a backdrop of lamentable 'progress' in the interim. Few residents had been permanently re-housed, little remedial action had been taken on the hundreds of vulnerable tower blocks identified nationwide, and nobody had been arrested. The retired judge appointed as chairman, an obvious Establishment figure if ever there was one, aroused little respect and some hostility from the community. The Inquiry Panel steadfastly refused to appoint to its ranks any Grenfell resident, bereaved relative, or local community representative. What was a little encouraging was that the media were able to witness and report the charade, and the involved public showed a healthy disrespect for the laughably arcane legalistic procedures. As they themselves said, it was their Inquiry, however the State sought to maintain otherwise.

John McDonnell, the Shadow Chancellor claimed that those responsible for failings over the Grenfell Tower should be held to legal account and I agree. My worry is that the powers that be will delay and generally use the law and its defects and uncertainties to protect the guilty, for that is our national ruling culture. It has happened many times before and doubtless will again, although the exact details of scandals and tragedies will obviously differ. Then he went on to claim that the wrongdoers had committed 'social murder', a clearly controversial claim which Conservatives denied. McDonnell explained about our long history 'where decisions are made with no regard to the consequences, and as a result of that people have suffered'. There obviously is no such concept as 'social murder' enshrined within our noble legislation, but isn't it about time, given that our powers to punish are so woefully inadequate?

Health

It is with trepidation that I turn my attention to the NHS, in that it is daily discussed in the media and is a sacred cow beloved of the British public. We all have a stake in it, whether now or in the future, and it is par excellence a topic on which people profess to 'know', or at least have a strong opinion about.

It was set up, the centre piece of the New Welfare State, by the Attlee Labour Government just after the war. And it was established as a cardinal principle that treatment would be free at the point of delivery. Since then, of course, there has been much back-sliding. The dental service, for example, has long been partly privatized, the opticians wholly so, and now people in employment under pensionable age must pay for their prescriptions. All the while a private health scheme has been in operation in parallel, with treatment paid for by the consumer, sometimes via insurance schemes, or through an employer.

So my first comments are that I support the principle of the NHS being firmly within the public sector. I do not approve of private medicine and would have it abolished, once the NHS has firmly guaranteed funding good enough to provide excellent quality. As a first step we could remove the right of the public sector doctors to run ancillary private practices. Secondly, I would naturally return dentists and opticians to the public sector fold.

And add a considerable extension of mental health, a glaringly scandalous current under-provision. We need ring-fenced expanded budget provision for mental health so that more professionals can be trained – from psychiatrists to counsellors. Treatment, even residential, should be in the locality where patients live. There should be mental health awareness courses for managers in public and private sectors, and for those in other relevant walks of life, like teachers and the armed forces. Part of what has to be a national plan and series of educational campaigns is to remove the national cultural stigma.

With the accelerating progress of medical science we are long past the point where moral dilemmas start to occur in relation to some of the things we could do. But the problems will mount and our law will have to keep pace. It will not be wise to rely on the general ignorance to inform the political deliberations either. Scientifically trained philosophers should always be consulted.

My own predictions include serious concern about the prolonging of life, at both ends of the age spectrum, when it has very little quality and a highly predictable likelihood that this situation will continue at best. Multi-handicapped children can be in such a category, as are those in a long-term coma. Charlie Gard, was one such child, whose cause became the big medical story in England during the summer of 2017. Although the medical experts gave him no hope of recovery whatsoever, from a situation where he was being kept alive by machines and unable to communicate even whether he was in pain, the parents refused to accept this. The result was frenetic activity between parents and the courts, the obtaining of alternative medical opinion from the United States, and the active involvement of the pro-life movement. All to no avail and desperately sad, no doubt, but to me it showed how the media can stir matters up irresponsibly for their own commercial ends and how pathetic is the effect of anti-social media opining on the basis of ignorance and emotion.

I think it right that we are moving in the direction of legalizing assisted suicide in certain highly restricted situations also. There is a lot of mush talked about alleged moral differences between allowing someone to die and actually commissioning it. Doctors need a better way of salving their conscience.

That we are living in a very nasty country is confirmed almost daily and we must not believe otherwise simply because we personally have been alright so far. Even that beloved of British institutions, the NHS, has untold horrors, it would seem, where the public has been deliberately deceived and damaged by deadly practices the authorities kept quiet about. I refer by way of example to the contaminated blood scandal of the 1970's and 1980's, which left 2,400 people dead and another 1,200 terminally ill. Essentially, what happened was that those suffering from haemophilia began to be treated with a new product, a powdered factor concentrate which produced blood clotting.

Unfortunately, this was bought from the United States, where the concentrate had been made in some cases from prisoners who were drug addicts. This introduced infections such as HIV and hepatitis. The allegations of victims and their damaged families included notably, that when this information came to the attention of the authorities, they covered it up. No government, health, or pharmaceutical body admitted liability and despite the independent Archer Report in 2007 little compensation was paid. The former health secretary under Labour, Andy Burnham, described the scandal as a 'criminal cover-up on an industrial scale'. What is also depressing is the fact that this story runs in parallel with those in other walks of British life, such as the Hillsborough enquiry into police conduct and the numerous institutional child abuse cover-ups. All have been characterized by enormous reluctance on the part of the government of the day to investigate, to make public the findings, to criminally prosecute the guilty, to put in place consequential reforms, to make what restitution is decently possible to the victims. It seems therefore fair to conclude that this is the way our society is governed, and that collectively we do not care enough about it to ensure that those responsible for such conduct and attitudes are denied the opportunity to take charge.

Collapse of the NHS has been much signalled for a long time. Recent developments do nothing to counter such dire prediction. Nurses, demoralized by the impossible working demands and resentful of being constantly on the receiving end of government's restraining pay policy, are leaving in large numbers. Brexit has probably unsettled potential recruitment from abroad at the same time.

Whilst conditions differ enormously across the country, (part of the so-called post code lottery) the Head of the British Medical Association pointed in 2017 to an inexorably rising demand on GPs which could see the 'collapse' of the system. Recruitment is problematic and inadequate numbers are being trained. Some practices are financially unsustainable, with smaller ones especially vulnerable.

'Your Life in My Hands' is the thought-provoking title of a book by Rachel Clarke telling of her experiences as a junior doctor in an NHS hospital. Ms. Clarke is singularly well-qualified to do this since she graduated from Oxford University reading Politics, Philosophy, and Economics, then embarked on a career as a television journalist before retraining as a doctor. She saw and lived first-hand the hectic life, the stress doctors are under, the long hours, the short-staffing, the anti-social shifts.

The Health Secretary, Jeremy Hunt, who tried to extend the service from five to seven days a week, was faced with a strike by the junior doctors as a consequence.

He tried every trick and spin to turn the public against them and sought unilaterally to impose a new contract on them. Rachel Clarke loathes the man with a passion. She could not do her job because of the ever changing rotas. Childcare cost her more than she was earning. When she left, to a specialist job in palliative care, 'up and down the country' services and beds were being cut and working conditions deteriorating.

There will be excessively high costs for the State to bear for quite some years owing to the disastrous Public Finance Initiatives entered into from Blair onwards. These had the effect of loading excessive costs onto the public sector for the benefit of private firms in contractual agreements for such works as building new hospitals. They are long-term, with high interest serving the loan debt annually over a generation. The private sector paid up front to build the public sector buildings very quickly and then leased them to the users on ridiculously favourable commercial terms. This does not just affect hospitals, of course, but such as schools too. The fine print frequently ensures that the maintenance bills are draconian and eat into annual budgets disproportionately, necessitating the sacking of staff in some instances. Simple replacement items like blinds or furniture can be charged in the thousands of pounds, extortionate amounts.

We should realize by now that the Conservatives are bent on a wholesale privatization of the NHS by stealth.

As the GP Youssef El-Ginghly said in the Observer in March 2013, the service is slowly being replaced by one

'bound not by a duty of care but by a contract and driven, not by what is best for the patient, but by the cost of the encounter'.

In 'The Extreme Centre – A Warning' Tariq Ali also quotes Allyson Pollock, Professor of Public Health Research and Policy at Queen Mary University of London. She claims that notably United States health care investors, with the collusion of the British Government, are moving in to exploit financial opportunities in concert with the wants of their shareholders, not the needs of our patients. According to Ms Pollock 'our public hospitals (are being) given over to private-for-profit investors'. And 'what remains of the NHS is a funding stream... (and the NHS) reduced to a logo'. Public ownership is being broken up by 'closing hospitals, closing services, and privatizing or contracting out'. 'England...abolished its national health services in 2012 with the Coalition's Health and Social Care Act'. This Act, among other matters, removed the 'duty to provide universal health care, in place since 1948'.

This privatization trend, needless to say I am wholly against and wish to see rapidly reversed before it becomes too costly for the State to pay out all the compensation for lost business. I am utterly convinced that insurance schemes are not adequate, that they are mostly unaffordable to ordinary people, who will increasingly lose out by reduced quality of treatment or maybe none at all.

There are, and would still be under a reformed public-sector NHS (for the status quo is too unstable and problematic to last politically unfettered), serious ongoing problems – notably of over-demand – unacceptable variations in quality across different regions – unavailability of services during weekends and other unsocial hours, lack of investment in medical and pharmaceutical breakthroughs. These will have to be addressed, but are too frequently used to smokescreen the endemic, fundamental failings. As usual the impacts of media commentary are inclined to be dangerously irresponsible and destructive.

Rationing is creeping into the NHS such that formerly routine operations are subject to longer processes and more exacting criteria aimed at deferral. For one thing, the pain threshold has to go up!

On the question of adequate funding we should look to spending the kind of proportion of GDP that Germany does and add elements as necessary to cater for a proportionately ageing population. A dedicated health and care tax, affordable to the public and means-tested, could be one help here. There has to be reinstatement of a training bursary for nurses and fair pay for them and the other paramedics to ensure a continued quality supply of indigenous applicants. We have to end 'health tourism', the exploitation by foreign nationals, who sometimes evade the lenient and retrospective fees.

One of the barometers people use is waiting time before surgery. In August 2017 some four million patients were on the list. Whereas under the Referral to Treatment (RTT) Scheme, waiting time should be no longer than 18 weeks from referral to operation, this aspiration has collapsed in reality with patients sometimes going longer than a year. The Royal College of Surgeons said it should be a wake-up call for the Government. Jeremy Corbyn, as Labour Party Leader identified one key reason as being the lack of social care availability, which led to people having to stay in hospital longer than their medical needs justified. He advocated, as is surely obvious, the imperative of funding more and better social care.

Education

Some will know that I have written on this subject before, in 'Radical Bureaucracy', and again in my 'Memoirs of an Educationalist'. My views have not changed, but a selection of them are included here nevertheless so that the book offers a reasonably comprehensive statement on the wider questions of welfare reform. I will try to be brief, and simply state my desired outcomes without further justification or argument. I am here concerned with ends rather than means. I do not know how we will get there and I don't believe we ever will, which is one reason I eventually gave up the struggles in my own career. Matters were mostly proceeding in quite the opposite direction by then. Some who approved of them will naturally regard my proposals as reactionary.

Starting with pre-school children it is clear we need far more organized state provision, and intervention to prop up failing families. There ought to be means-tested nursery education on the State from the age of two, as well as care, welfare and play provision virtually from birth. It should not depend on your pocket, or where in the country you happen to live. Qualified teachers trained in early years would be in charge in my world.

There are mysteries to me that there should not be concerning child care and education for the very young. They come from various sources. Firstly, there are different sorts of provision. And secondly government claims distort the true position. Time was when a Labour government under Blair could have legislated to make free nursery education a statutory requirement, along with the attendant child care. But they did not and Tory aspiration to strip down State help and encourage private companies to make profits out of the sector soon took root in default. The results are therefore uneven across the country. We have child minders, play groups, pre-school, soft play centres and any manner of outlets – at a price, to those who can afford it. Whilst there are government schemes to help with some of the costs they typically pay institutions less than cost, thus stimulating reluctance to participate. Meanwhile, Labour initiatives like Sure Start are whittled away.

Gingerbread and the Child Poverty Action Group have repeatedly warned government that tens of thousands of children have been plunged into poverty as a direct result of rising private childcare costs not fully met by government financial support to their families. This is from a combination of complex welfare rules, ongoing benefit and tax reforms, and slow administration, as well as underfunding (probably deliberate as part of the Austerity Programme).

Infant and extended (8 to 12) junior schools would be separate, well equipped and with teachers educated to at least advanced level in key subjects such as English and mathematics, Science specialists should also be recruited so that children receive a proper grounding. In general the education background of primary level teachers needs improvement, desirably to degree level beyond the B. Ed.

Secondary schools would be on the comprehensive model, without selective entry by ability, and would be, say, 12 to 18. GCSE 'O' and 'A' levels would be retained, but broadened to reduce early specialism.

The organizational arrangement and admissions would be via local authority control, with considerably enhanced delegated powers and finances from central government, such as the ability to decide capital funding. Private schools would be abolished, the best being absorbed into the State sector, as would education at home, academies, free schools, specialist colleges, grammar schools and the like, and all pupils would be required to attend State schools until fifteen. There would be no church schools, no single-sex schools either. Class sizes would be reduced to the twenties. Pay for teachers would be more competitive and reduced contact time would relieve pressure. Easter would be fixed and the long summer holidays more evenly spread at the end of the three terms.

Special education would be established for the first time on a regional basis within daily travelling distance as a combination of special schools and special units at ordinary schools, arrangements being adequate to meet demand, which has not happened nationally thus far and is a scandal of our age.

There will be all sorts of issues with academies and free schools run outside of local authority control, where central government is the only external source of authority and funding. They will attack the democracy inherent in school governing bodies and their carefully balanced representation moving to a system in favour of autocratic structures where one ruling body may cover all schools in the ownership chain and membership is skewed heavily towards the business community at the expense of parents, teachers, local interested worthies and politicians. National bargaining over teachers' pay will break down, ostensibly in favour of payment by results, but concerned more with disenfranchisement of unions and financial affordability.

Some of the new 'educational entrepreneurs' do not respect teacher professionalism. This, the decline in local authority control, and the inevitable shortage of teachers, in a critical culture where they are rather undervalued, has led already to 24,000 teachers being without teacher training qualifications. Of course, such niceties have long been dispensed with in private schools when it suited them.

The national curriculum concept would be applied at every stage and controlled by a multidisciplinary committee of experts independent of government, but representative of society as well as academia. Philosophy would be a core discipline from junior school to leaving age. Political science would be a requirement at secondary school. Teaching religion would be banned and left as a private matter at home. There would be no act of daily worship either. In general curricula would reflect the vocational and practical needs of pupils in a rapidly changing world. Accordingly, they would be less academic, more concerned with developing independent and critical thinking, creativity, problem-solving, practical household skills, emotional and social development, team and interpersonal aptitudes, financial management, understanding of the law. SATS would be abolished.

Colleges of further education need to be revamped, adequately funded, raised in status, catering for 14 to 19 in the main, vocational and technical in orientation, with systematic apprenticeship schemes in the different walks of life adequately linked to local industry, commerce, and the public working sector. This means delegation of funding to the local education authority again, so reversing the national control model currently stifling their efforts.

It is a terrible indictment of British culture that colleges of further education and their students have been relatively neglected and undervalued compared with the academic elite. But the standing of the whole teaching profession needs raising in prestige. This can only be done by educating them to a high level and paying them handsomely. Their professional training should be extended, conducted in universities, and given a strong proportion of practice in school classrooms with the aid of qualified teacher-mentors. What we can well do without, however, is so-called 'super heads' helicoptered in to trouble-shoot 'failing schools' at astronomical salaries. Who is kidding whom?

Universities have expanded too much. They can probably only really benefit about thirty percent of the population without a serious dumbing down, which is, of course, what we have been seeing. By the same token we must in all social justice suitably arrange matters so that all who can benefit intellectually do so. There must be flexible schemes to enable late starters and those who wish to better themselves in later life. This necessitates abolishing tuition fees and returning to the former grants system, means-tested, so that education and accommodation are paid for by the State as a national investment for the future. Existing graduate debt should be reduced by strong State subsidy. Interest on loans should early be abolished. Much more should be said about the many roles of universities, but it is important that they become neither poodles of industry, nor turn out graduates too unworldly for the demands of the world of work.

Whilst I do not wish to live in a society that expects its graduates to pay for their degree courses, affordability by the State is a serious problem. A happy solution for me would be if we returned to a much lower percentage of the cohort going to university – let's say around fifteen to twenty percent. There is ample evidence the country does not want and cannot absorb more than that into the kind of jobs commensurate with their talents and that students outside this ability band need other kinds of educational input.

Finally, in this whirlwind tour of the education sectors, I will make a plea for continuing adult education, not just vocational but also purely for leisure. It is fairly clear that only State provision will serve what I am looking for, namely local provision countrywide, including residential short courses in adult colleges, where these are needed to complement the parallel provision hopefully available in colleges of further education. Unhappily, the experience of recent years has seen many closures owing to financial starvation of anything non-vocational.

There is still yet another glaring gap. For those professions that require postgraduate or professional qualifications all we have now is some sponsorship by firms and the availability of private, costly loans. So many who have the ability do not make it.

I am deeply and profoundly opposed to the direction of travel of Tory educational reforms. They pay lip service to the poor and needy whilst advocating an expansion of grammar schools, selective by ability. Significantly, the grammar school programme had to be put on hold, as the unpopular proposal it is, when Teresa May failed to get elected with an overall majority. Encouraging those with enough money to set up 'free schools' outside the local government system has led to distortions of provision, with some areas up to twenty percent overprovided with places, whilst others experienced a shortage. At the time of writing the expansion was on hold, faced with the flak. The Public Accounts Committee discovered in April 2017 some were using buildings unfit for purpose, like redundant office blocks and police stations, without either playgrounds or sports fields on site. Democratic control of schools via government bodies has been weakened as claims of 'academy' schools have abolished governing bodies made up of parents, teachers, and local politicians in favour of a board of directors manned by professional finance and other business people, as I illustrated earlier.

The move to formula funding of schools by means of a nationally imposed formula seems on the face of it fairer than locally developed formulae until you realize that it makes wildly inequitable assumptions of financial need between pupils living in different parts of the country and that it is intended to reduce schools' resources even as it is introduced at a time of rising rolls and inflation. Again, May's weakened Government had to cut back on its free schools expansion programme to divert temporary money into this cocked up national funding formula after schools showed they could not cope.

At the heart of Tory education reforms is the belief that education is a commodity to be bought and sold. If it cannot make money for providers, then it has little value and is dispensed with. As we saw earlier, the gradual closing of the former residential and day-course adult education colleges is a case in point, their focus on liberal arts and crafts driving them to the wall. This inevitably means that the perceived needs of a working economy are paramount in subject selection, that State education has less money available since larger proportions of the budget are creamed off to the profiteers.

I was pessimistic about the plight of the underclass even before the Tory grip was tightened in successive governments from Thatcher on. Now I am convinced they have absolutely no hope whatsoever as the gap between the affluent and the rest increases remorselessly.

I see a nightmare in which family homes, suffering all their externally-imposed problems, get nastier. The children bring this dysfunctional unhappiness to schools, which get nastier. And the teachers, already under unreasonable pressures to perform, just leave or go through the motions.

Education at home should be made illegal and loopholes closed where children receive religious indoctrination in buildings not within the definition of a school.

Oddly, formal education in its traditionally understood modes of provision seems likely to be much less important in the future. For one thing, change is now too rapid for anyone to be kitted out at the start of life with all the skills and knowledge they will need to get through it. Secondly, computers have radically altered the way we do things and are affecting how we learn too. It seems ironical to me that computer courses, par excellence individual tools of learning, are increasingly being used with weaker students, those who were previously very reliant on human teachers. I cannot be optimistic about outcomes. Likewise there seems to be a movement among elite employers to lower formal entry qualifications and to recruit for in-house instruction from the elite schools instead of universities. At any rate, parental expectations that a good general education leading to a solid set of GCSE and 'A' level qualifications in a range of subjects, will in future culminate in well-rewarded careers seems highly dubious. Careers are being replaced by fragmented work experiences in less secure employment and with low wages and flat hierarchies. At the same time, the value of examinations of every kind and all age-groups are under attack. Governments endlessly mess about, without really knowing what they are doing, so kids are their perpetual guinea pigs.

Our society frequently displays a nasty streak towards the educated. It likes to take down graduates a peg or two. Yet it may be premature to announce, as the independent newspaper did in 2015, that we could be witnessing 'the death of the graduate'. In fact, the article was really about society moving to a realistic assessment of their worth following research that failed to link academic success causally with performance in the world of work. Movements are afoot in some quarters though, as hinted at earlier, for professional recruitment agencies to drop 'A' level and degree requirements from their hiring criteria, and it remains to be seen whether such practice becomes a norm. At least ability and diligence are still valued, apparently, however perceived and measured. All the same, it is hardly surprising, given these attitudes, which could be read as thinly veiled prejudice on the side of dumbing down, that by 2015 half of the United Kingdom's graduates were working in unskilled low-paid jobs. Admittedly, this is partly the result of about two in five of the cohort going on to a university education of some sort. We never had it so bad in modern times.

Culture

I am not going to attempt to define the word 'culture', which is something of a catch-all. Broadly, however, I shall use it in a conventional sense to mean art and crafts, the entertainment media such as television, film, and theatre, and the written word in fiction and non-fiction. It seems to me self-evident that there is at least a potential connection between culture and wellbeing. While some people are obviously more interested in formal culture than others, most will surely get some enjoyment out of parts of it. When you add in sports and games and quasi-social gatherings this becomes more obviously true, perhaps, and in all cases where participation is an option the interest could be deepened.

An early question, therefore, is whether culture is a phenomenon the State should be making a financial contribution to out of our taxation, and, if so, to what extent? It is one of the first areas to be cut back in times of austerity, of course. And since folk have decided cultural preferences you are never going to get complete agreement as to what is most worthy of support.

This is quite a test for Conservative governments, for their natural inclination is to subsidize nothing that has little chance of making a profit. Money-losing projects of all kinds, cultural and otherwise, are usually left to amateurs and volunteers. Minority interests and the highbrow are naturally somewhat at risk under such a regime. Even facilities arguably of benefit to most, like public libraries and community centres, have been ruthlessly chopped.

Over time this will have a huge effect and render Britain a much impoverished place for dwellers and visitors alike. And yet I can see it happening by degrees now. Sorrowfully to relate, it will not be a major issue for the unrefined masses whose tastes, being popular, will continue to be catered for.

Our lives are not only getting unhealthy faster, but they are also noisier too. Whilst some of the noise is perhaps inevitable, in the vicinity of big machines for example, a lot could be avoided with a bit of thought for others. As people get older they are inclined to notice it more and suffer the consequences in higher stress and hearing problems.

The culture of young people, regretfully, is much to blame. They tend to like loud pop music and little understand how their ears will be damaged by it, especially from exposure to loud speakers at pop concerts. In the right kind of environments, such as acoustically designed concert-halls, it is possible to hear pieces played by a hundred-piece orchestra and massed choirs in perfect comfort and safety, without being assailed by excessive decibel levels.

The older citizens are not catered for in public places like cafes and shops, where so-called music is thoughtlessly piped at high volume, thereby causing people to raise their voices in conversation to be heard. The noise on offer, or rather enforced by the policy of a largely absent management when you ask, tends to be mostly 'pop' tunes from the sixties and seventies, presumably of main interest to a rather small demographic. It is almost never ever classical music of any ilk since we are dumbed down. People do tend to 'switch off' in such environments, probably not consciously noticing for the most part, but this spineless acceptance of what ought to be intolerable is both irrational and antisocial, particularly when we are there to buy something.

Crime

I suppose I am going to sound a bit like a Liberal here. I do believe in freewill and thereby that we have a moral responsibility for our actions. And of the justifications for the punishment that this argument lets in I believe that of reform to be far stronger than either retribution or deterrence, albeit it is labour-intensive and costly. Retribution can speak to a mean streak of malice that brings society down closer to the level of criminality. Deterrence brings in the undesirable result that we fail to commit crimes not because we believe them to be wrong so much as we are (unhealthily) fearful of the consequences. And besides, does it work? No, rehabilitation is the positive option, the one with appeal to an educationalist and other humanitarians, whilst admitting that, sadly, some people are too evil, or mentally sick, or so lacking in self-control, that they cannot be reformed.

I have lots of worry about crime, like most people, I imagine do. Unlike the majority, though, whilst I believe it the first duty of government to keep us safe, I don't believe they can completely in these days of terrorists and nutcases, nor, I suspect, do they generally try very hard. Their immigration policies have imported problems for us for a start.

As it seems to me, the law is hopelessly inadequate and in need of reforms which it probably will not get, for example, laws to keep up with cyber-crime, financial fraud, pension swindles and tax avoidance, as well as changing technology. Individuals cannot gain justice, because only the rich can afford to pay for going to court. Sentencing policy is inconsistent and illogical, it's underlying value system far from explicit. Victims have few rights and poor treatment.

We have a partly corrupt, in part lazy, cowardly, and incompetent police force, racially prejudiced as well. We have judges drawn mainly from the top echelons in society. We have an adversarial system of barrister-led case-skewing which can conceal the truth. The prisons are increasingly privatized, de-skilled and demoralized, and under staffed, our probation service has also been cut back. Dangerous ex-cons roam the streets because they are let out by bad judgement which goes unpunished, or they simply abscond. Released prisoners'after care' is rudimentary. Whereas we should be aiming to equip prisoners with the skills and self-reliance to live successfully back in the community wherever possible.

The courts have very many faults, notably administrative inefficiency and daft procedures, but whilst advocating wholesale reforms I will single out only one. There is a deal of concern about the Court of Protection because of the institutional secrecy surrounding its operations. Government regulations, updated in June 2015, reaffirmed in spite of media criticism that hearings should normally be in private. This is especially worrying given that the Court of Protection deals with the mentally incapable. Evidence leaked out in 2013 that judges were able to make unilateral decisions, on care home residence and life-and-death health matters, without any sort of court hearing, following representation from a local authority. The vulnerable person is unrepresented in any ensuing discussions and these are often not written down either as evidence or decision.

Now I have chuntered about the Police before, in my book 'Radical Bureaucracy' and they remain a very deeply flawed and troublesome institution, whose resources and behaviour are hopelessly and woefully inadequate to discharge their tasks. The public seem largely impervious to the claims above, apparently unaware of, or indifferent to, the almost weekly examples of gravely serious police shortcomings being revealed. And what are more shocking still are the Establishment cover-ups which prevent allegations of police malpractice from being independently and transparently investigated. Important examples would include the Hillsborough case, where deaths at a Sheffield football match a generation ago were wickedly and systematically blamed by the police hierarchy on crowds of supporters, to deflect from the gross incompetence of the force. Even a tacit admission to the victims' bereaved families took several inquests over very many years to extract. The same process followed for the coal miners who suffered filmed police suppression at Orgreave during the union strikes, the Tory Home Secretary ruling against holding an official public enquiry.

Then there are the police atrocities. Every year people are killed in police car chases, including innocent bystanders. Suspects die in police custody in mysterious circumstances. Trigger-happy, nervous officers shoot people wrongly thought to have guns. All cases are investigated by another police force, instead of an impartial independent body. At the end of the day no police officers are convicted.

The police urgently require internal reform. For one thing they had a long-term bias against graduate recruitment, so their brains are in short supply. Graduates are especially needed in the detective force and for combatting cyber-crime. Recruitment from early-retired members of the armed forces could also be beneficial. In common with all public sector bodies that politicians don't trust and can't resist meddling in, so they are swamped with form-filling. But their operations too require careful scrutiny. To single out just one important malaise, police responses to incidents like motorway pile-ups and terrorist attacks prompt the thought that they are invariably top-heavy, their actions being mainly to freeze the scene for inordinate lengths of time and prevent people going about their lawful business, at perhaps considerable cost of time, money, distress, even health. There will be untold damage to business and commerce through loss of working. It is high time national media exposed this nonsense, where the balance is wholly on the side of getting evidence for possible court proceedings, with no regard to people's welfare at all.

A case could be made out for a radical structural overhaul, which might reduce the number of police authorities and thereby bring an improvement in uniformity of practice. Clearly they have been adversely affected by government targets and this has distorted police operations on a day-to-day basis. It has also arguably led to deliberate fudging of statistical returns on performance against crime, some attempted redefinitions of crime categories, and hard-nosed prioritization of efforts. This last has relegated many more minor crimes, such as burglary, to tokenism on prevention. But policing is supposedly by consent, and this is the most likely public interface, so it risks disaffection.

The common criticism from the public is that they want to see bobbies on the beat, a phenomenon which used to be the characteristic and now has disappeared altogether in places where the police themselves deem it appropriate (like Heswall, where I live). This is quite scaring, especially for women and older people, because there appear to be no remedies against abuse and physical attacks by youths and young men, whether on property or the person.

Finally, and I could go on, why don't we just abolish the new system of Police Commissioners. They are expensive amateurs with weak powers standing outside operations altogether and in the place of democratically elected local police committees. Some are beginning to spawn expensive 'executive 'officers and deputies, sometimes by patronage.

Even relying on the Ministry of Justice's own statistics, given here for the year 2013/14, Britain has a prison crisis at the time of writing. Prisons remain violent places, where there are high suicide rates among inmates (88) as well as attacks on officers and each other (14,500). The spending cuts imposed by the Conservative Government have resulted in severe overcrowding of cells. There are regular breakouts (225), including murderers, and every now and then riots which trash prison wings and overwhelm the local staff. Prisons are awash with drugs, which must at some point implicate individual prison officers. It goes without saying that morale among prison staff is very low, leading to strike action, against their own code of conduct, in 2017. Rehabilitation programmes, for drugs and sex offenders, are failing.

The Government has followed the highly dubious and publicly alarming policy of allowing selected prisoners out on licence, including rapists and murderers, but in June 2015 no fewer than 1,153 offenders who had been recalled to custody were still on the run: over 500 of them had remained so for over five years. We need serious sanctions against the nameless ones who make these terrible misjudgements with seeming impunity and we need transparency.

Enlightened attitudes notwithstanding what follows here should convince that we need more and better prison places rather than less. In July 2017 Peter Clarke, the Chief Inspector of Prisons, delivered a condemnatory annual report on the conditions in young offenders' institutions, described as 'dire'. He concluded that none of them in England or Wales was a fit establishment in which it was safe to hold young people. One major element in a rapid decline was noted to be a 'vicious cycle of violence'. But there is a recurring pattern here: independent surveys of prison conditions and their attendant recommendations for reform are routinely ignored by the Government.

We know that ex-prisoners have a high rate of re-offending, round about one in four. There is also something gravely wrong with the prison system from the deterrence point of view since our proportion of population jailed is one of the highest in Europe, whereas our crime-levels remain obstinately high as well. The privatization of growing parts of the service seems to have undermined prison safety as well as leading to the loss of experienced officers put off by the low-pay regime.

Levels of numbers in prison could rise dramatically, too, if the courts were to sentence in the way many believe they should. Presently magistrates hand down on average ten suspended sentences before they imprison a criminal. In Crown courts, which deal with the most serious cases, the figure was eight, according to official figures from the Ministry of Justice up to December 2015.

'Violence against the person' crime, according to the Office for National Statistics rose by 24 per cent from July 2015 to June 2016 compared with the year before. There were thousands of incidents involving knives.

Sad to say, another feature to watch out for will be the doctoring of figures, or regular changes to requirements and definitions for record keeping, to conceal the proper picture and trends. In 2017 crime was said to have almost doubled in a year, because fraud and cyber-crime were recorded in the released figures for the first time. The Office for National Statistics confirmed that fraud was now the second largest category.

The Home Office has failed utterly to deport foreign criminals, a complex system being the pathetic excuse given by them in 2015. Ministers have, naturally, given assurances over the years when press concern has been expressed, but the incompetence remains, leading one to speculate that the Government actually prefers our country to receive 'enrichment' in this way. Among former ministers who have signally failed in the matter it is interesting to record David Cameron and Teresa May. It obviously did them no harm.

There are so many unacceptable faults in the Prison Service, which has deteriorated ever since its partial privatization and financial cut-backs. One particular outrage which should be of public concern is that seventy-one convicted criminals or suspects were freed in error during the year 2016-17, which on average would be rather more than one per week! These are not escapees, but owed their liberty to administrative failings. By some kind of twisted logic the Ministry of Justice says they are not regarded as unlawfully at large!

There are, scandalously, some kinds of very serious crime that hardly ever lead to prosecutions, never mind convictions, because they are perpetrated by Muslims living in this country, and the authorities concerned, owing to the climate of political correctness fostered by the Government as well as racial fears, are reluctant to act. I refer to forced marriages and female genital mutilation, carried out in accordance with Sharia law and the customs of foreign lands, not our own. In the case of forced marriage schools are in a very good position to spot what is happening within the family and the community, but a national framework needs to be set up to ensure monitoring and multi-agency cooperation where suspicions are raised. Whether the Government's Forced Marriage Unit will be enough only time will tell. Owing to a quirk in our laws forced marriage was only made criminal in 2014, since when one whole conviction was attained in 2015, but the maximum penalty remained nominal – a prison sentence of five years.

By 2016 not even one conviction had been achieved for female genital mutilation, FGM, a fact called 'lamentable' by a Commons Committee. Here there is absolutely no excuse, because the practice has been illegal since 1985, yet it is employed on an industrial scale. There are even over 8,500 known cases in Britain today.

Slavery is alive and flourishing in Britain. In addition to the people trafficking activities that bring workers illegally into the country, we have indigenous slavers who prey on the homeless, those who would not be missed. One such case actually led to convictions for a whole family in August 2017 when it was proven that they had kept vulnerable adults in squalid conditions for years. They paid them a pittance, forced them to work in the family business and used violence in case of complaint. Drugs and alcohol also helped to ensure their victims' compliance. The National Crime Agency, NCA, was assisting with 300 police investigations into modern slavery, typically with children from Europe being sold to families here.3,805 victims were estimated in 2016, with every city and major town in the UK likely affected.

So I am nervous all right, fearful even. As I do not see us going in a direction I could begin to be sanguine about. Then cap it all with Government usage of the crime statistics, packaged and doctored unscientifically to soothe us into a false and complacent acceptance that all is well and getting even better.

Family

I suppose most countries interfere incessantly with the lives of their subjects, so family law is rather a good test of freedom and constraint. It is useless railing against marriage, though I personally detest the idea and consider it a subjugation of adult individuality and financial choice, mostly in the interests of children. I have written extensively on the subject in my sociology book 'Outside the Outcrowd', so my comments will be restricted here.

The first years of the 21st Century have witnessed quite a few changes owing to governments messing about. They moved to introduce the strange legal entity of Civil Partnership in order to improve the rights and social standing of 'gays', then later allowed same-sex couples to marry. We have travelled in my lifetime from a situation in which homosexuality was illegal and those discovered prosecuted or otherwise persecuted, to one where they are positively feted and encouraged. It may now not even be legal for me to express my distaste of homosexuality, its physical practice consisting in unhealthy, not to say disgusting acts – leastways among males. But I don't really care. Somebody should say it, the more explicitly the better. Let's not bum around the houses.

Civil Partnership is a curious legal status, poorly understood by the populace, not usually explained by the media, but it appears to have been invented by the Government at a time when they judged same-sex marriage out of the question. But now that has come into force the state of Civil Partnership seems an anomaly, the more especially as it is not available to single-sex couples. We have therefore arrived at the usual dog's breakfast that bad policy brings us to. Needless to say, I would abolish both.

Media do not help us obtain a balanced view of marriage, child raising and their realities, with much mush and gush stressing idyllic and romantic pictures. Whereas the excessive and unremitting pressures and workload are imposing intolerable strains on relationships in a climate where it is sometimes easier and less stigmatizing to just walk away.

Fay Weldon commented in March 2017 in the Daily Telegraph on the adverse consequences for women of feminism. As she saw it, the demand (and more latterly the expectation) that young women and mothers would and should go out to work had reduced job opportunities and wages for their male counterparts, so that they could no longer support a family alone. Similarly, female attitudes had been affected so that Weldon described a new generation of assertive women with a pronounced sense of rectitude and corresponding unwillingness to listen to alternative viewpoints (especially on topics like childrearing, no doubt). Such women, she noted, were extremely easy to offend. I have further heard the argument made that feminism has been a leading causative factor in the decline of the nuclear family...

I am also unhappy about the legal grounds for divorce. In 2017 the Appeal Court ruled against a woman's claim to be divorced on the grounds of her 'loveless and desperately unhappy' marriage. Many people, myself included, would think this a very good reason, but without her husband's consent, which could be quite vindictive and is not required to be justified by reason as evidence, she will have to wait five years of separation first. The other grounds, incidentally, are adultery, unreasonable behaviour, desertion, or a two-year separation if uncontested by the parties. Campaigns have been running for years to change the law to allow no fault divorces, but the Government would rather make people suffer the added stigma. Clearly, they are determined, on uncharitable grounds, to hold marriages together as a social good, whatever the misery inflected on the poor sods suffering this church-blessed status.

And when we reform marriage and cohabitation arrangements, to bring them into the field of simple contracts, let's keep the noses of religion out of it. They've done untold damage by encouraging moralistic straight-jackets in the past. Simply ensure all sign up to fair prior arrangements – a legally enforced prenuptial agreement – which makes provision for separation, property division, and finance – in clean-break settlements which may involve a short-term maintenance element if circumstances warrant, as where there are young children to consider.

Maintenance is a troubling area still. There are many cases of women expecting, and sometimes being granted by the courts, financial support for life from their ex-husbands. But why should they? Get them working for a living like most men have to. And what effect does this have on an ex-husband's sense of justice in society and his willingness to enter into formal relations with a woman in the future?

Turning now to cohabiting couples, it is amazing how many people don't know that unmarried heterosexual partners have no financial rights once cohabitation comes to an end. This is how the State deliberately encourages marriage, by legal vindictiveness and indifference to the plight of those who live together outside of wedlock. Here are two barbaric laws about living together.

The first is that where a divorced or otherwise unmarried parent has a child or children of dependent age he/she cannot remarry without surrendering a very substantial chunk of the legacy to the spouse's legally supported main claim. The spouse's own financial standing coming into the relationship is deemed irrelevant, whether well off or no.

The second atrocity is where the cohabiting partner of a parent thereby becomes legally responsible for the future maintenance of the partner's existing children, as well as any children they may subsequently have together. Unsurprisingly, the first law puts a lot of heterosexual people off marrying and the second law puts many more off even offering cohabitation. Does the State care? There is no evidence of it so far over many years.

They sometimes say that governments are for the family. Well, they pass some extraordinary legislation difficult to square with the claim, or with human decency for that matter. One instance is to look at the position of grandparents. Under English law they do not even have access rights to their grandchildren. If the parent refuses, grandparents have to 'seek the leave of the court' to make a formal application for contact. If they get over that hurdle they have to argue their claim in court, perhaps being opposed by the parents. Custody is a whole other ball park again!

I'm afraid that the country needs to get used to the fact that it is socially rotten. One major aspect of this is the endemic national practice of very large-scale child abuse. I say 'endemic' because it carries down the generations and has been going on for so long across the nation and inside numerous institutions, prominent among them under the current spotlight being religious bodies, notably Catholic and Anglican, local authority Social Services, care homes in both public and private sectors, and within the BBC itself, no less. The British Government has also been complicit, notably in the deportation of 'bastard' children and orphans to Australia after the Second World War.

The legal and establishment cultures of the nation have ensured denials, cover ups, and failure to convict and punish the many miscreants. They still do. The Police have traditionally deflected complaints. Victims, often inadequate individuals who feel shame and haven't the resources, have not been believed when they do pluck up the courage to come forward. Years go by. Some die before they can receive anything remotely approaching justice.

And when government eventually concedes by setting up an enquiry, years then pass whilst the committee gets its procedural act together, various chairpersons and lawyers resigning in the process. Terms of reference are the key to government tactics. They invariably rig proceedings so that the scope is limited. Institutions escape financial penalties or legally enforced reforms. Individuals escape prosecution, sometimes on the grounds of their old age, by the time due process catches up with them. So it is part of the fabric, part of who we are as a country.

Family Courts need exposing for what they are if the public are to be informed and reassured that children are being removed from their family only for the very best of motives, and into the proper kind of care, where they will not fall foul of abuse, unlike so many of their predecessors. We need transparency, written accounts, fully reported by the press, juries as well as a judge, accountability for decisions. Especially do we need to safeguard against social workers erroneously spotting 'danger signs' in ordinary, decent families and persuading judges behind closed doors to take their children away.

And who speaks for the families and where are their rights and powers?

The Children's Commissioner for England published in 2017 a damning report on the vulnerability of the nation's children. Some 670,000 children were found to be in problem families, with over 26,000 of them living with an adult carer undergoing drug or alcohol treatment. 1,200 children are discovered annually to be in slavery and in the case of over half a million the state has needed to intervene with direct care or other support. Not surprisingly over 800,000 children over five suffer from mental illnesses. The report also chillingly concludes that the known figures could be the tip of the iceberg!

Welfare

'Welfare' may be the wrong word, so negative are its connotations after years of slurs against it in the Tory press. 'Social Security' was the older term and it captures quite nicely the idea that people (perhaps all of us) are at some times of our lives in need of the umbrella of a caring State.

The area of activity has been hopelessly picked on in the Cameron years, from Coalition to Conservative government, as they sought to reign it back in favour of charities, unpaid voluntarism, or hive off any elements that could be made, maybe artificially, to turn a private profit. Welfare has been in danger of becoming, in its atrophied condition, piecemeal policy failing adequately to cushion against the crude roughness of unfettered capitalism.

What has made the Welfare State increasingly unpopular (with the exception notably of the NHS) is persistent media pillorying with effective Tory propaganda. Claimants have been disparaged as workshy, the poor as having brought it on themselves. So tougher conditions of entitlement have been imposed over the years, squeezing financial cuts out of the system. The means-testing regime, with accompanying bureaucratic difficulties and delays, has been linked to moral opprobrium, with the result that legions of people who are entitled to benefits have been stigmatized into not even applying.

Frank Field, a vastly experienced and respected MP for Birkenhead, has taken the plight of benefits recipients to heart. He alleged that the introduction of the universal credit benefit in the Government's long-running welfare reform introduction was flawed and has in practice had the effect of forcing claimants into poverty. He explained:

'a number of benefit changes have stopped people getting the help they need. Those benefits are meant to knit together and give us a safety net.(But) the welfare state is by accident being reshaped into an agent that causes destitution'.

Some would say it is no accident…One problem was the long delay – six weeks or more – between assessment and payment. Another involved rules such as the homeless being disallowed from Jobseekers' Allowance because they had no fixed address, or the exacting requirements on the paper evidence to be supplied by applicants.

So what is to be done? Well I for one do not know the answer to how you persuade vindictive and prejudiced people, the 'I'm All Right, Jack' brigade, those convinced of their superior worth and rectitude. The fact that formal opposition had to be raised speaks volumes for their caring nature. But I suspect that any significant amelioration in the direction of social justice must come with the sweeping away of current models in favour of a radical new system. Some such are already in evidence in civilized Western countries (always look to Scandinavia).

Such a new system would obviously have to have substantial public support (therein lies a major difficulty), but it clearly requires removal of the stigmatized means-testing, bureaucracy where it is unnecessary or unhelpful, and attitudes of corrosive moral condemnation. One touted method is called the Universal Basic Income, UBI, which would be paid to everybody, in or out of work, and irrespective of financial standing. There could be all sorts of variations on the idea, and clearly the benefits could be set at different levels for state affordability and individual wellbeing, but it seems likely that there would have to be a residuum of means-testing, certainly to cover the disabled and housing benefit.

Those who put forward UBI, and it is an exciting, positive idea that could eventually sit alongside the NHS, twin jewels in the crown, as it were, tend to play down its probable problems. It may seem to them a just solution, for example, but huge numbers are likely to see it as very unfair, giving equally to the rich. It would additionally be an inconsistent measure set alongside a taxation system which would make the rich pay their higher proportionate dues. Of course, massively redistributive as it would be at the start, it would not be long before the weak, the not very bright, the dishonest and so forth would again be relatively badly off, failing to use their UBI responsibly or appropriately. This is a common argument from the critics of redistributive wealth measures.

But I do like many of the predicted consequences of a UBI system – the payments to carers and others unwaged, who are more often women, the reductions in inequality, opportunity to be cushioned while you seek employment, more fulfilling employment, or studying for qualifications. Workers would be able to vote with their feet to a greater extent, forcing employers to pay decent wages and provide good working conditions. Just leave out the rich and the affluent middle classes.

Whilst definitions of a 'Living Wage' differ, and it is frequently subject to quantitative increases, nevertheless Jeremy Corbyn was able accurately to say in April 2017 that about six million people working in the United Kingdom earned less than it. So something in all human decency has to be done to stop such a state of affairs. Where does employer irresponsibility end and welfare begin?

In April 2017 the Conservative Government brought into force benefit reforms limiting child tax credit and child benefit to no more than two children and applicable to children born from then on. Whereas under the previous system the numbers of children per family for whom claims could be made was unlimited. This highlights a recurring dilemma for social policy:any financial cut-back will be perceived by the affected as an attack on families' 'rights' to have as many children as they wish. But the rest are reluctant to pay for them should they one day find themselves unable to. And surely governments have a responsibility to ensure that we do not become too many.

But under the Blair Government the Sure Start Scheme was introduced in 1998 to provide pre-school provision for the children from economically poorer families. Whilst there have been some mergers, the number of centres has decreased dramatically since 2010 when the Conservatives assumed power, by 1,240, or one third of the total. Areas like Swindon and parts of the North East have no such centres remaining. So this does look like an unjustifiable attack on the poor.

Jonathan Wolff, the political philosopher has subtly important messages about disability in his book 'Ethics and Public Policy' which I endorse. The first is that the varying views and attitudes of real people with disabilities must be listened to if we are to have effective policies. Secondly, there is no 'one size fits all'. There are various kinds of disabilities, and the abilities of those with the same disability vary so much, that we have to be very careful. We cannot allow our leaders to bring in tick box 'fitness to work' testing; actually a truly nasty way of saving money by denying benefit to those in dire need. Additionally some handicaps will have a higher lobbying profile and/or greater public understanding and sympathy. Clearly arguments of capability and resource availability will usually be relevant. Finally, equality may be unattainable given the severity of someone's disability, but we should not make the situation worse and should strive for realistic improvement. Stigma is a big problem, as is people's relative ease around the disabled. Sensitivity of handling is crucial to psychological adjustment, so clumsy or uncaring approaches by Government to their financial aid are absolutely unacceptable. Among other aspects of fitness to work is the need for Government to demonstrate to its people the high valuation it places on its physically and mentally crippled war heroes by providing the kind of generous and ongoing after care that would make us feel proud to live in such an enlightened and civilized country, rather than suffer the shame of their mean-spirited neglect as presently. The deep, media-driven hypocrisy of a nation that enthusiastically celebrates its Para-Olympic athletes' achievements every four years, then virtually ignores them in between times should be quite enough stimulus for reform with chastened humility.

Care

One sad issue that rose to near the top of the non-Brexit political agenda during 2017 when this book was being written was the realization that social care was being massively underfunded. The Government's declared policy was to integrate health and social care under a joint funding regime to be allocated regionally and locally. The trouble was that with government financial constraints within their long-term austerity programme, neither the NHS, nor the local authorities (responsible for social care) could cope with the increasing costs of demands from an ageing population. The results were very serious for the patients. Elderly people were kept in hospital after their treatment ended because the local authorities could not afford to look after them at home. This in turn drastically increased the waiting times for other patients needing operations, since beds were simply not available. The next development on the ground was private care providers rescinding contracts with over ninety of the hundred or so local authorities.

The Conservative Government responded in a brutal way, first claiming that resources were adequate, had never been better, and had not been cut; secondly, and more truthfully, admitting that a short-term stimulus was needed. It therefore took the extraordinary and hopelessly divisive patch-up decision to allow local authorities (who differ vastly in wealth) to increase their budgets by three per cent in the short-term with these proceeds of the council tax ring-fenced to social care. At the time of writing across-party clamour for proper and permanent adequate national funding had yet to gain a toehold.

We have a long way to go because care homes are struggling to keep financially afloat, given the government cut backs to local authority budgets means they can pay them less. And in July 2017 a report by the Care Quality Commission, following a three-year inspection of over four thousand nursing homes, concluded that one in three was providing 'poor care'. A quarter were failing on safety and adequacy of staffing levels.

Our care homes are in a growing state of crisis as the pressures of an ageing population mount, something the government should possibly have foreseen! Fortunately, we have the Care Quality Commission (CQC) to keep tabs on what is going on. Large private (for profit) firms dominate the market, whereas what they can be paid by local authorities for the care they provide has declined markedly as a result of the austerity cuts visited on them, so contracts are being repudiated. A consequential effect is that wages are low so that recruitment and retention become harder. Scare stories abound regarding abuses and neglect suffered by elderly inmates, about care homes that have closed suddenly, pitching the residents into unfamiliar surroundings detached from friends and carers alike. This can often be their death sentence.

An important aspect of social care is long-term residential care, where patients' conditions of health are too severe for them to continue living in their own home and so need to go into provision in the public or private sector. It has been a national scandal speaking volumes about our real values as a country – what we do rather than what we say – that in order to afford this care many elderly persons have had to sell their own homes. For example, a study published in March 2017 for the insurance company Royal London concluded on the basis of separate regional comparisons that an average length of stay of around thirty months in a residential home would incur costs equating to roughly forty to fifty percent of the value of an average home in the North-West, Midlands, Yorkshire, and Wales, some 56% in the North-East, where house prices tend to be lowest. By contract, the figure is a modest eighteen percent in London, so there is a veritable postcode lottery to add to the injustice of it all.

The national disgrace and shame of State policy inaction on long-term residential care is all the more disgusting when it is seen to have been ducked by the May and Cameron governments, the Coalition of Con-Lib, and the Brown and Blair Labour governments before that. This is despite the known ticking time-bomb of an ageing population so that decisive action becomes ever more urgent and unavoidable. The closest they got was to set up an across-party group to consider the matter and to commission the Dilnot Report, which reported as long ago as 2011. The Austerity years kicked in after the banking crisis in 2007, with financial uncertainty then compounded by Brexit.

Dr Nick Taylor, a researcher from the Commission on Care, reflected usefully on the state of play. A main object of Dilnot was to protect older people from having to sell their homes to pay for care. His recommendations included a cap on the costs an individual would be expected to pay. There would be a means-tested scheme with quite a high threshold of assets before personal payment became mandatory. But, implementation kept being deferred and is nowhere in sight at the time of writing.

The Government's stated intention was in my view deceptive. They talked of a threshold of £72,000 above which the State would foot the bill, whereas what they did not say was that accommodation costs were not included. The effect of that would mean people having to pay £140,000 before receiving any financial support from the State at all!

The nature of the law regarding payment for long-term care costs was thus woefully bad from the point of view of all but the very rich and the very poor at the point when Teresa May called a snap general election in 2017, as has previously been outlined. Although she mostly uttered benign, anodyne, or not very revealing remarks about her future intentions in most policy areas, with long-term care she unwisely declared a bold new plan in the Conservative manifesto. Details were somewhat confused, but she generously said that although old folk would have to pay for their care home stay, they could keep their last £100,000. So, although the value of their existing owned home, if any, would be taken into account in assessing liability for costs, the payments back to the State would not start until after their death, when if necessary the house would be sold. But she also introduced a new, nasty feature wherein old people receiving care but continuing to live in their own home would have to pay for it from day one, albeit in the same manner, the money being reclaimed from their estate post mortem.

The flak she received was considerable, and not merely from the public and opposition parties. Under pressure she next introduced a cap, although helpfully its value was left unstated. This would set a maximum figure beyond which recipients of care were not required to pay. Further criticisms inevitably followed, some to do with the appalling disparities in the market values of homes in different regions of the country. In the end, the policy was quietly dropped from the Government's legislative programme, the Queens Speech merely referring to an intention to hold all-party talks on the way forward. At least here was a political recognition that the current system was unjust and needing reform. But this was in effect a return to the situation of several years earlier, when all-party talks had broken down. There was then no political agreement on how these undoubtedly rising costs could and would be funded and that remained the case.

Various ideas have been put forward, all to be shot down, over the problem of paying the burden. National insurance contributions (income-related) could be levied on pensioners, the better-off ones could have their 'perks' removed, such as free local transport, winter fuel payments, and free prescriptions, a modest estates tax could be levied at death. More positively, there are those who see the costs being met out of general taxation and claim it would be a wise investment, boosting jobs and improving skills. But most of all would it not help to demonstrate that we are after all a civilized society, one in which we value our older citizens for their humanity, and because we will be old ourselves one day? And why should we be deprived of giving our children the legacy and helping hand they will need and we worked hard to create?

My own suggestions for reform would go much wider. If social care is to be funded like health costs, removing the artificial distinctions designed to save the public purse, local authorities as agents need to be adequately funded, care homes require renationalizing so that the wasted profit element is removed from costs and the suppliers can be better relied on to adopt humanitarian and caring values. Support for independent living at home, which is overwhelmingly what people want, would not only be encouraged by rhetoric but would be enabled through a professional, locally-based army of qualified carers.

Politicians sometimes claim we are a caring society. It depends what you mean by this. The Treasury-driven State is mean and parsimonious in its public support mechanisms of provision, as we have seen. By shining contrast, millions of ordinary citizens are daily engaged in deeds beyond the call of any duty our society has a right to expect. Our hidden and largely silent army of carers extends from young people to the very old. Over four hundred thousand octogenarians in 2016, for example, cared at home for their partners. Then there are those with severely disabled children and adults, not to mention, of course, the legions of mothers and housewives. Everyone gets tired and down-hearted from time to time. All need respite periods to recharge their batteries. Many require financial support unforthcoming, support and counselling networks and centres of expertise to help them cope.

There is a terrible truth about our so-called community: we tend to leave caring for the old, the sick, the young, the disabled or mentally ill, to family, whether or not equipped to do it, and, of course, mostly without support and entirely without pay. It saves the country billions, but it also puts an intolerable strain on some of the carers. One typical piece of State nastiness is that those who can claim a carer's allowance have it stopped or cut when they reach pension age. They typically exercise self-denial, dip into their own pockets, forego their own rest breaks and holidays, so that they are themselves in danger of, and some actually become, in need of care themselves. So it is no surprise that in July 2017 research by Carers UK put frightening figures to the above account, warning that their dedication had a 'catastrophic impact'. The trend to State reduction of respite care and the increasing charging for services to the cared for would have to be reversed, it said…

Cohesion

My final observations relate to the 'social glue' at the core of our wellbeing as communities. The Labour Party is divided on immigration, their middle-class elements tending to emphasize the economic and cultural benefits, the working class worried about threats to their jobs and changing the English culture in alien ways: a dilemma indeed for them. And as immigrants outbreed the natives the problems will loom ever larger and more urgent.

I have my observations on social cohesion. I have seen it weaken from the time of my childhood upbringing in the West Riding of Yorkshire. People were nosy, but they cared and helped each other out. Whilst areas no doubt continue to differ markedly, far too many so-called communities nowadays are such in name only. I live in one now. Neighbours will speak, some occasionally pass the time of day if you are out there gardening, but no real feeling or interest exists beyond a little gossip. They are largely self-contained in their group of family and friends, detached from the local community itself let alone wider society. They do not seem to notice the litter, the dog crap, illegally parked cars – on pavements and road junctions-the vehicle-damaged verges, the neglect of municipal trees, roads, and sidewalks.

And I am talking about a virtually white-only area above half-way in the financial scale. In parts of the country where there are mixed race areas, however, we have 'multiculturalism', which to me means segregated groups from given nationalities sticking apart with their own separate cultures, religions, customs, language, and sometimes laws. At best there is peaceful co-existence and a trading relationship.

'Social' does not have the depth of emotional attachment I believed in my younger days existed. People come together fleetingly for a common purpose in a class or meeting group sharing some interest or situational stage in life. They rarely meet, as strangers, to talk and get to exchange personal information and views. Relations are shallow, self-serving and transient, competing for airtime in over-busy lives. There is no help.

So as folk grow old their family and friends progressively die or shut down. One after another they become more and more isolated, more alone, lonely, more helpless. For the extended family has broken – geographically and in terms of a sense of moral responsibility – and the institutional caring organs of society have been remorselessly cut back financially by a cruel and very short-sighted Government. Local Government, for instance, is a major case in point. The deep irony is that because of its ever tighter budgets a local authority will have to impose what may seem heartless restrictions on entitlements to help. It can no longer be your friend.

In spite of all this, community does not seem like the natural state to which this nation aspires, or the Labour party extols as high values, so I cannot end this treatise on an optimistic note, as I would love to do. We could yet draw back from the jungle we seem bent on creating, but is there the collective wisdom and personal self-denial it would take?

As a direction of travel towards social cohesion, it is high time we stopped paying lip service to our anti-discrimination laws, 'brought in' during the 1970s, but sternly enforce them in both public and private sectors by an empowered Equality Commission, with individual commissioners responsible for specific groups – the aged, women, children, the disabled. Heavy fines and imprisonment should be available sanctions, with legal aid available for all who could not otherwise afford justice. Tribunal fees should also be abolished.

I have mixed feelings about the furore caused by the BBC's July 2017 revelation of women 'talent' being paid vastly less than their male counterparts in similar jobs. Yes, that is a scandal and there should be zero tolerance over it and very quick remedial action. Yet the much bigger scandal, for me, is the astronomical salaries these so-called 'stars' get in comparison with better qualified, hard-working and skilled practitioners in essential roles within the community. It comes down, once again, to the nation's value system, which disgusts me.

Ever since the financial crash of 2008 the high streets have been in decline, obviously more so in some places than others. There are other factors at work apart from soaring private rents and public rates, naturally. The British weather can have a marked effect, as can the counter-pull of supermarkets and trading estates out of town. When retail experts like Mary Portas come up with remedial proposals they largely fall on deaf ears. Central Government is far from committed or interventionist on the subject and local authority resources have been crushed by the same Government. What we do see are lots of empty premises, coffee shops, betting shops, and charity outlets. Redcar has a telling response. Artists have been encouraged to paint facades so that we have virtual shops instead of blanks. Might I suggest that where private enterprise has failed or cannot see a profit we could have voluntary and public centre attempts to build diverse community facilities.

Some, like Julia Hobsbawm, in her 2017 book 'Fully Connected' are convinced that our efforts to communicate in the modern world are causing us overload, stress, and considerable unhappiness. It is a combination of factors like the internet, smart mobile telephones, social web sites, computer technology that puts our social health at risk as we try to keep up and lead a balanced life, where change and knowledge explosions surround us. I agree and I like her slogan 'tune out is the new burnout', except she does advocate our switching off for one replenishing day per week. It is a commonplace that our personal identity security is compromised, but do we also realize that machines are being allowed to dictate to us how we work? She is praised for her grasp and the 'solutions' she offers, but they would not provide the complete answer for the likes of me. As she puts it, relationship quality deteriorates when we are no longer face to face, but social media can help slow this process down. Not if we were never part of that brave new world, it can't. And in any case it does only slow it down. The atomization and fragmentation continue apace. We communicate more in a remote and distant, virtual way, but interact in person less and less.

Finally, there is stress, which is increasing in the modern world owing to many unfortunate factors concerning our way of life. There are pressures on the young to gain qualifications sufficient to get a job. There is the insecurity of employment, leading to anxiety about their financial stability. Credit is too easy to obtain and very difficult to pay back, especially at the draconian interest rates the law allows, so rising debt compounds the problems and bears down corrosively on personal relationships. Some jobs are particularly stressful-nursing and teaching spring to mind. They are characterized by tough deadlines, box-ticking, high levels of managerial and Government interference and lack of trust. Family life no longer has the social cement of the extended family and wider community that once held it together in times of difficulty. Ongoing strife and estrangements can make it far from a restful haven of sanity, especially with the added demands of children. Having said all this, to some extent the remedy lies in each of us. Stress is a collection of negative thoughts often based on unlikely worst-case scenarios. We may prop ourselves up with drugs. But we may also choose to view things that get us down differently. Nicer and more realistic perceptions are a powerful answer, though you first have to cultivate strong-mindedness and don a Teflon coat, never an easy matter, unfortunately.

POSTSCRIPT

While the book has been in publication a lot of water has flowed under political bridges. And although the book is not meant to be a pot boiler, and does not depend on current events to give it relevance or significance, a few major things have happened which are worth mentioning, if only to consolidate some of its messages.

Regarding Trump, the fascinating exercise in popularism continued without resolution, but well illustrated the democratic dangers of the ignorant having their way. Michael Wolff wrote an insider story of the early days of his new Government which is widely regarded as reasonably accurate. The picture that emerged was curiously comforting because, for all that Trump appeared aggressive and unstable, he could not do a lot. As an individual his history shows him to be a rich father-made man, eventually inheriting charge of a real estate empire he had neither the wit nor the application to run. An extremely self-centred individual, as well as an insecure one, his reaction to others was invariably to find them wanting at some point and fire them. Few of the White House staff he appointed had any previous political experience or administrative acumen. As the firing went on it became harder to find people of quality willing to serve. Staff were so busy with their in-fighting and ill-defined roles that Trump would pass an edict and there would be no implementation follow-through. Planning and detail were beyond him. Very good at alienating the media, and indeed anyone he did not like or was suspicious of, he constantly received bad press. This, and his hopelessly poor grasp of reality, meant that he fought back by dismissively accusing them of producing 'fake news'. The big issues were saved from his attention for the most part because he could not grasp a complex brief. He did not like reading, had a very short attention span, and would not listen to others. As far as he was concerned, nobody else deserved credit and nobody else could occupy centre stage.

Yet a major worry persisted, that he could perhaps be manipulated to extreme ends, and that other members of his hands-on family, notably his daughter and her husband, could exert an unfortunate influence beyond their democratic non-status. Another was that, despite the daily demonstrations that he was palpably not up to the job, he apparently continued to receive blind support from many millions of Americans. This second point needs emphasis in the context of the book, for it sadly demonstrates serious defects of the de facto democratic system in America. Not only are the people incompetent to elect a decent government (also true in England), but their knowledge is distorted by media. The USA system also limits the Presidency to a narrow cohort of the very rich and has inadequate safeguards over recruitment and dismissal of White House staff.

On the Brexit front matters became ever more entangled, and an increasing worry whatever your stance over the question of leaving the European Union. Teresa May's lack of authority meant that Cabinet Ministers publicly briefed against her and each other. Media coverage, though intense, was not informing, and so time passed with intermittent negotiations, from which the impression was gathered that the British side lacked both competence and clear direction, whereas the EU side was inflexible. Outcomes thus remained very uncertain. Several major events were possible at this stage, any one of which could have made a big difference. To list prominent ones: the leader could be replaced, the Government might fall, a general election could have a variety of results, including stalemate or a new Labour Government, Parliament might vote against a negotiated settlement, there might be no deal at all, or the people could be given the opportunity of a second referendum. All this, of course, assumed that there was no economic calamity in the meantime.

One hunch I had was that Brexit, if it occurred at all, would have to be soft. This was because all the political parties in both Northern Ireland and Eire were implacably opposed to a hard border between them. Since EU rules required all regions of the UK to have the same border arrangements with it, the outcome was especially likely, given that the DUP votes were required to keep the minority Conservative Government in power here.

On the international front beyond Brexit, Britain became enmeshed in a major scandal involving the charity, Oxfam, and no doubt others of its ilk. It was revealed that many of their overseas staff, including senior managers in the field, had been accused of sexual abuse, exploiting their position of trust to have sex with local prostitutes. The practice had evidently been going on for a long time. Haiti and Chad were particularly mentioned, but the feeling grew that the practices were widespread. Additionally, some stood accused of abusing more junior charity staff from their poorly monitored positions of power.

When the story broke the International Development Secretary acted quickly to meet with charity sector leaders and demand explanations. It was said that Government funding could be withdrawn if the answers were not satisfactory, but in the event Oxfam agreed not to bid for more until they had put their house in order. What emerged was the fact that Oxfam central management had covered up the allegations for years. The Deputy Chief Executive of Oxfam, Penny Lawrence, tried to take full responsibility, since she was in charge of Overseas Aid at the times under scrutiny, and accordingly resigned. Priti Patel, the former Overseas Minister, then claimed that her Government had been complicit in the cover-up and the culture of denial. Over three hundred cases had come to light in the last year alone, she said.

A further development saw the charity's former head of safeguarding, Helen Evans, revealing that over a hundred cases in a ten-year period had occurred in Oxfam's UK shops, of staff being accused of sexual abuse, including rape, against young teenage volunteers. She eventually resigned in exasperation because her bosses ignored the evidence and the Charity Commission was subsequently very slow to act.

So what was becoming clearer was the usual denials and reluctance to act that has characterized the lovely leadership culture of the United Kingdom for at least a generation in so many walks of life. The reputation of the organization, and in particular its ability to raise money, has been the paramount concern, not the plight of victims. Of course, they will say that was then and we are cleaning up our act. Sadly, it would be ingenuous to believe them. If you are a paedophile looking for safe and easy opportunities they have shown that they do not care enough to stop you. So here we have a fitting addition to what was said early in the book about the charitable sector. We will get token resignations, shallow reviews, bland assurances, contrite statements, promises, but little of the no doubt costly reforms required for ongoing vigilance. Long before that most media will have lost interest.

A final illustration relates to pseudo-capitalist elements of the economy much beloved of the Conservative Government. Carillion was one of the favoured contractors frequently invited to tender for public sector contracts. There seemed to be no end to their claimed expertise, for they ran projects to do with such operations as rail, schools, aviation, military homes, university student accommodation, prisons, roads and hospitals. They also outsourced much of it to myriad small firms. So when they suddenly and spectacularly collapsed into liquidation it generated a national crisis. Not only did all these services need to be kept going, but the jobs of thousands of workers were no longer funded. Whilst tears were not publicly shed for the shareholders, an angry populace demanded further and better particulars.

What emerged immediately was not pretty. Opinion was inflamed by such facts as the cover-up of their financial position by Carillion, the pathetic trust and naïve lack of monitoring by Government. The fat cats were taking out enormous salaries and bonuses, and tendering for yet more contracts, whilst knowing that the company was in financial difficulties and that the deficit in the workers' pension fund amounted to billions. As Anthony

Hilton remarked, writing in the **i** newspaper, 'British construction firms have always behaved as if they could defy financial gravity. It's also the consequence of the relentless application of a neo-liberal political philosophy that for years has elevated financial engineering above real engineering; off balance- sheet finance above paying for things openly; and lauded the private sector above the public sector. It has fostered the belief that there is no financial challenge that cannot be solved by a deal, a sleight of hand, a willingness to screw suppliers and a taste for creative accounting. Thus the collapse of Carillion is an indictment of management, but one in which the Government, Whitehall, City bankers and even investors are also complicit. Taxpayers (employees and the service users) are the victims'.

My concluding remarks relate to the political climate we are living in, the rapid pace of topics coming and only apparently going. Every day the serious press reports on newly emergent stories about major problems at home and abroad. They surface, wave after wave, and it is difficult to maintain a sense of balance and optimism in the face of them. Then the media move on and we are left wondering about later developments.

To name but a few at the time of writing, there is the Facebook scandal, where millions have had their data misused without their knowledge or authority in a business deal involving a firm called Cambridge

Analytica. We know we are powerlessly caught between unfettered big business and censuring big government once we become part of the digital data world. Will a suitable balance ever be struck?

Then we have GKN, a British firm involved in Aerospace, which is being taken over in a hostile action by Melrose, a company with a past record of asset stripping. The Government, which has an attitude that almost any business is good business, true to form refused to prevent it.

A final omen will now have to suffice about the very unpleasant business world we inhabit. Joel Bakan, author of 'The Corporation: The Pathological Pursuit of Profit and Power', points out that psychopathic tendencies can be a real advantage to people in the corporate workplace. Character traits like being unemotional, ruthless, confident, ambitious, power-seeking, self-interested, amoral, can win them promotions denied to nicer people. But this is our capitalist system and the one the country has adopted. Do you begin to feel a chill?

Meanwhile, John Worboys, the notorious serial sex offender, was granted release by the Parole Board, and it was left to victims to pursue a self-financed group action to overturn the decision. Their success is historicall unique and threw rare light on a secretive system unfit for purpose. The scapegoat political sacking of the

Parole Board chief, when he was merely complying with their law, did not in itself address any of the underlying problems. It was revealed that unconnected legal measures brought in earler to limit police bail had effectively caused the release onto the streets of many violent criminals, even if Worboys would now remain in prison after all.

On the foreign front a little emphasized article carried a warning from a director of the UN World Food Programme relating that ISIS militants were regrouping and recruiting in the Sahel region of Africa with a view to mass migration, continuing the steady invasion of Europe which has been ongoing for some years past and which our leaders mostly deny.

And the much covered incident of the Russian spy Sergei Skripal being poisoned with nerve gas in Salisbury reminded us again of the menace posed by foreign political tyrants like Putin. It is symptomatic of the new world of computer warfare when we will not be quite sure where the enemy is coming from, or what to do about it beyond the symbolic gesture. We could hardly confiscate the London-based wealth of Putin's friends, Russian business leaders, since Britain benefits financially from its own corrupt regime of money laundering.

My pleas end here with an exhortation to beware the mealy mouths of politicians in power and the rallying

words they use for their gutless and toothless penalties-
name and shame, call to account, sanction, freeze the
assets, and self-regulation.

BIBLIOGRAPHY

Note: Acknowledgement goes to the **i** newspaper for all press references and its noble attempts to be unbiased.

Chapter 1 – Our Sham Democracy

Garcia, Beatriz, Consultant Researcher, Liverpool University.

Graham, Gordon, *The Case Against the Democratic State*, Imprint Academic, Thorverton, 2002.

Grayling, A.C, *Democracy and Its Crisis*, Oneworld, 2017.

Jones, Owen, *The Establishment and how they get away with it*, Penguin, London, 2015.

Kellerman, Barbara, *Followership*, Harvard Business Review Press, Boston, Massachusetts, 2008.

King, Anthony, *Who Governs Britain?*, Pelican Books, UK, 2015.

Naim, Moises, *The End of Power*, Basic Books, New York, 2013.

Whyte, David, *How Corrupt is Britain?,* Pluto Press, London, 2015.

Chapter 2 – The Trouble with Politics

Atkinson, Anthony, B., *Inequality – What can be done?,* Harvard University Press, Cambridge, Massachusetts, 2015.

Bacon, Richard and Hope, Christopher*, Conundrum,* Bite back Publishing Ltd., London, 2013.

Bauman, Zygmunt, *Liquid Times*, Polity Press, Cambridge, 2007.

Clegg, Nick, *Politics Between the Extremes*, The Bodley Head, London, 2016.

Crosland, Anthony, *The Future of Socialism*, Jonathan Cape, 1964.

Finlayson, Lorna, *The Political is Political*, Rowman and Littlefield International, 2015.

Hare, R.M., *Essays on Political Morality*, Oxford University Press, U.S.A; New Ed. edition 1991.

Head, Tom, *Civil Liberties*, One World Publications, Oxford, 2009.

Honderich, Ted, *Conservatism*, Pluto Press, London, 2005.

McNay, Lois, *The Misguided Search for the Political*, Polity, Cambridge, 2014.

Mishra, Pankaj, *Age of Anger – A History of the Present*, Allen Lane, Penguin Random House UK, 2017.

Paxman, Jeremy, *The Political Animal*, Penguin Michael Joseph, London, 2002.

Rawls, John, *A Theory of Justice*, Harvard University Press, U. S. A., reissue edition, 2005.

Walzer, Michael, *Spheres of Justice: A Defence of Pluralism and Equality*, Basic Books, New York, edition 1984.

Wolff, Jonathan, *An Introduction to Political Philosophy*, Oxford University Press, Third Edition, 2016.

Wolff, Jonathan, *Ethics and Public Policy: A Philosophical Inquiry*, Routledge, Abingdon, Oxon, 2011.

Chapter 3 – Dreams and Directions

Arriaga, Manuel, *Rebooting Democracy: A Citizen's Guide to Reinventing Politics*, Thistle Publishing, London, 2014.

Badiou, Alain, *The Century*, Polity, Cambridge, 2007.

Bourdieu, Pierre, *Key Concepts*, Ed. Grenfell, Michael, Routledge, second edition, 2012.

Harari, Yuval Noah, *Homo Deus: A Brief History of Tomorrow*, Harvill Secker, London, 2015.

Havel, Vaclav, *The Power of the Powerless: Citizens against the State in central-eastern Europe*, Routledge, Revivals, Abingdon, Oxon, 2010.

Hilton, Steve, *More Human: Designing a World Where People Come First*, W. H. Allen, London, 2015.

Kent, Edward, *Law and Philosophy*, Appleton-Century-Crofts, University of California, 1970.

MacDonald, Margaret, *'The Language of Political Theory'*, Meeting of the Aristotelian Society, Oxford, 1941.

Markovic, Mihailo, *'The Idea of Critique in Social Theory'*, 1983.

Tett, Gillian, *The Silo Effect*, Abacus, London, 2016.

Unger, Roberto Mangabeira, *Politics: The Central Texts: Theory against Fate*, Verso, London, 1997.

Williams, Zoe, *Get it together: Why We Deserve Better Politics*, Hutchinson, London, 2015.

Zizek, Slavoj, *Living in the End Times*, Verso, London, 2011.

Chapter 4 – Other Countries and Us

Bew, John, *Realpolitik: A History*, Oxford University Press, 2016.

Bootle, Roger, *The Trouble with Europe*, Nicholas Brealey Publishing, London, 2016.

Goldin, Ian, *Divided Nations: Why global governance is failing, and what we can do about it*, Oxford University Press, reprint edition 2014.

Grayling, A. C, *War-An Enquiry*, Yale University Press, New Haven, United States, 2017.

Nicholson, Michael, *International Relations*, Palgrave Macmillan, Basingstoke, Second Edition, 2002.

Singer, P. W., and Friedman, Allan, *Cyber Security and Cyberwar*, Oxford University Press, 2013.

Chapter 5 – Controlling Capitalism

Ali, Tariq, *The Extreme Centre: A Warning*, Verso, London, 2015.

Browne, John, *Connect: How Companies Succeed by Engaging Radically with Society*, W. H. Allen, Penguin, London, 2016.

Fulcher, James, *Capitalism*, Oxford University Press, 2004.

Halliday, Michael D., *Radical Bureaucracy*, New Generation Publishing, London, 2014.

Hickson, Kevin, *Rebuilding Social Democracy: Core principles for the centre left*, Policy Press, University of Bristol, 2016.

Hudson, Michael, *The Bubble and Beyond*, Update edition, Islet, 2014.

Mason, Paul, *Post-Capitalism: A Guide to our Future*, Allen Lane, U.K., 2015.

Mazzucato, Mariana, *The Entrepreneurial State: Debunking Public vs. Private Sector Myths*, Anthem Press, London, 2013.

Orrell, David, *Economyths*, Icon Books Ltd., London, 2010.

Steger, Manfred, *Globalization*, Oxford University Press, 2003.

Tormey, Simon, *Anti-capitalism*, One World Publications, Oxford, 2004.

Turner, Adair, *Between Debt and the Devil*, Princeton University Press, New Jersey, 2016.

Chapter 6 – Saving the Planet

No references.

Chapter 7 – Our Wellbeing

Halliday, Michael D., *Memoirs of an Educationalist*, Matador, Kibworth Beauchamp, Leicestershire, 2016.

Halliday, Michael D., *Outside the Outcrowd*, Authors on Line Ltd., Gamlingay, Sandy, Bedfordshire, 2013.

Hobsbawm, Julia, *Fully Connected: Surviving and Thriving in an Age of Overload*, Bloomsbury Business, London, 2017.

Lightning Source UK Ltd.
Milton Keynes UK
UKHW02f0806130518
322505UK00005B/142/P

9 781789 013184